VOLUME I

The Reminiscences

of

Captain Henri Smith-Hutton

U. S. Navy (Retired)

U. S. Naval Institute
Annapolis, Maryland

1976

Preface

Volume I of the memoirs of Captain Henri Smith-Hutton, U.S.N. (Ret.) covers the first half of his notable career as an Intelligence Officer in the United States Navy. Captain Paul Ryan, U.S.N. (Ret.) of the Hoover Institution in Stanford, California has been the interviewer. This volume takes us through Captain Smith-Hutton's confinement along with all members of the U. S. Embassy Staff in Tokyo after the Japanese attack on Pearl Harbor. The story concludes with the Captain's return to the United States on the SS GRIPSHOLM for duties on the staff of COMINCH. The balance of his career is covered in Volume II of the Memoirs.

Captain Smith-Hutton has read the transcript and made the necessary corrections. The entire MS has been retyped. A subject index has been added for the convenience of the user.

John T. Mason, Jr.
Director of Oral History
U. S. Naval Institute
Annapolis, Maryland

June, 1976

CAPTAIN HENRI HAROLD SMITH-HUTTON
UNITED STATES NAVY, RETIRED

Henri Harold Smith-Hutton was born September 8, 1901, in Alliance, Nebraska. He was appointed to the U.S. Naval Academy in 1918, was graduated and commissioned Ensign in June, 1922, and by subsequent promotions in grade attained the rank of Captain to date from June 21, 1942. His transfer to the Retired List of the Navy dates from June 30, 1952.

After graduation in 1922, he served in the Asiatic Fleet, consecutively in the USS HURON, flagship; USS BLACK HAWK; USS PEARY, and the battleship IDAHO, until May 29, 1926. During the following three years, he was a student of the Japanese language, attached to the American Embassy, Tokyo, Japan.

Returning to the United States in the fall of 1929, he was on duty in the Office of Naval Intelligence, Navy Department, Washington D.C., from November, 1929 until June, 1930. He then reported in the Newport News (Virginia) Shipbuilding and Dry Dock Company for duty in connection with fitting out the USS HOUSTON, commissioned on June 17, 1930. That cruiser later became flagship of the Asiatic Fleet, and he served aboard as Aide and Flag Lieutenant, and later as Aide and Fleet Intelligence Officer on the staff of the Commander in Chief, Asiatic Fleet. He then had shore duty at the American Embassy, Tokyo November 1932-April 1935, as Assistant Naval Attache, and when detached he returned to the Navy Department, for brief duty in the Office of the Chief of Naval Operations.

After serving the year July 1935-1936 as Executive Officer of the USS LAWRENCE, he was assigned as Communications Officer of the USS AUGUSTA, flagship of the Asiatic Fleet, serving until February 8, 1937, and thereafter for two years as Fleet Intelligence Officer on the staff of the Commander in Chief. Returning to the American Embassy, Tokyo, Japan, in April, 1939, he became Naval Attache and Naval Attache for Air, and was so serving when the Japanese attacked Pearl Harbor, T.H. on December 7, 1941, precipitating the United States' entry into World War II. He was interned, but in June, 1942 was repatriated and returned to the United States.

He reported in the Office of the Chief of Naval Operations, Washington, D.C., and had duty at the Headquarters of the Commander-in Chief, U.S. Fleet as an Intelligence Officer on his staff. For "outstanding services" while serving in that duty, from December 18, 1942, to October 12, 1944, he was awarded the Legion of Merit. The citation in part states: "...In charge of the Operational Information Section until July 1943, (he)...organized the Combat Intelligence Division...and served as Head of the new division until his detachment... By his skill, perseverance and highly specialized knowledge, together with his effective plans for the prompt dissemination of intelligence, Captain Smith-Hutton contributed materially to the successful prosecution of the war."

From October, 1944 until June, 1945, he was Commanding Officer of Destroyer Squadron 15, Pacific Fleet. His squadron was then converted to Mine Squadron 21 which he commanded until August, 1945. Later that month he was assigned to the staff of the Commander in

Chief, Pacific Fleet (Admiral C. W. Nimitz), and ordered to the Pacific Fleet Liaison Group, Headquarters of the Supreme Commander for the Allied Powers in Japan, and when that group was dissolved in February 1946, he became Chief of Staff to Commander, Naval Forces Japan (Vice Admiral R. M. Griffin). In June, 1946 he was ordered as Commanding Officer of the cruiser LITTLE ROCK, serving in that command until February, 1947.

He returned to the Navy Department, and had temporary duty in the Office of the Chief of Naval Operations, and was assigned as Naval Attache and Naval Attache for Air to France and Switzerland, in residence at the American Embassy, Paris, France. He remained there on duty until May 31, 1952, when he returned to the United States and had temporary duty in the Office of the Chief of Naval Operations, Navy Department, until his retirement became effective on June 30, 1952.

In addition to the Legion of Merit, Captain Smith-Hutton has the Victory Medal; the Yangtze Service Medal; the China Service Medal; the American Defense Service Medal, Base Clasp; the Asiatic-Pacific Campaign Medal; the American Campaign Medal; and the World War II Victory Medal.

Official home address of record: Fairfield, Connecticut.

— — — —

DECLARATION OF TRUST

The undersigned does hereby appoint and designate as his (her) Trustee herein, the Secretary-Treasurer and Publisher of the United States Naval Institute to perform and discharge the following duties, powers, and privileges in connection with the possession and use of a certain taped interview between the undersigned and the Oral History Department of the United States Naval Institute.

1. Classification of Transcript.

   (√) a. If classified OPEN, the transcript(s) may be read or the recording(s) audited by the qualified personnel upon presentation of proper credentials, as determined by the Secretary-Treasurer of the U. S. Naval Institute.

   (√) b. If classified PERMISSION REQUIRED TO CITE OR QUOTE, the user will be required to obtain permission in writing from the interviewee prior to quoting or citing from either the transcript(s) or the recording(s).

   ( ) c. If classified PERMISSION REQUIRED, permission must be obtained in writing from the interviewee before the transcribed interview(s) can be examined or the tape recording(s) audited.

   ( ) d. If classified CLOSED, the transcribed interview(s) and the tape recording(s) will be sealed until a time specified by the interviewee. This may be until the death of the interviewee or for any specified number of years.

2. It is expressly understood that in giving this authorization, I am in no way precluded from placing such restrictions as I may desire upon use of the interview at any time during my lifetime, nor does this authorization in any way affect my rights to the copyright of my literary expressions that may be contained in the interview. *I agree to have a complete copy of my oral history provided to 1) US Naval Historical Center 2) US Naval Academy Library (Special Collections)*

Witness my hand and seal this _____ day of _May_ 1975.

_____

I hereby accept and consent to the foregoing Declaration of Trust and the powers therein conferred upon me as Trustee:

_____

Interview with Captain Smith-Hutton

Place: Palo Alto, California

Date: December 6, 1973

By: Captain Paul Ryan, USN (Ret.)

Q: Captain Smith-Hutton, you've had a distinguished career, and I see that it started in Alliance, Nebraska, around the turn of the century. Could you tell me something about your early life?

Captain Smith-Hutton: I was born on 8 September 1901 in Alliance, Nebraska, where my parents had a small farm. Shortly after that, however, my father was employed by the Burlington Railroad as an engineer and we moved to the Black Hills in South Dakota -- that is, a few months after my birth. My family stayed there from that time.

So my boyhood was spent in the western part of South Dakota, in the Black Hills. I went to school there, attending the local schools. I graduated from Deadwood High School in the spring of 1917.

My boyhood was like that of other boys in the Middle West at that time. Because of the northern latitude and the elevation, there is heavy snowfall and it is cold in winter, so all of us were interested in winter sports, and we became quite skillful at skating and bobsledding. We introduced skiing to South Dakota. One of my classmates in school had relatives in Austria - since he was of Austrian extraction. One year, he went to visit them in the Austrian Alps, and on his return brought skis and told us about skiing. That was a new sport, so we took it up. I made my first skis in high school.

There was an abundance of game in the area and the mountain streams were full of fish. Several of us built a log cabin in the hills above the town, and pretended that we were hunters and trappers and could live on the animals that we killed and the fish that we caught. It was a very healthful life.

I can't remember anything else worth mentioning. The schools were good for a small Midwestern area. I must say that at a very early age I became interested in the sea, and I read everything I could find about the Navy. I was especially proud of the history of the Navy, during the Spanish-American War, which had ended just about the time I was born . . .

Q: . . . may I interrupt here, Captain, to ask if there were any naval veterans in your neighborhood?

Smith-Hutton: None that I can recall. I can't say now why it was that I became so much interested in the Navy, but we had a good library, and there were many books by naval officers. I remember one by Fighting Bob Evans who became my hero. I knew all about Admiral Dewey and the Battle of Manila Bay and Admiral Sampson and Commodore Schley of Santiago Fame. When I was about ten years old, I decided that if I could, I was going to the Naval Academy.

I found out how one got an appointment and had our family doctor give me a physical examination, because I learned that was important. When the doctor told me that I could qualify physically, I began to study subjects which would probably be most useful at the Naval Academy.

Q: Captain, you went to school in the town of Deadwood. Would you describe the size of the high school and the nature of the community?

Smith-Hutton: There were approximately 350 students in the high school, although the town itself was only about 5000. It was a well-to-do community, largely because of the gold mines in the area, which include the famous Homestake Mine, which is still a producer of gold. The hills are covered with pine trees so lumber is produced. The schools are perhaps better than you find in an average Midwestern town of that size. The school principal was a distinguished graduate of the University of Edinburgh, Scotland.

Q: Did you participate in any high school sports?

Smith-Hutton: I was particularly interested in swimming and tennis. Unfortunately, when I was a sophomore in high school, I hurt my knee badly in football, and the doctor suggested I give it up in order not to jeopardize my chances of getting in the Academy. I became fairly good at tennis, although my leg has always bothered me. I was graduated from high school in 1917 and was too young to go to the Academy, so I went to a small school called the Columbian Preparatory School on R Street in Washington, D.C. during the winter of 1917-1918.

Q: I believe it still exists, does it not?

Smith-Hutton: I believe it does. I took the examinations for the Academy in February 1918, and I entered in June 1918, having an appointment from Senator Sterling of South Dakota who was a family friend.

Q: Captain, would you tell something about life at Columbian Prep during wartime Washington days?

Smith-Hutton: The school was a well organized and well run prep school. There were perhaps 50 students in all. We lived in a dormitory! About half of the students were preparing for West Point and half for Annapolis. We were intensely interested in the progress of the war in Europe, and we used to hold discussions late at night, keeping maps of the various battlefields and battle lines in Europe.

I roomed with John Jay Pierrepont from New York, who became my greatest friend. We entered the Academy on different days and were assigned to different companies but after graduation we went to China. I remember him with great affection and admiration. Unfortunately, he developed a bone infection and died in 1950, when he was in Boston.

The spirit of the prep school was excellent, and I think that the preparation and the training that I got in the school, although not comparable in any way to that of the Academy, was very good preparation for the Academy when I eventually entered that summer.

Q: Captain, you entered the Naval Academy just when World War I was in its last days. At the end of every war, there tends to be a slackening of discipline in the armed forces; mainly I think because with the expansion of military forces, standards tend to go down. Now, when you were at the Naval Academy, did you have occasion to observe this particular thing happening?

Smith-Hutton: Perhaps to some extent, but in looking back, I think that one of the reasons that we had comparatively little, as far as the class of '22 was concerned, was the fact that such outstanding officers as Admiral Edward Eberle and Admiral H. B. Wilson were Superintendents, and the Commandant of Midshipmen for the first two years was Captain W. H. Standley who later became Chief of Naval Operations. These officers were able to inspire even young undisciplined groups of officers. So I would say that we may have had some postwar problems, but comparatively few because of this leadership.

The class was a large class. There were approximately 950 when we entered. That was because in 1918 many youngsters who would normally enter civilian life were attracted to the service. Shortly after peace came, there was a slackening, and some of the class resigned, but comparatively few, at least to begin with.

I remember one of our problems during the fall of 1918 was

the world wide flu epidemic. Only about 20% of the regiment were up and around and able to attend classes. There were several deaths, all in the upper classes.

But 1922 was a class with a great deal of enthusiam, cohesion, and class spirit. Some of the outstanding members of the class were the president who was Clyde King, a football player, Francis Whitaker, who became an outstanding naval engineer, was the vice president. We had men such as Vincent Gallagher, and as a matter of fact, these men that I'm talking about were all football players, and there were six members of the crew which won the Olympic championship in 1920, who were in the class.

With promotion to youngster, that is, to third classmen, after our youngster cruise, that class spirit became even stronger, and I must say that it exists even to this day. Our first midshipmen's cruise in the summer of 1919 was to the Caribbean and Panama. There were six coal burning battleships and these ships were not only very old but there were very few experienced men in the crews. I was too young and too inexperienced to realize it at the time but later I heard officers say that the captains expressed doubts that the ships would be able to reach Panama. They said frankly that the midshipmen did such excellent work that they were responsible for the success of the cruise.

I can recall firing the boilers, hoisting ashes, and then going down and firing boilers again, doing the work that would normally be done by firemen. But it was very interesting and we did good work. The second cruise we went to . . .

Q: . . . excuse me, Captain. You were talking here about

midshipmen manning the fire rooms and dumping the ashes. When we were talking previously on this topic, you happened to mention that one of your co-workers was Hyman Rickover, who was a classmate of yours. Can you comment on how you and Admiral Rickover served as ash heavers?

Smith-Hutton: Rickover and I were assigned to the same fire rooms, and we worked together firing one of the boilers. And when it became our turn, we went on deck to man the ash whip. This consisted of catching the heavy buckets of ashes as they came up from below, carrying them to the side of the ship, and throwing the ashes down the ash chute.

Rickover and I got better and better at this, and I remember that at first, I thought he was not very strong. But, by the end of the cruise he was a very good man on that ash whip.

Q: You kept up your association with Admiral Rickover throughout both of your careers, I gather, and we'll touch on that later, if that's agreeable to you.

Smith-Hutton: I consider him a good friend and wonderful officer.

Q: Captain, the Naval Academy goes through various social changes, and we see some of them today, in changing haircuts and relaxation of certain standards that we observed in former years. When I was a midshipman, all midshipmen could smoke, but I know that some time in the early Twenties, smoking was forbidden. Were you ever a victim of this no-smoking ban at the Naval Academy?

Smith-Hutton: Unfortunately, I got caught smoking twice. For the first offense, I got 20 demerits and was sent to the "prison" ship, the old Reina Mercedes, for two weeks. For the second offense, I got 50 demerits and was sent to the ship for six weeks. So I spent two months of my plebe year on the prison ship for smoking, and of course, lost the privileges of going into Annapolis. I couldn't attend any athletic events for that period but I did attend classes.

I can't recall that it did me very much good, because I took up smoking again youngster year and second class year. Of course, in first class year we were allowed to smoke in Smoke Hall, after lunch.

I can't remember that there were many of my classmates who were caught for other offenses, but I'm sure there were, and that's perhaps because I wasn't quite as old and quite as mature as some of the others and wasn't tempted to French out and do some of the more exciting things.

Q: Would you define the term French out?

Smith-Hutton: It means to leave the Academy on unauthorized leave. It comes from the British Navy; "to take French leave" of course, that means to just sneak away. Curiously enough, in France, "filer a la Anglaise" is to do exactly the same thing.

Q: Captain, in your career, particularly as a Naval Attache, you did considerable writing of reports and analyses and the like. During your years as a midshipman, did you find time to do any writing for the Log, Lucky Bag, that is, the yearbook or some of the literary magazines?

Smith-Hutton: I was an associate editor of Lucky Bag, and worked very hard on that the entire time I was at the Academy. One of the prominent members of the class was Jerry Olmstead, who stood #1 in the class. He had been appointed the editor of the Lucky Bag shortly after we came to the Academy and got a class organization going. As I say, I was an associate editor, and Olmstead and I worked closely together for three years.

My main work was to see that the biographies of the class were submitted in an acceptable form; while I did comparatively little of the writing, I was in charge of correcting and editing the biographies. That was an interesting job, and although I hadn't thought much about it, perhaps it did have something to do with the fact that I was later able to correct reports and prepare them more easily than if I hadn't had that early training on the Lucky Bag staff.

We had the usual successful Lucky Bag in most ways, and though I haven't seen a copy for some years, I believe it's still interesting.

Q: You have demonstrated that you're a linguist, having learned Japanese fluently, and you speak French, having lived in Paris as an attache, too. At the Naval Academy, did you study French?

Smith-Hutton: No, at the Academy I studied Spanish, which was comparatively easy for me. I had spoken French considerably at home, since my mother was part French-Canadian, and she spoke French to me frequently. As a result I've always felt quite at home in French. In Japanese, I had to work very hard as all of us do, and I learned it after three years of hard study. It's very different from any other language. While I don't feel that I have a special gift for languages, I feel that I can do quite well in almost any of them if I study.

Q: You did star in Spanish or "Dago" as it was called in those days.

Smith-Hutton: Yes, I did. It was one of the subjects that I didn't have to worry about, fortunately.

Q: Captain, you've mentioned that your mother was part French-Canadian. Then she obviously did not come from South Dakota. Where did your family orignate?

Smith-Hutton: The family was originally from Maine, not far from Portland, although there are no members of the family living there now. I never have visited the area. It was something I hadn't thought about until very recently, and of course, they've all left Maine.

Q: Your father, being an engineer, was drawn to the West because the railways needed his assistance?

Smith-Hutton: Yes. As I have mentioned, he was employed by the Burlington Railroad and worked in the Nebraska-South Dakota area for a considerable time, until his death in 1946.

Q: Well, thank you, Captain, for a most interesting description of your early years.

Interview with Captain Smith-Hutton

Place: Palo Alto, California

Date: December 13, 1973

By: Captain Paul Ryan, USN (Ret.)

Q: Captain, in our last interview, we discussed your cruise to Panama, where you mentioned your friendship with Midshipman Rickover. There were two other cruises you made, one to the Pacific and one to Europe. Would you describe your experiences on these cruises?

Captain Smith-Hutton: Our second class cruise was in 1920, and I was in the old battleship Kansas. There were six battleships of the vintage of the Kansas in that squadron. We went through the Panama Canal, where we coaled ship, and from Panama to Hawaii. I remember Hawaii rather well. Fifty years ago, Honolulu was a very different city from present day Honolulu. Pearl Harbor was under construction, but there wasn't room for battleships.

We were most hospitably received. The people took us to their homes. The excursion that impressed me the most was a trip that several of us made to a pineapple plantation. Afterward we went to the factory where they canned pineapple. It was the Dole Factory, of course. And on leaving, we were given armloads of pineapples which we took back to the ship with us. Incidentally, Rickover and I were on that same excursion.

We coaled ship alongside the dock, and that, as usual, was an all-hands evolution which took a day to clean up.

Then we went to San Francisco, where the people were most hospitable. There was a dance organized for us at one of the city halls and the midshipmen had a wonderful time. San Francisco is, of course, a beautiful city, with the hills and the magnificent bay.

We realized too, that San Francisco is different from many American cities, since large numbers of San Franciscans are recent arrivals from Europe. Then there are remnants of the gold rush days.

From San Francisco we went to San Pedro and Long Beach, from where we went by that electric tramway to Los Angeles where there were several receptions and balls and dances in our honor. The people of the West Coast were indeed hospitable.

After another exercise at coaling ship, we returned to . . .

Q: . . . excuse me, Captain, may I interrupt and say, did you anchor out at Long Beach, or did you go into San Pedro Harbor?

Smith-Hutton: We went into San Pedro Harbor. That is, the four senior ships went alongside the pier and two anchored out, as I remember.

Q: I see. Thank you.

Smith-Hutton: Then, back through the Canal. We stopped at Guantanamo, which has been a Navy port for many years. Ashore in Guantanamo there is little to do. But swimming and baseball

and other games on shore near the harbor are possible. I don't
remember exactly, but it seems to me that we were not allowed to
go to Santiago or Caiminera or the other pleasure places in the
area. And then back to Annapolis, where we anchored and went
on leave.

Q: Captain, one of the major products of Cuba has been rum.
Did the midshipmen sample this major product?

Smith-Hutton: I'm sure they did, but I didn't like it. I had
tried it in Panama but the weather was hot and one drink made me
so that I couldn't walk and my entire day ashore was spoiled.
I remember thinking the taste was good but the after effect was
terrible.

Then, our first class cruise was to Europe. We sighted the
coast of Ireland and then headed north. I remember the heavy
fogs - since it was in June. Our position was not accurate because
when the fog cleared a little the flagship was headed
directly for St. Kilda Island.

Then we went through Scapa Flow and across the North Sea to
Oslo, which at that time was called Christiania. The Norwegians
received us very hospitably. My recollection of it was that it
was a beautiful place, in hills covered with pine trees the
moment you got out of the city. At that time of year, that is
the end of June, it was light even at midnight. So we had
difficulty sleeping.

Q: Did the midshipmen use hammocks? What was your diet like

Smith-Hutton #2 - 15

aboard ship? You didn't have the deep freeze and the refrigeration facilities that ships have today.

Smith-Hutton: Well, actually, midshipmen are always hungry. We had many tinned things, but as I recall it, our diet was good.

Q: You had potatoes and onions?

Smith-Hutton: We had potatoes and onions, yes. And beans, of course, canned and dried navy beans and plenty of ham. They baked bread on board ship. Also we had canned pears and canned peaches for dessert much of the time. We rarely had ice cream. The pastry was only fair on the Kansas. But none of us really complained.

Q: What time did the working day start, 5:30?

Smith-Hutton: 5:30 was the usual time.

Q: Did they serve morning coffee?

Smith-Hutton: Always morning coffee. And then we had breakfast at 7:30.

Q: You were swabbing down the decks, that two hours?

Smith-Hutton: And shining brightwork. From Oslo, that is, from

Christiania we went to Lisbon. Portugal was a very different place from Norway. We thought then that the Portuguese were not very clean, and although the city was a beautiful city, it wasn't as well kept, wasn't as spotless as Christiania. However, we had a good time, and there was plenty to do in the vicinity of Lisbon, at Estoril and other places along the coast.

Q: Let's talk about Estoril for a minute. This is a favorite watering place now for jet-setters and deposed European kings. What was it like back in the early Twenties?

Smith-Hutton: It was a sleepy little place, a bit dusty, and we went there by cart. There were few motor cars although finally several of us got a taxi to get there. Later they did organize bus trips. And there was a place to gamble, even then, but it wasn't very flourishing or prosperous. Of course, there were few tourists in 1920-21.

Q: They did have a beach?

Smith-Hutton: The beach is beautiful. Oh yes, the swimming is good. Although the Portuguese were very particular about what the girls wore in swimming. Their swimming costumes were very much like the costumes they wore in 1890 in the United States -- they had to be practically dressed to go swimming in Portugal and, of course, in Spain also.

Q: The Catholic Church culture is very dominant in Spain and

Portugal still, I imagine.

Smith-Hutton: Yes. Although they've relaxed some of these rules to attract tourists.

From Lisbon, we went to Tangier, and Gibraltar, and had a pleasant stay there. However, it was for only two or three days and I don't remember anything except that Tangier was a smelly, odorous sort of place, full of dust and camels and people in shrouds.

Q: Captain, during your midshipmen cruises, did any officer impress you as being an outstanding popular personality?

Smith-Hutton: The officer that I remember best was our battalion officer, Lieutenant Commander LeBourgeois. He had been with us at Annapolis. He was very popular because he was fatherly and sympathetic to our problems. He never seemed too busy to receive a midshipman, even though the problem was a very minor one, and he didn't harass us by being too severe for minor infractions. I don't recall that there was any major problems that he had to decide because I'm sure he wouldn't have let his sympathy for midshipmen keep him from doing his duty. But fortunately, this didn't happen. We found him a splendid officer. I look back with a great deal of affection on Lieutenant Commander Le Bourgeois.

Q: You know, Captain, that he's the father of the present Rear Admiral Julien Le Bourgeois in the Navy.

Smith-Hutton #2 - 18

Smith-Hutton: Yes, I knew that, although I'd forgotten it. I've never had the pleasure of meeting his son.

Q: Captain, when you graduated in 1922, there were only 4200 line officers in the Navy. You were in a class which graduated 394 for the Navy, and 26 midshipmen for the Marine Corps. You then received your orders, and I see you have them there. Would you read them for us?

Smith-Hutton: Yes. These orders are dated 27 May 1922, from the Bureau of Navigation, to Ensign H.H. Smith-Hutton, USN, U.S. Naval Academy, Annapolis, Maryland, via the Superintendent, Subject, to duty on the USS Huron. "Upon graduation you will regard yourself detached from duty at the U.S. Naval Academy, Annapolis, Maryland and are authorized to report on 28 July 1922, to the Commandant of the 12th Naval District for duty on board the Receiving Ship at San Francisco, California, pending transportation via Army transport for Manila, Philippine Islands. 2) All transportation for yourself and dependents involved in connection with the above shall be without expense to the government. 3) In case you do not desire to bear this expense, you will regard this authorization as revoked and return this letter to the Bureau for cancellation. 4) Upon arrival at Manila, P.I., you will report to the Commandant of the 16th Naval District and by letter to the Commander-in-Chief of the U.S. Asiatic Fleet for such duty as may be assigned to you on board the USS Huron. Signed, Thomas Washington."

Q: Captain, I note that in paragraph 2, these orders say that the travel shall be without expense to the government. Did you bear the expense of traveling cross country to San Francisco?

Smith-Hutton: Yes, I paid for that personally. It was my understanding that due to the small allowance for travel at that particular time, if I had desired to go by government transportation, these orders would have been canceled. I probably would have been ordered to report to New York or Norfolk for transportation via Navy transport to the West Coast, and from there on, by Army transport for Manila. I paid for the rail transportation across continent because I wanted to see my parents who lived in South Dakota before going to San Francisco.

Q: Captain, not many people travel cross country by train in this age of aircraft. Would you tell us about your trip cross country?

Smith-Hutton: I like travel by train and it was a pleasant trip. To South Dakota I went via the Pennsylvania Railroad and the Burlington. Then on leaving for the West Coast, I went via the Union Pacific to Salt Lake City. It was most comfortable to travel in those days on Pullmann trains. Then, on the Western Pacific through the northern part of California, and the beautiful Feather River Canyon to San Francisco. The scenery is beautiful and it was certainly a most comfortable trip.

My parents decided to take advantage of the fact that I had

to go to San Francisco to come as far as they could with me, and my sister, who is somewhat younger than I, also came along. I had a few days leave and we went to Yosemite Park to see that beautiful area. I said good-bye to them in San Francisco to report to the Commandant for transportation in accordance with my orders.

It was a very pleasant trip, and I look back on it with a great deal of pleasure.

Q: Captain, as a young ensign in San Francisco, you had to report to the Naval District Headquarters. Where was it located?

Smith-Hutton: I reported to the headquarters and to the receiving ship at San Francisco. We went through the Ferry Building and got a launch to Yerba Buena Island in the Bay. (Yerba Buena means "good grass", "good herbs".)

There, I was on the receiving ship in San Francisco until 11 August. Then I boarded the Army transport Thomas, which sailed that same day for Honolulu, then Guam and the Philippines.

I might add that Yerba Buena in San Francisco Bay was the site of the original Naval installation which was taken over by the Navy as soon as the Naval District was established. The island was enlarged by the addition of Treasure Island, which is a man-made island adjacent to Yerba Buena.

Q: You boarded an Army transport, Captain, and sailed away on a month's cruise to Manila. Would you describe that?

Smith-Hutton: The U.S.A.T. Thomas was a transport which the Army had already had in service some 15 years at that time, but she was very comfortable. She made about 12 knots. The ocean was so very calm that we had little movement on the ship. We spent our time playing cards, bridge, acey deucy, and cribbage. There were a number of young officers and their wives on board. I remember a Navy couple, an officer in the class of '21, Ensign Thomas Dell, and I formed quite a friendship for him and his wife. I still correspond with them. There was an Army officer, Lieutenant Farrell and his wife. He later became a lieutenant general in the Army. We had the usual food, neither very good nor very bad. But the old Thomas was a comfortable ship and I can say that we had a pleasant cruise. We passed our time pleasantly.

Q: Captain, you arrived in Manila on 7 September 1922, and you were looking for the Huron, I imagine. What happened?

Smith-Hutton: On arrival in Manila, we got orders to report to Pecos for transportation to North China. The Pecos was a very large oil tanker commanded by Commander William Glassford. She carried oil for the destroyer squadron and for the submarines. She was in Manila having brought oil from Borneo so when we reported on board, the ship got under way very soon for North China.

We found the Huron at Chefoo, on the north coast of Shantung Province. And on 12 September I reported to the Captain with 11 of my classmates who were also assigned to the Huron. She was the old armored cruiser originally named the South Dakota.

All of us were sent to the flagship for a short time for indoctrination, and, of course, joined the junior officers mess. Only four of us, the senior four, got state rooms. I was one of those lucky ones and roomed with a classmate, Miltone Miles who later became a vice admiral. The other eight had to stow their gear and sleep on cots in the passageways outside the mess. A young writer who is preparing a book about Vice Admiral Miles wrote recently that only two officers of the group are still alive.

Q: Captain, the USS Huron, your first ship, was an armored cruiser. We have a tradition of singing a song in the Navy that has to do with the armored cruiser squadron. Was this one of those ships?

Smith-Hutton: Yes. Her original name was the South Dakota, changed to the Huron, the name of a city in South Dakota. She was built in San Francisco at the Union Iron Works in 1907, and therefore, not one of the original armored cruisers. Many of them were built years before that -- for instance, the New York, which became the Saratoga, was built ten years before. But she certainly belonged to that famous armored cruiser squadron. She was a 15,000 ton ship, could make 22 knots, was about 500 feet in length, with a 27 foot draft. That was a problem in navigating along the China coast. The complement was roughly 1000 men. She had two 8-inch gun turrets, so there were four 8-inch guns, with a secondary battery of 6-inch guns. Her main armor belt was about six inches thick with 6½ on the face of the turrets, and a four-inch armored deck. She was sold in 1930, as scrap.

Q: Captain, I see you have an ensign's journal here. I recall in the Thirties that we had to keep journals also. Would you describe who your mentor was and what was his method of instruction for young officers?

Smith-Hutton: We had periodic discussion groups, meetings approximately once a week, and were always given an assignment by the senior watch officer, who was Lieutenant L. P. Lovett, in the class of 1918. He was later a Vice Admiral and the author of a very well known book on service customs and etiquette.

Q: I believe the title is Naval Customs and Traditions.

Smith-Hutton: That's the book.

In these meetings we were free to discuss anything and to ask questions, as long as they concerned our duties. We didn't get far afield, although from time to time there were political discussions, particularly in regard to China and the Philippines. Since I was the junior officer in Number 2 turret on the quarter deck of the old Huron, I stood watches. Several of the officers were in communications and not watch standers but they still took part in these discussions. As I say, the methods of Leland Lovett was very informal, but quite effective.

In looking through my assignments here, I find that some of them pertained to my special duties in the turret and in second division. This one is on foresighting and sub-caliber problems.

Then, in connection with Woosung and Shanghai -- this assignment gives information in regard to the tides and currents, including a sketch of the Yangtze . . .

Q: . . . excuse me, Captain, what was the reason for your being required to draw this sketch of the river mouth?

Smith-Hutton: Lieutenant Lovett wanted us to become familiar with the configuration of the lower Yangtze, and to be sure that we had some idea of the navigation problems.

Interview with Captain Smith-Hutton

Date: 20 December 1973

By: Captain Paul Ryan

Q: Captain, in our last session we were discussing your junior officer days aboard the USS Huron, an armored cruiser. One of your mentors on board was Lieutenant Leland P. Lovett, the famous author of Naval History and Traditions. Now, did you as a junior officer, have a general appreciation of the political conditions in the Far East and its effect on the operations of the U.S. Asiatic Fleet?

Captain Smith-Hutton: Yes. Lieutenant Lovett was a Southerner. He was well liked, easy going, flamboyant, and much interested in international politics. He spoke fluently and well, and in discussions we often touched on the political situation in China. We followed the movements of the various armies and commands, and discussed the political implications, including the strength of the Communists and their growing influence in Southern China, particularly. The British, who were the principal targets of the Communists in Southern China, were alarmed by the spread of Red influence, and watched developments very closely. We weren't entirely familiar with what was going on, but we had more than a general knowledge.

Q: I must say, Captain, Lieutenant Lovett sounds like a very interesting type of officer-instructor. I wish I'd served under him.

Turning to another point, I'd like to ask you about the type of enlisted men that you ran into on board the Huron on the China Station. For example, the annual report of the Secretary of the Navy asserts that for that year of 1922, only 35 percent of applicants for the U.S. Navy were accepted. Did you feel that the average enlisted man in the mid-1920's was high caliber?

Smith-Hutton: There were many enlisted men in the Huron and the Black Hawk that I would call Asiatic theatre types -- that is, professional sailors who liked the romance of the Orient, who drank more than the average, and who liked exotic women. Almost none of them had gone to high school, and they had no intention of going back to school, but they did like the Navy and the service, and intended to remain, especially in the Asiatic Fleet. They became good bos'n mates, gunner's mates, signalmen and the best of them were very good petty officers, not necessarily educated men but good, solid, old-fashioned sailor types.

I think that in the Asiatic Fleet at that time, we had complete peacetime complements, and about the time I was sent to China, there was never a shortage of volunteers for duty in the Far East.

Q: Captain, at the end of World War I, the Navy was going through the usual curtailment of funds in the Navy budget. For example, the Navy was reduced from 115,000 to 86,000. There was also a fuel shortage. The operations of various fleets were suffering.

How did this pinchpenny policy affect the Asiatic Fleet?

Smith-Hutton: There was no shortage of fuel oil that I can remember in the fleet, and certainly the destroyers and submarines were required to carry out regular engineering competitions, full power runs and smoke prevention runs. Of course, the Huron and many of the coastal and river gunboats were coal burners and were not included in these competitions, since many of them were one of a kind, but they were required to carry out the regular competitions in their classes, and were expected to keep ready for any duty in any emergency.

Since these coal burners required fine coal which was not available in the Philippines, the Navy bought coal from China and Indochina, and while I don't know about prices, it was certainly cheaper than coal in the United States. The oiler Pecos made regular trips to Borneo in the Dutch East Indies, and I am sure that the Navy bought fuel oil cheaper than in the United States. In fact, there was no pinchpenny attitude in the fleet as far as fuel was concerned. I do remember, however, that the destroyer squadron commander and his staff required all ships to exercise great care not to over-expend the allotments for repairs and upkeep. Economy and efficiency with no waste was the order of the day. But one certainly couldn't characterize this as a pinchpenny attitude.

In sum, the Atlantic and Pacific Fleets which were operating at home were given very little fuel and had to exercise the greatest economy, whereas the Asiatic Fleet and perhaps the

Mediterranean forces, which also were operating abroad showing the flag and protecting American interests, were given more means to carry out their duties. For the Asiatic Fleet, there was no question of drastic economy measures.

Q: Captain, the Chinese Revolution was in full swing when you arrived in China in the early Twenties. What impact did the Revolution have upon junior officers and upon ship's operations of the USS Huron?

Smith-Hutton: While I can't say that we junior officers had any great appreciation of the historical significance of the Chinese Revolution, we soon realized that if there were disturbances in coastal or river areas and if the lives of U.S. residents were endangered, the ships of the fleet were sent at once to protect them or to evacuate them. And we talked about this frequently in our discussions in the JO mess, and with Lieutenant Lovett. The junior Marine officer in the Huron had won a Navy Cross in Nicaragua. He had been in the Asiatic Fleet for several years and had been ashore with landing forces several times in China. He told us of his experiences with excited Chinese mobs. These mobs were almost always very cruel and bloodthirsty. Victims of mobs seldom lived to tell of their experiences.

The ships' landing parties were drilled frequently, and during inspection were given a thorough going over by the inspection officers. Landing parties and fire and rescue parties were supposed to be ready within a very few minutes from the time they were called away, and during drills were usually actually embarked and landed. They were very efficient.

Q: You're familiar with the book or movie Sand Pebbles? Have you seen the movie or read the book?

Smith-Hutton: Yes, I saw the movie and read the book.

Q: Was this a fair depiction of U.S. naval operations in China?

Smith-Hutton: To some extent. Normally the situation was quiet and the Chinese were friendly and smiling. They could and did become warlike and then they felt and acted toward our ships and men as shown in the movie.

Q: Captain, did you have an opportunity to go ashore on any landing expeditions or landing parties, during your stay in China?

Smith-Hutton: Yes, when I was in the Peary in Shanghai in 1925, I was with the landing force for about two weeks, and I'll have occasion, I think, to describe that in more detail later.

I have here a fleet general order which outlines the policy of the fleet, as set forth in 1929 by the Commander-in-Chief. This was renewed each time there was a new CinC but the policies changed very little. I think this is a very interesting resume of what the fleet was supposed to be doing.

Q: Yes, I agree. I notice this was signed by Admiral McVay, Commander-in-Chief of the Asiatic Fleet in 1929. With your permission, I propose that this document go forward with the tape, for inclusion in the typewritten version. It describes how the Asiatic Fleet supported U.S. policy in China, for example, the Open Door Policy and aloofness from interference in the internal affairs of China and the like.

Smith-Hutton: Splendid.

Q: Captain, I note that one of the objectives of the U.S. Asiatic Fleet was to maintain and improve friendly relations with the Chinese people. Could you tell me, what was the attitude of the average U.S. naval man toward the Chinese people?

Smith-Hutton: It isn't easy to describe the feelings of the officers of the destroyers and submarines toward the Chinese, because our relations with the people were so limited. Very few officers could make friends with the Chinese because there was a lack of common problems and there was no Chinese middle class. Then there were language difficulties.

It may have been different with the coastal and river gunboat officers who spent long periods in the same ports, but with the fleet ships it was impossible.

For instance, we joined the <u>Huron</u> in Chefoo in September, 1922, and were busy with ship duties but could go ashore after working hours. That meant going ashore for tennis or swimming, or having dinner or a drink at the Chefoo Club. There weren't any good restaurants in Chefoo. And there weren't any Chinese members of clubs in the coastal ports. In fact, Chinese were not allowed in the clubs except as bar boys or waiters. Of the Chinese officials, that is, the governors, mayors, navy or army officers, which we met officially, few spoke English and none of us spoke Chinese, so an interpreter was necessary. When we met one who spoke English, we got to know and like him quickly. The merchants visited the ships with their wares, and we met tailors and shoemakers ashore, but if any of them had families, we didn't know about it.

In the various ports there were dance halls with Chinese dance partners. About 1923, there began to be Russian dance partners. Then there were bars and houses of prostitution. But these are much the same from Suez to Shanghai.

Married officers also met very few Chinese. Then after two weeks in Chefoo, the Huron sailed for Shanghai. The opportunities to meet Chinese in Shanghai were about the same as in Chefoo, even though Shanghai is a huge international city. It is an amusing city with clubs and golf courses, horse racing, dog racing, night clubs, and dance halls. Shanghai's reputation of being a wicked city was well deserved in that there were many wealthy businessmen and a curious intermingling of great luxury and great poverty.

But there was no real intercourse and no chance to make friends with the Chinese. When I learned to speak some Chinese, I made a few acquaintances, but no real friends.

Q: Captain, I think your remarks concerning the difficulty of an average naval officer who is afloat to make friends in foreign places is well taken. I myself have noticed the same condition.

I'd like to turn now to your thoughts on health conditions in China in the early Twenties. Going from port to port, with conditions not as sanitary as they might be, did you encounter poor health conditions or were there any health problems on board?

Smith-Hutton: There was always a need to exercise great caution in Chinese ports because of epidemics. There was a cholera epidemic in Shanghai in 1922, and the crews of all the ships had to get cholera inoculations. And all personnel were ordered to stay out of the native city, to drink only bottled water and to eat only food that was cooked at reputable places. There were frequent smallpox epidemics and several typhus epidemics. Also, it was necessary to guard against dysentery and stomach disorders at all times.

But in general, I must say that our crews were young and vigorous, and I don't recall that any of these epidemics affected our ship. But the medical officers were very alert and careful.

For example, I remember that the crew of the destroyer Peary was vaccinated five times in one year against smallpox, because if there was an epidemic in the port we were about to visit, the division doctor preferred to repeat the vaccinations rather than risk an outbreak of the disease, even though the crew had been vaccinated just a few weeks before.

This was apparently effective, because none of us caught smallpox. The VD rate was not high, but there again the medical officers deserve the credit for this. Instructions and lectures on VD were given frequently and all hands were alerted with regard to prevention measures.

For example, for a while in Chefoo all men going ashore on liberty were required to carry prophylactics, and on return to the ship had to sign a register in sick bay if they had been exposed. If they had been exposed and hadn't used the prophylactic, they were restricted to the ship for considerable periods.

One year, in spite of everything, there were several cases of VD reported, and the Shore Patrol established a prophylactic station at each end of the street on which almost all of the brothels were located. All men leaving that street were required to enter the station and apply a prophylaxis. And there were no exceptions. Even officers were required to take one.

I recall that a petty officer came out of the street with his wife and assured the patrol that they had just been sight seeing. He was required to visit the station along with the others. When he protested to the captain, he was told that perhaps he should not go into that area, especially with his wife. Of course, not all of the ports could be handled in this fashion because of the location of the brothels, but it worked in Chefoo. Naturally, the men gradually became indoctrinated and learned to protect themselves. It wasn't any great problem with old hands, although accidents can always happen, especially if the men were intoxicated.

Q: Captain, fleet training wherein ships operated as a fleet received a lot of emphasis in the early 1920's. But I suspect that with the China situation and the need for Asiatic fleet ships to operate singly or in small detachments, that all this ruled out much fleet training. How did you keep up the operational efficiency of each ship?

Smith-Hutton: The standards of training of the fleet flagship and the destroyers and submarines were quite high, all things considered. I think the individual ships would certainly compare favorably with those of the fleets at home. Also, as far as the destroyers were concerned, division training was good.

The gunnery exercises for individual ships were carried out both in the winter, when the ships were normally in the Philippines, and in the summer in the Chefoo area. All the required exercises were completed every year, as were the torpedo exercises. Engineering competitions included full power and smoke prevention runs, and every possible opportunity was used to take advantage of the cruises between ports to conduct division maneuvers or maneuvers with any ships in company. In the three years I was in the fleet, there was no fleet exercise as such, so that we could say that there were no fleet drills, operations, or training. There were comparatively few changes in officers and enlisted personnel on the individual ships, and that made it possible to train the crews and keep them efficient.

I would like to point out that Lieutenant Commander W. H. P. Blandy was the squadron gunnery officer of the destroyer squadron, and that Commander Holloway Frost, who was the captain of the Ford, had an additional assignment as squadron tactical officer. They were very competent officers. So the squadron didn't lack for excellent technical supervision and control. But as far as fleet exercises were concerned, there weren't any.

Q: Very interesting, Captain. Would you identify Lieutenant Commander Blandy and his subsequent career for us?

Smith-Hutton: Lieutenant Commander Blandy became Chief of the Bureau of Ordnance and later an admiral, as Commander-in-Chief of the Atlantic Fleet.

Q: This is during and after World War II.

Smith-Hutton: After World War II, yes.

Q: And Holloway Frost is a familiar name to people, students of naval history. Could you identify him?

Smith-Hutton: He wrote an excellent study of the Battle of Jutland, and was the author of another book which was widely used in destroyers entitled On A Destroyer's Bridge, when he was a commander. Unfortunately, he died as a comparatively young officer.

Q: Captain, on 30 August 1923, the Tokyo earthquake took place, and I think something like 80,000 people were killed. As you know, Admiral Anderson took part of the Asiatic Fleet up to Japan. Could you tell me, where was the Peary during all this excitement?

Smith-Hutton: In August of 1923, I had been transferred from the Black Hawk to the destroyer Peary (DD-226), the flagship of the 43rd destroyer division. The whole squadron was in Chefoo completing summer gunnery exercises and training, preparing to leave for the Philippines, stopping as usual in the Chinese coastal ports. We were still in Chefoo when the earthquake took place. The Huron, Black Hawk and 13 ships of the squadron sailed at once for Japan. However, the Peary and the other five ships of the 43rd division were ordered to the Yangtze River area to show the flag, and to show the Americans in China that they weren't abandoned. The British Navy always had many more ships along the China Coast and in the Yangtze River than we had, so that the ships of the division formed a welcome addition to the usual Yangtze patrol. This also, marked the beginning of great unrest in the Yangtze Valley and in South China. Also there was exceptionally high water that year, and vast areas of the Yangtze Valley were flooded.

The Peary went up the river about 600 miles as far as Hankow and stayed there a month. Hankow was a very flourishing industrial city, and of course, still is an important area. At 1923, however, it was the center of large British interests, and the factories and international concessions made it a great international city. It was very interesting to see how the city had developed. There were British, Russian, French, German and Japanese concessions with many banks and business houses. We enjoyed our stay there very much and, fortunately, there were no incidents to spoil our summer cruise.

The city later became the scene of several bloody incidents, and finally, in 1927, it was surrendered to the Chinese. For years it stagnated, although under communist China it may have become a great city again.

One of the problems of destroyers operating in the Yangtze was that their ground tackle was not large and strong enough to hold them well. In order to be sure that the ship could hoist her anchor, we sighted our anchors every four days. I think that of the six ships in the division, each ship lost one anchor during our stay in Hankow.

Q: Captain, you mentioned that each of the six ships on the Yangtze lost an anchor. Could you describe in some detail what the conditions were?

Smith-Hutton: There was much silt in the river; so in four days the anchor becomes stuck in the mud. The problem is to pull it from the mud, hoist it to the waters edge, then drop it again. But this is delicate and may break the anchor chain. If you break the chain, you have lost your anchor. You haul in the chain slowly, then go ahead slowly on the ships engines. Since there is a river current, you can swing the ship a little to put pressure on the chain, trying to free the anchor from the mud. Working carefully, constant pressure is kept on the chain. With good luck the anchor gets loose and comes up. With bad luck the chain breaks and that anchor and some chain is lost. Of course, when the river falls in the winter, the Chinese recover the anchor and chain and sell it back to you.

Q: Very resourceful people. Captain, in 1923 in December, Sun Yat-sen, the President of the Republic of South China, threatened to seize the customs office in Canton, then under international control. Do you recall the incident, and were you present?

Smith-Hutton: One Saturday morning when we were in Manila, preparing for our usual weekend, we received orders to fuel to capacity, take on fresh provisions, and proceed at best speed to Hong Kong. That message was addressed to the 43rd Division. We did as ordered and had worked up to 29 knots by the time we passed Corregidor at the entrance to the bay. Shortly after that, however, on leaving the bay entrance, especially when we left the lee of Luzon Island, we found a strong northeast monsoon, which was really heavy at that time of year. The sea became so rough that we had to slow to about eight knots. It took us three days to go the 600 odd miles to Hong Kong, and even at eight knots, there was considerable storm damage to the fo'c's'les of the ships. The awning stanchions, among other things, were bent so that they had to be replaced.

We stayed in Hong Kong three days. I recall that there was a difference of opinion between the British Commander-in-Chief and the British foreign office authorities, because the Commander-in-Chief was very anxious that we not have all six ships of the division go to Canton at the same time. He said that Canton Harbor was rather crowded, and secondly, he felt that there was nothing which two or three ships couldn't handle. There were already British, French, Japanese, American and Portuguese ships in Canton Harbor. Our Commander, South China Patrol agreed two ships was enough.

The Chinese were very much excited about this concentration of ships which they said was a threat to their sovereignty. They announced that ships proceeding to Canton would be sunk by the forts at Boca Tigris where there was a battery of 10-inch guns.

However, the division commander had orders from the Commander, South China Patrol, who was Commander J. O. Richardson, later Commander-in-Chief of the U.S. Fleet, who was already in Canton said that we would proceed in spite of this Chinese threat. We cleared ships for action and went through the mouth of the Tiger at 25 knots.

We had service ammunition at the guns and we were going as fast as we felt we could.

The Chinese soldiers near the batteries stood at attention and waved to us as we went by, but no shots were fired. Our introduction to Canton was a very peaceful one.

Canton Harbor was indeed congested, but our ships went right to their buoys in a very seamanlike manner. I think Commander Richardson was pleased and I recall later that the British and the French officers at the Canton Club said they were much impressed by the way in which our captains had handled the destroyers on arrival at Canton.

We stayed two weeks, and we were relieved by two other ships. We went back to Hong Kong, and then about the end of February we returned to Manila. The whole incident was solved peaceably, and there were no problems, but I believe that the threat was thwarted by the large numbers of foreign ships that assembled in this small harbor in Canton. Commander Richardson was commended by the Commander-in-Chief for his handling of the situation.

Q: That's a very interesting account, Captain. The threat by Sun Yat-sen to seize the customs office in Canton obviously was part of a nationalistic movement that was rising in China, and I believe that the Chinese customs had been put under control some years ago. Perhaps you can tell us the background on this.

Smith-Hutton: As a result of the debts of the Chinese government and particularly the reparations that they had to pay for damage done to foreign interests during the Boxer Rebellion in 1900, the customs revenues in China was placed under international control. There were nationals of all countries connected with the Boxer reparations in the customs offices. The head was a British officer whose name was Hall and he gave the customs a very efficient management. He was the senior customs officer for many, many years. It was an entirely honest organization and while a large part of the revenue collected went to China, certain parts of the monies were payable to a foreign account in payment of the damages done and in repayment of the loans which had been given to China. It was perhaps one of the few honest organizations in

China.

Q: Thank you, Captain. I have one other question. Who was the division commander who made the decision to steam past the Boca Tigris?

Smith-Hutton: That was Commander J. S. Abbott, who I believe was in the class of 1907. He had been commander of the Destroyer Division since it left the United States in 1922. But more importantly, Commander J. O. Richardson was the officer who really decided.

Q: Thank you, Captain. One more question before we leave Canton. Who was the Commander-in-Chief of the Asiatic Fleet during this incident?

Smith-Hutton: The Commander-in-Chief was Admiral Thomas Washington, who had taken the command in October of '23, but I am sure he left the final decision to the man on the scene, that is, Commander Richardson.

Q: In March of 1924, the War Department organized a round-the-world flight. This operation upset a few of the fleet deployment schedules, and particularly that of the Asiatic Fleet. Were you involved in that operation?

Smith-Hutton: Yes, the 43rd division was responsible for the escort and safety of the fliers, from the northern Kuriles Islands to

Shanghai. The destroyer Pope (DD-225) with Captain McLaren, went to the northern island, which is Paramushiru, with gasoline and some spare parts, and he waited until the four fliers arrived from Alaska. On arrival there he provided them with an anchorage and refueled the planes. Fortunately, the weather was clear so that they had no problems, although Kuriles Island weather is usually very bad. Their next leg was to Hakodate in Hokkaido, the largest northern island of Japan. At Hakodate another ship supplied gasoline and was prepared to give any services that they required. I think all they needed was oil and gasoline. The Peary had visited Hakodate and Captain Abbott found that everything was in readiness for the IR arrival.

When we returned to Tokyo Bay, and on arrival there, we provided the same services for them. They stayed in Tokyo a day or two, and then were ready to fly to Kagoshima, the next stop. I recall that they passed directly over us, while we were waiting off the southern coast of Shikoku. We had received word that they had taken off from Tokyo Bay, so we made smoke that could be seen easily, and they passed overhead. We steamed in the direction of Shanghai to indicate the correct course and that was the last we saw of them. They landed without incident at Kagoshima, and the following day took off for Shanghai.

At Shanghai our responsibilities ended, but the other two divisions escorted them as far as India.

Q: Captain, the Peary met the round-the-world fliers at Hakodate and Tokyo. Would you tell us some of the details of how you supplied gasoline, food and even sleeping accomodations to these tired aviators?

Smith-Hutton: We had 50 gallon gasoline drums which we stowed on the fantail. I think that we had 50 or 60 of them, and we also had some spare parts. I believe they didn't need any spare parts. We loaded gasoline drums into the motor launch, and towed it alongside the aircraft, which were secured to the buoys which we had planted. We saw that the aircraft were fueled properly and we provided guards. We also gave them lodging for the night. They slept in the officers' quarters in the wardroom. We gave them hot meals while they were on board the ships and prepared sandwiches and snacks for them while they were in the air. Of course, they were in the air a comparatively short time, only four or five hours between the stopping points of the flight, so they didn't need large quantities of provisions. I think that the fliers enjoyed working with us, and except for the fact that we were not able to do anything except to take care of them, we were glad to be able to help.

Q: This concludes what has proved to be a very interesting session, Captain. Thank you very much.

Interview with Captain Smith-Hutton

Date: January 4, 1974

By: Captain Paul Ryan, USN (Ret.)

Q: Captain, we were in China when we concluded our last session, and you were en route in the USS Peary to Chefoo. This is in the spring of 1925, when all of a sudden your operation plans were disrupted. Could you tell us what happened?

Captain Smith-Hutton: A violent anti-British propaganda campaign was launched by the Communist branch of the new nationalist Chinese Cantonese government, that is, the Kuomintang. The Russian communists aided this campaign because they desired to eliminate all British influence from China. The British had large interests in South China and this anti-British campaign developed into a general anti-foreign movement. Since the armies of the Kuomingtang were also gradually moving north to the Yangtze Valley area, there developed a combination of anti-foreign and internal military struggle. Shanghai, being the largest and most important Chinese port, both for foreign and domestic commerce, was one of the main communist targets. Early in the spring it became evident that if the Communists could carry out their plans, they would start a general boycott of all foreign commerce in the Yangtze Valley.

About the end of May, when the squadron was, as usual, en route up the China Coast to Chefoo, we had word from our Consul General in Shanghai that the situation was getting serious. As a result of his warnings, the Commander of the Yangtze patrol force, who was then Rear Admiral Charles McVay, came to Shanghai, and on his recommendation the Commander-in-Chief ordered the squadron commander to detach the 43rd division and place us under orders of Commander, Yangtze Patrol.

The Peary, which was the flagship of the division, went into Shanghai and took the usual anchorages in the middle of the Whangpoo River. After we had been there about ten days, the landing force was ordered ashore. The British also became alarmed and sent a battalion of troops, from the Seaforth Highland Regiment in Hong King to Shanghai, to assist in the protection. The authorities also mobilized the Shanghai Volunteer Force. Many of the foreign residents of Shanghai had served in the British, Italian, American or Japanese armies. From these veterans, they organized a volunteer force to handle emergencies. Naturally, the Shanghai volunteers were not strong enough to defend the city against an organized military attack, but since the threat was usually from Chinese mobs, the volunteers could handle internal security problems and even attacks by guerilla forces.

The Peary landing force was under the command of the gunnery officer and was about 40 men strong. The commander ashore was a Lieutenant Commander, the commanding officer of one of the gunboats.

It was customary to erect barbed wire baricades around the entire perimeter of the settlement and to man these baricades with riflemen and machine gunners. They had orders to prevent mobs from entering the settlement.

This whole incident, although it was fairly ugly and lasted several weeks, never did develop into active fighting.

Q: Captain, tell us, how were the landing force equipped? What did they carry ashore?

Smith-Hutton: The Peary's landing force was four squads of riflemen and one machine gun squad. In this force in Shanghai, they took no tools, such as entrenching tools or other equipment, since they were quartered in buildings which were commandeered by the Shanghai Municipal Council. They had their own personal equipment, canteens, and rifles, ammunition, pistols, and as I say, one machine gun squad.

Q: Probably a Lewis or a Browning machine gun.

Smith-Hutton: It was a Lewis gun.

Q: What about rations? Did they take rations ashore?

Smith-Hutton: The ship supplied rations and after a short while, messes were organized by the Municipal Council and the volunteer forces, aided by the ladies of the settlement. The men said that they were very much pleased with the food that they were given while they were ashore in this landing force. Some of it came from the ship and some of it came from local sources.

Q: Otherwise they would have been eating hardtack and canned corned beef and canned peaches, probably?

Smith-Hutton: Yes, that would have been it, but they were very well provided for in this particular instance.

Q: Captain, you mentioned in our informal talk that a Shanghai Volunteer Corps also participated in this security patrol. What was that Shanghai Volunteer Corps?

Smith-Hutton: The Shanghai Volunteer Corps, which was organized shortly after the international settlement was organized in the middle of the 19th century, was for the purpose of keeping Chinese mobs or guerilla forces from attacking and getting control of the settlement. By the beginning of the 20th century, there were at least 3000 men who volunteered and who were organized in companies by nationals. For instance, there were several British companies, several American companies, several Japanese companies, as part of the force. All were men who had been soldiers. Many of them were very competent because of the experience that they had had in the armed forces of their own countries.

Q: And their objective was to prevent looting and the threat of mobs?

Smith-Hutton: Yes, and, of course, to assist the police to maintain order and peace in the settlement.

Q: Thanks. Captain, while the Peary was in Shanghai on this mission, where was the ship moored? Did you have communication with the beach? Did you allow the officers and crew to go ashore?

Smith-Hutton: The ship was moored just below the point where Soochow Creek flows into the Whangpoo River, and off the Whangpoo docks. It was close enough so that the Peary had visual communication with the Isabel, which was Admiral McVay's flagship. While we had no direct radio communication with the landing force ashore, that was maintained by the Commander, Yangtze Patrol who was, of course, in constant communication with them.

For the first few days, when the situation was tense and the mobs outside the settlement perimeter were very threatening, there was no liberty for the crew. But that subsided after the first week, and so it was felt that the crews could go ashore. They were required to stay inside of the settlement. Sports, such as baseball games were organized at the Shanghai racetrack, which was inside the perimeter. The men went ashore, fairly early in the afternoon with the understanding that they had to be back on board by sunset. It was summer and the days were long, so that gave them a good recreation period. They were free for six or seven hours.

Q: Captain, about this time, in June of 1925, you had received orders for detachment, and at the same time you were studying for examinations for promotion to lieutenant junior grade. Your days were rather busy then, weren't they?

Smith-Hutton: I was indeed. My orders came from the Commander-in-Chief to leave the Peary to go back to the United States, if I could sail by 30 June, and in the meantime my examinations for promotion to lieutenant junior grade had arrived. So I took the the exams on the Peary in the midst of all the excitement. I finished them in three or four days, and since there was no change in the situation or in my orders, I was actually detached on 30 June and sailed on a Dollar Liner for Seattle.

Q: Captain, what did your orders say?

Captain Smith-Hutton: To embark on the steamship President McKinley to Seattle, and upon arrival there, to await further orders from the Bureau of Navigation.

These orders involved two months' delay in reporting to the 11th Naval District in San Diego, then upon the arrival in a West Coast port of the battleship Idaho, to report to the Idaho for duty.

I went home on two months' leave, reported to San Diego on 21 September, and was instructed by the Commandant to report to San Francisco where the Idaho was expected. I reported to the ship on 24 September. We were in San Francisco for about one week, and then joined the other ships in the Battle Force in the San Pedro-Long Beach area for exercises and gunnery training.

Q: Captain, in the Twenties, the United States Navy was going through a transition of moving the bulk of their naval strength on the East Coast to the West Coast, presumably because of the threat posed by growing Japan. The cruisers and destroyers were sent to San Diego, and the battleships as I understand it, were sent to the Long Beach-San Pedro area. When I was a young officer in the Thirties, we anchored off Long Beach behind a breakwater, but in the 1920's the breakwater didn't exist. So, where did the _Idaho_ moor and what was life like for the enlisted men in that area?

Smith-Hutton: During the time I was in the _Idaho_, that is, from the fall of 1925 to the early summer of 1926, the _Idaho_ anchored in San Pedro Harbor, with the rest of the battleships. As I remember, one or two of the battleships did go alongside in San Pedro. The flagship of the fleet and the flagship of the battle force, but the other ships anchored out in the stream. There were no buoys that we had to pick up, and the traffic in and out of the port was not heavy, so there were no problems in that connection.

The liberty boats went into San Pedro. There were very few facilities for recreation in San Pedro, but, of course, from San Pedro it was not far to Long Beach or to Los Angeles by the electric tramways that ran between the cities. There were also buses, and while I can't recall that there were athletic facilities in San Pedro, the men enjoyed themselves -- one could swim and there were movies.

The officers made use of a small municipal club with tennis courts in San Pedro and it wasn't long before many of them had friends throughout Southern California.

Q: Captain, turning to the international implications of the transfer of the bulk of the U.S. Fleet to the West Coast, was there any feeling or conversation in the wardroom of the _Idaho_ concerning this move of the fleet to the West Coast? Was the significance apparent?

Smith-Hutton: There was general acceptance in the wardroom and among the officers of the fleet that the reason for the shift from the East to the West Coast was because of the growing strength of Japan. They knew that the shift was based entirely on the international political situation.

However, I must say that there wasn't much information available to us about the Japanese. The general opinion of Californians was that the Japanese were not friendly people. Bad feeling had developed during World War I.

Incidentally, this was one of the reasons why I, shortly after I reported to the Idaho, decided that at the first chance I was going to go to Japan to study Japanese.

There was no feeling of hostility toward the Japanese among our officers, it was merely a question of knowing very little about them.

Q: It was at this time then, Captain, that you made the decision to apply for language training. Did you shortly submit a request?

Smith-Hutton: Shortly after I reported on board, I submitted a request via the Captain to the Bureau of Navigation to be assigned to Tokyo to study Japanese.

Q: Captain, do you recall any officers or your shipmates in the Idaho who later became famous?

Smith-Hutton: Among the junior officers, yes. One was Lieutenant Dan Gallery who is a well known author, and a distinguished aviator.

He was the First Division Officer. Lieutenant "Deke" Parsons, a classmate, was the Fire Control Officer. He was responsible for dropping the atomic bomb on Hiroshima. Those two officers were among my very good friends.

Q: When you mention Dan Gallery, I am reminded that he captured a U-boat in World War II and that you were in operational intelligence on Admiral King's staff. As operational intelligence officer, did you have any contact with Captain Gallery?

Smith-Hutton: I remember very clearly one afternoon, Captain Gallery, who then had command of a hunter killer group, came to see me at the Commander-in-Chief's headquarters. He announced that his group was going to capture a German submarine on their next cruise and he asked if I would help. I told him that I would give him all the information we had.

After this conversation, we went to the Office of Naval Intelligence, and got all available documents on German submarines. I promised to give him the positions of submarines at sea and the rest, of course, is history. He actually did make the capture -- the first foreign ship captured by an American ship in more than a hundred years.

Q: Captain, when you mention Dan Gallery, I also consider him one of my friends. I know him as a man of many parts. Did he do anything to impress you younger officers aboard the Idaho?

Smith-Hutton: He did indeed. Of course, he impressed us

professionally, but also he impressed us one evening by bringing on board several Hollywood movie stars, including Miss Zasu Pitts and several of her colorful friends. As a result, Dan Gallery became the outstanding officer of our wardroom.

Q: This concludes the session on 3 January 1974, and a very fine session it was.

Smith-Hutton #5 - 54

Interview with Captain Smith-Hutton

Date: January 10, 1974

By: Captain Paul Ryan, USN (Ret.)

Q: Captain, last week at our session, you were aboard the Idaho, and some time in the spring of 1926 you received orders to language instruction. Could you describe what the orders said?

Smith-Hutton: Yes. I have my orders here. They were dated 26 March 1926, from the Bureau of Navigation to Lieutenant (j.g.) H. Smith-Hutton, USS Idaho, via the Commander-in-Chief, Battle Fleet, Subject, Change of duty. "You will regard yourself detached from duty on board the USS Idaho and from such other duty as may have been assigned to you at such time as will enable you to proceed to San Francisco, California, and on 1 June 1926, report to the Commandant, 12th Naval District and the commanding officer of the USS Chaumont for passage. Upon arrival at Shanghai, China, you will proceed to Tokyo, Japan and report to the American Ambassador in person, if he is present, otherwise by letter for duty as attache at the American Embassy for the purpose of acquiring a knowledge of the Japanese language. 3) You will also report to the Naval Attache at Tokyo, Japan, who will have supervision over all matters connected with your study, and will make quarterly reports of your progress. 4) You are hereby authorized to perform such travel from time to time in connection with your duties as may be directed by the Naval Attache, and you will be entitled to reimbursement for expenses other than the actual cost of this travel at a rate not exceeding $7 per day as specified in the act of 10 June 1922. 5) You will submit on the last day of each month a written report to this bureau showing the amount obligated by you for transportation and subsistence for that month in connection with the above mentioned travel. This report is to be submitted in addition to any reports that you may be required to submit to other bureaus, see Article 815, U.S. Navy regulations, paragraph 15. The Naval Attache at Tokyo is hereby directed to take up your accounts, and is authorized to spend for your tuition, textbooks, stationery and so forth the sum not to exceed $50 per month, cumulative within the fiscal year from the current appropriations, pay, miscellaneous. 7) The Secretary of the Navy has determined that this employment on shore duty beyond the seas is required by the public interest. Signed W. R. Shoemaker."

Q: Thank you, Captain. I notice that you received $50 a month to pay for your instruction, which seems ridiculously low now. When we get along in the narrative, perhaps you can describe how the money was used.

Now, I'd like to ask you to describe your voyage to the Far East.

Smith-Hutton: I was detached from the Idaho on 29 May 1926 and reported to the Commandant of the 12th Naval District for passage on the Chaumont. The voyage we made by Honolulu and Guam and Manila was uneventful. My fellow passengers were Navy and Marine officers en route to the Philippines and China. Upon arrival at Shanghai on 14 July 1926, I was detached from the Chaumont and reported to the Naval Purchasing Officer for commercial passage to Yokohama.

Q: Captain, may I interrupt -- I note that our Purchasing Office in Shanghai was evidently there to support our naval forces in the Far East. Could you comment on its mission?

Smith-Hutton: The Purchasing Officer bought supplies for our Yangtze Patrol ships, as well as other ships of the Fleet. He was in contact with not only the local merchants, but with the shipping companies. If ships required supplies, they got information in regard to costs and probable time of delivery, from the Purchasing Officer. He was a Commander in the Supply Corps, and a very efficient officer. The office was well run with a motto of service to the fleet.

Q: Thank you, Captain. Sorry I interrupted you, but that's very interesting and I did want to get it in the record. You now proceeded to Tokyo.

Smith-Hutton: On 23 July 1926, I reported to the Office of the Naval Attache, and on 24 July to the Embassy. Since our Embassy had been burned in the earthquake in '23, the two offices were not together. The Naval Attache's office was in a small room in his residence, and the Chancery of the Embassy was in an office building in the center of Tokyo.

The Ambassador was a distinguished lawyer from New Hampshire, who had been in Tokyo about a year when I arrived. The acting Naval Attache was Lieutenant Commander R. H. Hein of the class of

1910. Since it was late July and hot and humid in Tokyo, both the Ambassador and the acting Naval Attache were in the summer embassy in Chuzenji.

At that time, there were four language officers studying Japanese, and I made the fifth. The others were Lieutenant Commander F. B. Melandy, class of '11, Lieutenant D. W. Roberts, class of '21, Lieutenant W. J. Sebald of '22, and First Lieutenant J. S. Monahan, USMC. The three Navy officers had a comfortable summer house in Karuizawa and they asked me to live with them. Karuizawa is about 90 miles west of Tokyo in the mountains, and is cool and pleasant in the summer. That summer the mother of Lieutenant Roberts had come from the United States, and as she liked Japan, decided to stay. The officers asked her to keep house for them. She engaged a Japanese cook and a maid or two, so it was a pleasant household.

Karuizawa is a typical Far Eastern summer place, with many tennis courts, a nine hole golf course, with riding horses with some 2000 European and American diplomats and businessmen and their families. The missionaries also spent their summers there. During World War II many Europeans who remained in Japan were required to live there and even today it's a very popular resort.

The house was a ten minute walk from the village, and since there were a number of British language officers, missionaries and civilians studying Japanese, there was no shortage of instructors.

Lieutenant Roberts had already arranged for me to start lessons with one of his instructors, so I began at once. The prescribed course, a difficult grammar written by a German.

Students learned to read using children's readers used in the Japanese public schools. Since children even of six or seven years old already know how to speak Japanese, these readers are not suited for adults who do not speak the language.

My teacher was Professor Naganuma, who was a man of unusual talents. He was a graduate of Tokyo Commercial University, and a good linguist who had been assistant to a Professor Palmer, a British language expert who had been invited to come to Japan by the Ministry of Education. Naganuma liked the Berlitz method of language instruction, and he decided that, if possible, he would prepare a course such as the Berlitz course to apply to the study of Japanese. He asked me whether I would be the guinea pig and follow such a course as fast as he could prepare it. I agreed and we worked together.

Mr. Dooman and other embassy experts were astonished at the progress I made. As a result, Naganuma and his courses were much in demand in later years. He engaged several assistants to teach not only the Navy but the State Department and Army language officers. With the Naval Attache's permission, he used the readers and other materials we had prepared since we had actually paid for their preparation. He continued to teach all through the Thirties, up to the outbreak of the war. After the war he started a school for the occupation personnel, diplomats and foreign residents in Tokyo. I received word just last month that he died in the spring of 1973.

Q: Most interesting, your description of serving as a guinea pig for language instruction. Could you tell us specifically, what was this new technique?

Smith-Hutton: The technique that Naganuma used was not really new. He used the natural way of learning which a child uses to learn to talk and to always explain the entire lesson in Japanese, to never use English, to introduce two or three new words and phrases in a paragraph, and then to repeat them over and over again until the pronunciation as well as the use is easily recognized ask a series of questions, very similar but with one or two words changed, so that the questions and the changes are repeated time and again, so that you have perhaps ten new words in each lesson, and you talk for half an hour, much as children do when they learn or hear words for the first time.

Of course, in Japanese, the writing is similar to Chinese writing. The Japanese adopted the Chinese characters, ideographs, a thousand years ago; although the pronunciation is quite different, the meaning is generally the same. So writing is a combination of learn those sentences, and then learning how to write them, using a new series of characters every day. It is a natural method, and avoids long grammatical explanations until the student is able to understand that in Japanese rather than have an English translation. It may seem complicated, but actually it is a natural method which is easily followed, although there is, of course, considerable work. Japanese is perhaps the most complicated and difficult language of any of the world's great languages.

Q: Thank you, Captain. Did your instructor, being Japanese, hate to tell you of your mistakes, for fear of offending you?

Smith-Hutton: I should say he didn't. He was very severe with me, and as a result I was as exact as an American could be in pronunciation and in usage. He was very severe and very critical of any mistakes I made, so there wasn't any question of trying to hide.

Q: Captain, it has been said that the Japanese language lacks a system, that it's illogical and imprecise. Would you agree?

Smith-Hutton: Certainly, it is imprecise, and it is capable of being interpreted in several different ways, particularly if you try to hide your real thoughts or your real intentions. It's been said that Japanese is just a very cumbersome and difficult means of communicating or hiding your thoughts. I think that it is more correct to say that, rather than that it's illogical. But there are very few rules, and there is very little grammar to learn. Now textbooks use English and French terms to explain Japanese grammar, but they don't really apply as they do to another European language.

Q: Captain, I notice that there were very few language students assigned in the 1920's to Japanese language instruction. Could you comment on that?

Smith-Hutton: I think there were several reasons. The first reason is that there seemed to be no real need for many language officers. Another reason may have been lack of funds, even though our allowances were small and the course didn't cost much. There were not many officers on active duty, and thirdly, there was the difficulty of finding suitable candidates. Quite a number of officers were sent to Japan, to study the language, but several made very mediocre progress. There seemed to be no efficient way of weeding out those who might fail. I think all of these were good reasons.

However, in 1927 more officers were sent and the policy was to have officers studying at all times, three naval officers going each year for the three year course, and one Marine officer, so eventually the number was increased.

Q: Thank you, Captain. Then as I understand it, up to the year 1927, one naval officer per year was sent and after that three officers a year were sent.

Smith-Hutton: That's correct.

Q: Captain, did this policy of one officer, then three officers per year, apply to the U.S. Army also?

Smith-Hutton: No, the Army sent more officers than the Navy. It seems to me that there were perhaps twice as many Army as Navy language officers.

Q: Captain, did you enjoy diplomatic status in your assignment in Japan?

Smith-Hutton: Yes, we were ordered as attaches, and that applied to the Army language officers and State Department language officers. We were given diplomatic privileges, and as attaches we were invited to various ceremonies and parties that were of an official nature.

For instance, at New Year's we attended, with the Ambassador and his staff, the ceremonies at the Imperial Palace, bringing up the rear of the line in the American Embassy staff.

Q: What was the uniform for this ceremony, Captain?

Smith-Hutton: We wore full dress uniform with gold striped trousers, fore and aft hat, and epaulettes and sword.

Q: Well, they don't do that any more. I remember that we did away with that uniform, just about the time of Pearl Harbor.

Looking back on your stay as a language student, I think it was a case of total immersion in the life of the country, and also the lack of academic pressure. In other words, you were self-motivated and you determined your own progress. Were there any naval students there who did not make the most of this opportunity?

Smith-Hutton: Unfortunately, several officers were not well selected, and soon became discouraged with their studies and their lack of progress. In certain cases it seemed to me that they just stopped studying and became interested in doing other things, in athletics, playing golf or tennis or reading, and as a result they failed on the periodic examinations that we had every six months. It should be recognized, however, that not every naval officer is interested in studies of this kind and yet may be a fine officer. Also, some very enthusiastic officers who want to be good at the language just don't have the ability to learn. That doesn't mean for one minute that they aren't fine naval officers. It's hard to realize but this is a special assignment that requires special selection. But there was so much to learn, at least for me, not only about the language but about the manners and the customs and the art, the history, the literature, that I never lacked for something to do. And if I got tired of studying one phase of Japanese life, I could shift to another. It's a beautiful country. There are plenty of places to relax, if I was studying too much and tired of sitting in front of my desk learning Japanese ideographs. So the three years I was there passed very quickly, and I regretted when I had to leave.

I recall now that it is a question of knowing what to do, how to do it, and having the intention of continuing to apply the pressure until you've learned all of the characters and done all you could to master the course.

I must say this, though, that the more one studies Japanese, the more difficult it becomes, because one realizes that there are more things to study. For instance, even old men in Japan -- Japanese -- spend hours practicing writing beautiful characters with a large brush. So you see, the course doesn't end just in three years, and you can't master the language that quickly.

Q: This concludes the session for 10 January. Thank you very much, Captain, a most interesting session.

Interview #6 with Captain Henri Smith-Hutton

By: Captain Paul Ryan, USN (Ret.)

Q: Captain, in 1926, the health of the Emperor became a matter for national concern. Do you recall the circumstances?

Smith-Hutton: The state of health of the Emperor, as indeed anything in connection with him, is always a matter of great concern in Japan, and this was especially so in both the Twenties and Thirties, when great efforts were made to strengthen his position as a spiritual and as a political leader. The Emperor Taisho was the son of the great Emperor Meiji, who ruled from 1867 to 1912, and who was given much of the credit for the extraordinary changes which took place during this period, when Japan changed from a Medieval feudal state into a modern world power.

Although Emperor Taisho had been in poor health for years, took no part in national affairs and lived in complete seclusion, the patriots were determined to keep the imperial cult strong, and they have no publicity to his disability.

In December, 1926, he began to fail and daily bulletins in regard to his health were issued. The whole country waited anxiously for news of his health. He died on Christmas day in 1926, and of course the country went into deep mourning, including the diplomatic corps.

Several nights after his death, we went to the Imperial

Palace in full dress uniform with mourning badges. The ladies wore black dresses, and the palace and the grounds were lighted only by candles and lanterns. We filed in single file through one of the vast halls in the palace where the Emperor's body lay in a large coffin, covered with rich brocades. We had to bow in Japanese fashion every three steps.

After bowing in front of the coffin, we backed toward the exit facing the coffin and continued to bow.

Several nights later, we went again to the Palace, again in full dress, to be presented to the new Emperor, Emperor Hirohito who still reigns. The Ambassador was presented first by a court official, and he in turn presented each of us, and the Emperor   our hands. I think that set a great precedent, being the first time that foreigners were allowed to shake hands with the Emperor.

Again we backed away as we left his presence.

After several weeks of preparation, all was ready for the funeral, which was also held at night at a site near the Meiji Shrine on the outskirts of Tokyo. Again the diplomatic corps and Japanese officials assembled in full dress uniform, in open stands, along a tree-lined road leading to a ceremonial hall made of beautiful white unpainted wood. The funeral procession with officials and priests in elaborate robes, followed by a large wooden carriage drawn by oxen, came slowly up the road to the hall. It was very simple but very impressive. There was a blend of Oriental religious meaning and ancient display. Even the wheels of the carriage, the cart, as they turned made a weird creaking sound, as though they too were mourning for the Emperor.

It was certainly a unique spectacle, and I'm sure that anyone who saw it, in the dim light of the lanterns and candles, will never forget it. Unfortunately it was a very clear cold night, and since it is forbidden to wear overcoats in the presence of the Emperor, the diplomats and Japanese officials in European dress got chilled to the bone, especially the ladies. Japanese costumes which permit under garments to be piled on one another, then covered with an ordinary outside kimono, lend themselves to a midwinter ceremony in the open.

However, it was an unforgettable experience, and I might point out that there has not been another such funeral ceremony since 1926.

The coronation of the new Emperor which took place about 18 months later in Kyoto was also a colorful ceremony. I might talk a little bit about that later.

Q: Captain, you spent three years in language study in Japan. Now, did you spend this time living 90 miles north of Tokyo in that village of Karuizawa? Or in the city of Tokyo itself?

Smith-Hutton: After the summer in Karuizawa, we rented a most comfortable house in Tokyo, which was large enough to house all of us, and we continued our studies with the same instructors that we'd had during the summer. We did however all return to Karuizawa for the second summer, and at the end of that summer Lieutenant Commander Melandy and Lieutenant Roberts and his mother returned to the United States, having completed the course. Since our small household was breaking up, I decided to try an experiment and arranged with one of Professor Naganuma's group to go with me into the country where I would speak and hear only Japanese, and where I could study with him all day if I wanted to. I told him that he could select a place, and he picked Odawara, a village on the coast two hours south of Tokyo. The Naval Attache gave me permission to go, said that as long as I gave my address, I could live where I liked.

Odawara, being on the coast, is several degrees warmer than Tokyo and is noted for sunny days in winter, and is sheltered from northerly winds. I rented a small but pleasant Japanese-style house with a beautiful garden, and hired a cook and began to study in earnest.

About this time our Hydrographic Office learned that the Japanese Coast Pilot had been completely revised, and they asked Commander Courts, the Naval Attache, to arrange to have it translated into English.

Q: Will you define for the lay reader, what is the Japanese Coast Pilot?

Smith-Hutton: The Pilot is a detailed description of the entire coast, giving all the lights and buoys, a description of the harbors, the piers, and it really is the sailing directions enabling ships' captains and masters to navigate along the coast and enter the ports in safety, if they have charts that are corrected up to date.

Q: So this would be a very valuable navigational aid for a U.S. mariner?

Smith-Hutton: Of course our old Coast Pilot was based upon previous Japanese editions, but this was a corrected edition, so they wanted to bring our navigational information up to date.

And so, when they said that they would like to have it translated into English, they also said that they would be willing to pay for some of the translation. But the Naval Attache couldn't find any competent persons to do it, for the comparatively small sum that had been appropriated, and he said his own office couldn't do it without neglecting all other office translations for several months.

So he called me in and asked me what I thought. I was very reluctant to say yes because I knew that it would take a long time, but finally I did agree. Then, in a few days, my instructor and I worked out a system whereby he read the book sentence by sentence, and soon I was writing as fast as I could in English, and we finished the pilot in about six months, working about three hours a day, seven days a week. Everybody seemed pleased, but I was certainly glad to have it finished!

It might be of interest, when I mention that Japanese can be very difficult, especially when it comes to place names such as the proper reading of the name of a cape or headland or hill or small island. The Japanese Navy told me that if I ever came across anything that I wasn't sure of, they'd be glad to help, because, of course, the Japanese Navy Department knew I was working on the Pilot. So every few weeks, I would send to the Navy a list of places and request verification of the readings of the characters. Frequently they would tell me that they weren't sure what the reading was, but they would check with the local mayor or chief of police and let me know later.

Q: Captain, I think you should have received the Legion of Merit for that translating work.

Getting back to Odawara, did you ever meet any of the leading citizens of the hamlet?

Smith-Hutton: Yes, indeed. It so happened that two famous elderly men lived not far from the small house I'd rented, and I found that out a month or so after I got there. There was a magnificent estate about a quarter of a mile away, with a beautiful garden and several houses, on a small hill overlooking the ocean and the beach, and on inquiring I learned that this estate belonged to Baron Masuda. He had been the head of the famous Mitsui Trading Company which is still in business, as one of the greatest commercial enterprises in the world. It has immense shipping, banking and manufacturing interests.

Also interestingly enough, Masuda, who was in his eighties, had gone to the United States as a boy, with the first official Japanese mission to visit our country.

Q: This was termed the first embassy to the United States, which took place, I believe, before the Civil War, and they came to the Washington Navy Yard in the District of Columbia. Are you referring to that?

Smith-Hutton: That is the one, the one shortly after Commodore Perry's visit. It was in 1854 or '55.

Q: And I think Commander Franklin Buchanan is very prominent in the photograph taken of the group at the Navy. Later he was an Admiral in the Confederate Navy.

Smith-Hutton: Yes, I'm sure of that. Well, Masuda was a young boy at the time of the mission.

I called and left cards at his home, and a few days later, I was invited to tea, and I was certainly most cordially received. To my surprise, I was introduced to Admiral Baron Soto Kichi Uryu, and his wife. They lived in one of the other houses on the estate, being related to the Masuda family. The Admiral was a graduate of our Naval Academy, class of 1881, and his wife was a graduate of Vassar of the same year. Admiral Uryu was famous in the Japanese Navy, in fact in all Japan, as a hero of the war with Russia, having been one of Admiral Togo's colleagues and friends. He had commanded the Fourth Division of the Combined Fleet which escorted troops landing in Chemulpo in Korea, and he had sunk three Russian ships the very first day of the war. He and his wife and Baron Masuda had very pleasant memories of their days in America and loved to talk about them, and during my stay of Okawara I visited them frequantly and I always enjoyed seeing them. I corresponded with them occasionally until they died in the middle thirties.

Q: Captain, he obviously was disposed in friendly fashion to the United States. Was he alone in the Japanese Navy in this sense?

Smith-Hutton: No, indeed. Of course Admiral Uryu had been in the United States and he had been well received and he liked the United States, but there were many naval officers in exactly that situation, including Admiral Nomura, Admiral Yamamoto, later who commanded the combined fleet, Admiral Yonai, who was the Navy Minister. There were a great many Japanese naval officers who felt that the United States was the country of all the foreign countries with whom Japan should be friends. They were sincere in this opinion.

Q: Captain, that's most interesting, to hear that. You recall that in 1924 the U.S. Congress passed the Japanese Exclusion Act, and this generated much resentment, I'm sure, in Japan. Did you encounter some sign of that?

Smith-Hutton: Yes, indeed. The Japanese people were always indignant whenever this subject came up, and considered that the United States had insulted Japan by excluding Japanese from the United States, making it impossible for Japanese to become U.S. citizens. It was because of California insisting that the law was passed and all the Japanese resented it. We could have handled it better and still had the same result since it harmed relations between Japan and America.

Unfortunately, the law had little practical effect, since even if Japan had been put on the same quota as other nations, which could have been done, only about 170 Japanese would have been admitted each year. To cause international ill feeling of that kind just to prevent 170 Japanese from entering the United States seems ill advised. It's also possible that this discrimination made the Japanese Navy more determined than ever not to accept an inferior ratio as concerned their Navy. The exclusion act did much harm and no good.

Interview with Captain Smith-Hutton

By: Captain Paul Ryan, USN (Ret.)

Q: Captain, in your stay in Japan as a language student, did you ever have a chance to visit some of their naval installations?

Captain Smith-Hutton: Yes, indeed. The Naval Attache or his assistant visited most of the Japanese naval bases, the air stations and the aircraft factories once a year. This was done under an understanding of reciprocity and in return for permitting us to visit their installations, the Japanese in Washington were allowed to visit ours.

There were a few exceptions. For example, we didn't allow the Japanese to see the Naval Gun Factory or factories where torpedo parts were made; Dahlgren and other stations where we tested bomb sights were also not open for inspection. In this connection, it's ironic that Japanese naval torpedoes were much superior to ours, at least at the outbreak of the war, and their optical equipment was superb.

When I was a language officer, there was an Assistant Naval Attache who was a Naval aviator, so Commander Courts, the Naval Attache, arranged with Commander-in-Chief, Asiatic Fleet to send an aviator for a period of two months to assist in inspecting Japanese naval air stations. The first officer so detailed was Lieutenant J. J. Ballantine, class of '19 at the Naval Academy, who was an unusually well-qualified officer, and he did all the actual inspecting. However, he spoke no Japanese, so a language officer was detailed to accompany him, and I was detailed.

The two of us inspected all the Japanese naval air stations and sent in detailed reports on shore-based naval air. We wouldn't allow the Japanese to visit our carriers or observe operations at sea, so we were not permitted to see theirs. Lieutenant Ballantine, who commanded the carrier Bunker Hill during World War II and then commander carrier task groups and later commanded the Sixth Fleet, was well liked by the Japanese naval aviators. He considered them to be good pilots and so reported.

Later it became the practice to send an aviator as Assistant Naval Attache and Lieutenant Commander Ralph Ofstie, a classmate of Ballantine's, was the first. He went to Japan in '35. He was followed by Lieutenant Commander Bridget (1921) but when I was ordered as Naval Attache in '39, Lieutenant Commander Bridget, who was senior to me, was relieved by Lieutenant Stephen Jurika, of the class of '33. He was my assistant until 1941, when Lieutenant Phares, in the class of 1932 came. Phares was in Tokyo only about six months, since just before war broke out. I asked that he be detached for duty with the Asiatic fleet.

Q: Captain, as a former Naval Attache, I know that ONI used to prepare specific requests for intelligence, but I'm sure from the 1920s on it was so small that instead of specific requests, they sent more or less general instructions regarding reports. In connection with your visits to the naval air stations with Lieutenant Ballantine, is this the way you operated, and what were your impressions? What information did you gather?

Smith-Hutton: Each time we visited an air station, we studied previous reports to see that they were as complete as possible. Then when we were there, we compared what we saw with the data in the previous report, so that we could bring the data up to date.

In general, our impression of Japanese naval aviation was that they were several years behind us because of lack of money, but we found a high morale and a great determination to improve. The spirit of the officers and men in aviation was good.

The training was done at Kasumigaura, a fine station about 40 miles north of Tokyo near a large lake where there was ample room for a landing field. There were several hangars for both land and sea planes. They used the lake for seaplane operations.

There were perhaps 15 instructors and each year 50 to 70 officers, warrant officers and enlisted pilots were trained.

Lieutenant Ballantine considered that the training, which followed patterns used in our Navy or the British Navy, was quite adequate. The original courses of instruction had been prepared shortly after World War I by a group of British officers from the Fleet Air Command who had been hired by the Japanese to organize their naval air force training command.

The weather in that area was good and there was plenty of room. There was no reason why the standards of training couldn't equal those of Pensacola. I recall that some of the instructors at Kasumigaura had visited Pensacola and talked to Lieutenant Ballantine about our training.

There was great enthusiasm about this time in the Japanese Navy for aviation. This may have been due to the fact that Rear

Admiral Yamamoto, who had been Japanese Naval Attache in Washington, had returned to Tokyo in 1925. He was a very intelligent and dynamic officer, and he was convinced, and had in turn convinced the Japanese high command, that the future of forces at sea depended on developing carrier aircraft and in strengthening the naval air force.

After his return in '25, he went to command the carrier Akagi and then was promoted to Rear Admiral. He was given a special assignment in the Bureau of Aeronautics, under which he had charge of aviation training.

Commander Courts had met Yamamoto and liked him, and several times invited him to receptions at his home. Yamamoto was a very outgoing officer. He liked to play cards and was a skillful card player. I remember listening to him enthuse about the future of naval aviation, not only in Japan but in all the navies of the world. Of course, he became Commander-in-Chief of the Fleet and actually planned the attack on Pearl Harbor.

Q: Captain, did you and Lieutenant Ballantine obtain written material from the Japanese naval aviators such as training courses, curricula, things like that?

Smith-Hutton: No, we didn't. It was our understanding that these were classified materials in the Japanese service, in contrast to many of our training manuals which are unclassified. I think that the Japanese did obtain much unclassified material in Washington and perhaps from our Government Printing Office, which has no counterpart in Japan. The result was that while they talked to us quite frankly and freely and seemed to make no effort to hide information that we requested, we got no classified material, or written material, I should say, in regard to training.

Q: Captain, judging from what you say, then, it would be highly unlikely that you or Lieutenant Ballantine would be invited to visit a Japanese carrier.

Smith-Hutton: No, we were never invited, and by the same token, we were quite careful not to invite the Japanese to visit an American carrier because we felt, rightly or wrongly, that they were behind us by several years, and that they had much more to learn by looking at one of our carriers than we had to learn by looking at one of theirs.

Q: Well, Captain, in hindsight, would you have any comment to make about the superiority, real or supposed, of U.S. carriers over Japanese carriers about 1941?

Smith-Hutton: I think that the Japanese carriers, particularly with their experienced personnel, were as efficient as ours, and also their personnel were good.

In that connection, I recall that during the Shanghai incident in 1937, when the Japanese were attacking the Shanghai area, they established an airfield just to the south of the city not far from the Shanghai Power Company. This was a 50 million dollar American enterprise and we had a landing force there to protect it during the fighting.

I arranged to have Lieutenant J. P. Walker, a Naval aviator (USNA, 1927) sent to command that landing force. For a period of approximately three weeks, he observed the operations of the airfield which was used entirely by carrier planes. Walker reported that if we had sent an air group ashore to establish a field as the Japanese did and operated it in the fact of enemy attacks as well as they did, our officers would have considered that they had done a fine job. From that I was convinced that Japanese naval aviation was an efficient service.

Q: Captain, that's most interesting, your observations on naval aviation. I find that while you were very conscious of the state of superiority of Japanese naval aviation, that Captain William Puleston and Fletcher Pratt, who both wrote books on the coming war in the Pacific which came out about 1940, presented a different view. This view was built on many myths, that the Japanese were not good aviators, that they were near-sighted, that they copied U.S. engines such as the Pratt and Whitney and even British flying boats. In the light of all this, it appears that your reports to ONI did not reach the fleet, because in the fleet wardrooms there was again a feeling that the Japanese were not as good as we were in naval aviation. Do you agree with that?

Smith-Hutton: Yes. It is most unfortunate that the reports sent back to our Navy Department by experienced observers such as Lieutenant Ballantine and Lieutenant Walker didn't receive wider circulation, and that the officers of our Navy didn't know about the opinions of our experts.

In that connection, there was the case of the Japanese aircraft called the Zero which was developed about that time. It turned out that the Zero, which was in use in China before World War II by the Japanese, had been in combat with the Flying Tigers, the group of American aviators flying American aircraft led by the famous General Chennault. General Chennault had had some rather sad experiences with the Zeros, as we all did for a while. But he and his pilots worked out tactics by which they could at least be on even terms with the Zero. This was because our aircraft were basically more **steady** and could stand considerably more punishment than the Zero.

Chennault sent detailed reports back to the Army Air Corps Headquarters as to what American aviators must do in order to overcome the superior climbing ability and superior speed of the Zero under certain conditions. However, it wasn't until the war had been going on for a year that these reports were found in the War Department files.

It's a great pity that we sometimes get fixed opinions and are unwilling to change them.

Q: Thank you very much, Captain. A very fine session.

Interview with Captain Smith-Hutton

Date: January 24, 1974

By: Captain Paul Ryan, USN (Ret.)

Q: Captain, in the 1920's Japan was stepping up its activities in Manchuria. At the same time, the Prime Minister, then General Baron Tanaka, presented a memorial to the Emperor regarding Japanese policy. It was a somewhat fiery document. Do you recall how your embassy colleagues and yourself viewed the Manchurian situation and the Tanaka memorial in those times?

Captain Smith-Hutton: Shortly after General Tanaka presented this document, or is reported to have presented the document to the Emperor, it was published in China. It was denounced, of course, by the Japanese and was said to be false. Even to this day, I've never seen any reliable or official evaluation of the document that would prove that it was written by a high Japanese official. But in looking back, Japanese policies during the 1930's show that, whether the document was true or false, Japan followed the recommendations contained in the memorial and among them, of course, was the seizure of Manchuria by the Army.

I've already mentioned that the Army had decided that Japan couldn't continue as a great power unless she did control Manchuria, and so she viewed with alarm the increased influence of the Central Chinese government in Manchuria. The influence of General Chiang Kai-chek had spread gradually northward and the Japanese made no attempt to hide their fear that the Manchurian warlord,

General Chang Tso Lin, might declare that he would follow the instructions of the Central Chinese government.

If that happened, Japanese control of the entire area might be very much weakened, because Chiang Kia-chek was anti-Japanese, and, as a matter of fact, anti-Japanese feeling was growing throughout China.

In addition, Chinese from outside Manchuria, south of the Great Wall, were being attracted in great numbers by the availability of land and work, and the relative prosperity in Manchuria brought by the Japanese presence.

Also, the Japanese armies hoped to induce Japanese citizens to leave their very crowded homeland and migrate to Manchuria.

All of these considerations influenced the thinking of the Japanese Army, and it was evident that the high command was trying to decide on the best policy in regard to Manchura.

Q: Captain, the Tanaka Memorial was highly nationalistic, and at the same time, there existed what we know as the Black Dragon Society. Do you recall any of its activities and what your reactions were?

Smith-Hutton: The Black Dragon Society was the name of one of perhaps a dozen patriotic societies which flourished in Japan especially during periods of political excitement. It was certainly the best known abroad, perhaps because of the sinister romantic name. The origin of that name is interesting. When the society was founded, about 1901, it was a nationalistic society that favored war with Russia. They decided to advocate war, their aim being to get the Japanese Army and people ready to drive the Russians out of Manchuria, and to advance to the Amur River, which is the boundary between Siberia and Manchuria. So they named their society the Amur Society. The Amur River is the name used by the Manchus, and the world in general, to denote the river, but the Chinese don't use it. They call the river Hei Lung Chiang, and those three characters mean the Black Dragon River.

Since the Japanese use the same characters as the Chinese, this proper name, when written in Japanese, becomes the Black Dragon Society. It has nothing to do with romance nor is it sinister. It's just the Amur Society. It's all very simple.

Many of these patriotic ultra-nationalist societies had their real origins in the discontent which remained after the restoration of 1868, when about two million samurai lost their privileges and much of their influence. In reality most of them were mere gangs of excitable men, working for what they thought was the good of the country. Most of them were loosely formed, had no real organization, and in quiet times they had a tendency to fade away to nothing. They reappeared during times of unrest when they could raise money and even organize formally. That was true of the Black Dragon Society.

Mitsu Toyama was connected with the Black Dragon Society, and with many other societies, but actually his principal disciple was Uchida. He was probably more influential than Toyama was. Both were gang bosses, who used blackmail and fraud and threats of assassination to influence political figures. Uchida was more of a politician and he made speeches and wrote articles, even a couple of books. He organized the publicity campaigns.

However, it's recorded that at a society meeting in 1906 there were only six members present at one of the meetings of the Black Dragon Society.

Uchida once spent 18 months in jail for threatening the life of Prime Minister Kato, but he continued to write books and articles and to make speeches.

One of the main branches of this Black Dragon Society was the Great Japan Production Society, which was also led by Uchida. He called it a labor party based on Japanism, which advocated reaction at home and aggression abroad. Actually, the more militant army and navy officers advocated much the same program, so there was probably a connection, but which influenced the other the most is very difficult to say.

Another of these patriotic societies was the Jimmukai. Jimmu was the first human emperor (his ancestors were gods), according to the ancient legends and this society advocated that Japan gain control of all Asia. It was perhaps the strongest patriotic society, and many of the younger Army officers on active duty were connected with it from the outset.

Another influential patriotic society was the National Foundation Society, the Koku Honsha, which was a society with important political figures such as Baron Hiranuma as a director. The main purpose of that society was to educate young students along proper political lines, and was probably the most respectable of all the so-called patriotic societies. Another was called the Great Japan National Spirit Society, that is, the Dai Nippon Koku Suikai. It included Toyama and many other racketeers and leaders. They engaged in the usual gang practices.

In the final analysis, many of the Japanese connected with these societies were genuine patriots who were loyal and good citizens but many were misguided young men and women.

Q: Thank you very much for that very complete description, Captain. I have a question regarding the influence as you saw it, of the secret societies upon the Japanese Navy. Did any naval officers or did the Embassy ever comment upon such influence?

Smith-Hutton: I remember once hearing Admiral Nomura say that he felt that the newspapers treated the activities of these societies in a sensational way, and in many instances, the activities didn't justify this treatment. He felt that he himself had been somewhat radical, or would have been classed as a radical as a young officer, and that many of the young officers who were considered radicals would certainly outgrow these tendencies as they became older. This is perhaps so, but on the other hand, most of the Embassy staff who were close to the Japanese felt that they had a sinister and bad influence on the country as a whole because of the criminal activities of some of the leaders, especially when they used blackmail and fraud, as they frequently did. This certainly had a corruptive influence on youth and on Japanese society in general. We looked on these patriotic societies as gangs of thugs.

Q: Captain, in the social life of Tokyo there were various clubs, the American Club, the British Club, probably some Japanese clubs. Was there any racial aspect to membership in these clubs?

Smith-Hutton: In Tokyo, there was none whatever. Of course, in the American Club most of the members were Americans and in the British Club, most of them were British, but that was because they were places where men, with similar ideas, could get together and have meals or could have parties. However, if an American or a Britisher wanted to bring Japanese guests to the clubs, there was no objection. Perhaps the best club in Tokyo was the Tokyo Club which was established shortly after the restoration. The officers of the Tokyo Club were largely Japanese, although a few distinguished diplomats were members of the board of directors and considered themselves honored to be members of the club. I know our ambassador used to go frequently to the Tokyo Club and meet his Japanese friends there for talks. There was no social problem at all, as far as the clubs in Japan were concerned.

It's true that we had comparatively few Japanese at the American Club, but if a member invited Japanese guests, there was no objection.

Q: That's very interesting, Captain. Could you contrast the situation that existed in Japan regarding clubs with that that existed in China?

Smith-Hutton: In China it was quite another matter. The Chinese were not allowed in the foreign clubs in Shanghai or in Peking or other Chinese cities. There were clubs for Europeans or Americans, and some even had signs on the doors saying that no Chinese guests were allowed in the clubs. After World War I, the Chinese began to resent these restrictions but that was the way the clubs were organized and they remained that way throughout the time I was in China.

Q: Thank you, Captain. It still existed in Hong Kong, I recall, as late as the 1950's.

I don't want to belabor the discrimination aspect of our conversation, but could you tell us what you considered to be the feeling of the Japanese and Chinese toward Westerners?

Smith-Hutton: It seems to me that both the Chinese and the Japanese had a general superiority complex with regard to Europeans and Americans, although to a somewhat different degree. The Chinese considered China to be the center of the universe. Outside this center were barbaric countries inhabited by outer barbarians. In the Chinese language, China is the Central Flowery Kingdom. However, the Chinese did fear peoples who came to China in ships, and had much less dislike and fear for peoples who came overland to China. Perhaps this is because the first visitors to come were pirates. They came by ship, and they could also leave by ship and thus leave China easily. The Chinese have felt for centuries that they could deal better with the Russians who came overland to China than they could with the British, the Americans and the Japanese who came by ship.

The Japanese especially consider that white men and women have a disagreeable body odor. They say that we smell like butter. The super-patriots used any white race supremacy idea to cause ill feeling and to make the Japanese people dislike us. Throughout their history the Japanese have felt superior to others, and have stood ready to do their best to prove it. Anti-Japanese immigration laws were effectively used by the patriotic societies to foster anti-American feeling, as has already been mentioned.

Q: Captain, I notice that you're not a smoking man, and I wonder if in your days in Japan during the Twenties, did you smoke? How did you find the native tobaccos?

Smith-Hutton: Yes, I smoked. The tobaccos weren't good but there are several different brands. The Japanese made a tobacco called Sakura, that is, "Cherry Blossom", and, of course, there were various British type tobaccos made by the British-American Tobacco Company in China.

I remember one brand of cigarettes that was rather popular with the Japanese Navy, in any event, and it was called the Five Five Five Cigarette. They used to consider this to be one of the best brands. They smoked it because they were against the 5-5-3 naval ratio. They said navies should be like this cigarette, 5-5-5.

Q: Captain, I see the Japanese Navy had a wry sense of humor. Was this uniformly true or only on rare occasions?

Smith-Hutton: Only on rare occasions. Their sense of humor is always difficult for us to understand, and things that amuse the Japanese don't necessarily amuse us.

Q: Captain, with regard to the situation in Manchuria, there were many controversial things going on there. Was it possible for you to discuss with your Japanese naval friends any of these matters, or were they not disposed to do so?

Smith-Hutton: The older officers were quite free in talking about what was happening in China, and expressed their ideas of what Japan and China and the United States should do, but I found the junior officers, the officers of my age, for instance, were reluctant to talk about it. I recall that they said frankly that they didn't know much about China and Manchuria and they weren't anxious to talk because it might give a wrong impression. They weren't anti-Army and they didn't want to have me feel that they were against the Japanese Army, so they would prefer not to discuss the situation. It was a political, rather than technical and professional situation, and they felt that political discussions were not proper between military men especially with foreign officers.

We sometimes felt, too, that they were conscious of the fact that there might be security problems. It depends on where the discussions took place, but, for example, sections of the Imperial Hotel were thought to have microphones. Especially the rooms where senior diplomats and senior foreign officials might stay, and perhaps certain sections of the lobby and dining rooms. Of course, it was quite different in France where almost all of the hotel rooms in the Hotel Crillon, for instance, had microphones, and it was frequently joked about in Paris. That wasn't so in Japan but the discussions were kept to a minimum by the Japanese themselves.

Q: Captain, it's been said that U.S. foreign policy in the Far East in the 1920's and '30's was influenced heavily by U.S. "friends of China", that is, missionaries and oil people and shipping firms, and even friends in the Department of State. These people might have been motivated by U.S. self-interest, or by love of China, or by a delight to see Japan placed in the position of the devil. On the other hand, Japan had no such resource; there were no "friends of Japan" in the USA. As you look back in hindsight, would you agree with this thought?

Smith-Hutton: It is certainly true that our State Department in the Twenties and Thirties tended to favor the Chinese cause as opposed to the Japanese, and part of this sympathy came from the fact that Dr. Hornbeck, who was the most influential figure in Far Eastern affairs, was sympathetic to China, had lived in China, and his principal assistants were pro-Chinese. There were no officers who could be called "old Japan hands" that I recall.

But it must be said that the Japanese were their own worst enemies, in that all through this period Japanese actions in China were aggressive and open to criticism. The 21 Demands, the capture of Tsingtao, their efforts to harm the interests of all European countries, so Japan was on the defensive, and had been forced to give up many of their plans at the Washington Conference, however, it was agreed that the powers would not interfere in disputes between China and Japan, and therefore the Japanese position had a legal basis. Japan's first aim was to try to break the restrictions of the Washington Naval Treaty including the 5-5-3 ratio, and, of course, the only possible reason for that was to secure her position in case of an attack in the Western Pacific. Then Japan tried to hold on to Eastern Siberia and was very reluctant to evacuate this area. Of course, Japan could have made a better case for herself in China, because the Chinese were really difficult to do business with, but the Japanese aren't very skillful at presenting legal cases.

So even friends of Japan in America had difficulty in arguing their case, because the Japanese acted aggressively and in a most un-Christian manner. Also, American business interests in China suffered from Japanese actions. There was a feeling in America that there were immense trade possibilities with China and these were being lost to Japan.

Curiously enough, during most of this period, our trade with Japan was actually much larger than our trade with China, but even when this was pointed out to Americans, it seemed to make little impression. Americans did have a romantic sympathy for China and hated to see her attacked and abused by her smaller but more powerful neighbor. And during World War I, German propaganda used Japan as a possible enemy on our West Coast.

Of course, anti-Japanese feeling in the United States was also strengthened by the dislike of Californians for the Japanese farmers and the fact that they might be spies and agents.

Finally, I think State Department officials have legal training, and it was very easy to indict Japan as a breaker of the treaties and agreements. However, I do believe the State Department merely reflected American public opinion in being pro-Chinese.

Q: Captain, referring to the Japanese Navy of pre-World War II, I understand and it was my observation as a young officer that the Japanese naval enlisted men and officers were a higher type than the Japanese Army. Can you explain that?

Smith-Hutton: There were approximately 70,000 enlisted men and 7000 officers on active duty in the Japanese Navy, and incidentally, there were about 35,000 reserves. About 75 percent of the enlisted men were volunteers, and about 25 percent were conscripts. The naval officers were always very proud to be able to say that they could keep up to full strength with volunteers only, and that they could select these volunteers carefully, as intelligent good physical specimens. However, since there were very few volunteers from the provinces farthest from the sea, and since the Navy wanted to have reserve units everywhere, they fixed the conscript numbers at about 25 percent of the total strength. Almost all of the conscripts came from the mountainous areas.

They had no problems there either, since all young men were liable for military service and when inducting young men into the services, the Navy requirements were so small, that they were given their choice. The Army recruiters seemed to make no objection.

The result was that the Navy really was a special service, and they also could get excellent men for the air arm of the Japanese Navy. The Japanese Naval Academy is at Etajima near Kure. Young men were examined each year and about 150 between the ages of 16 and 19 entered for a three year course. Again the entrance examinations were difficult. There were always many more candidates than they could possibly use, so that the selection process was very severe.

It is interesting to recall that the Engineering Academy was at Naizuru on the coast of the Sea of Japan, with a course very similar to the course at Etajima. My feeling was that these Academies were not very different from our own, but our Bureau of Navigation seemed reluctant to let the Japanese Naval Attache visit Annapolis, although I can't understand why. Since it wasn't of great importance, we never asked to visit, and therefore, I have never seen the Japanese Naval Academy at Etajima. On looking back, I'm sorry that I never did get that chance because I understand Etajima was a very interesting place.

Q: Captain, you spent three years in Japan, from 1926 to 1929, we're nearing the end of that three year period in this account. To put the matter in historical perspective, this is the period when Japan had moved strongly into Manchuria. She'd increased her defense problems and she would probably help to isolate herself from the world community. At the same time, the London Naval Conference was being planned, and she knew that she would have to negotiate again with the great powers on her naval strength. In Japan at this time, I understand that the Japanese Navy was split into two factions. One was for a strong fleet and the other one was more moderate in tone and was willing to consider treaty limitations. Do you want to comment on that?

Smith-Hutton: It was, of course, true that there were great differences of opinion, because the more aggressive officers, which were later called the "fleet faction" were very outspoken, and they had friends and supporters both in the Japanese Diet and in the press. Their arguments, which were for a large and greatly expanded naval building program, were aired in papers such as the important Tokyo daily, the Nichi Nichi. One of the outspoken advocates of a large fleet was Admiral Kanji Kato, who had been the chief of the Naval General Staff. This group presented their arguments forcefully, and they were eloquent. They attacked England and the United States, saying these nations were attempting to keep the Japanese from their proper historical place in history and in Asia. They accused the United States and Great Britain of having aggressive intentions in East Asia.

The weakness of their arguments was that Japan had limited resources, and particularly in 1929, the amount of money Japan could spend for the Navy was considerably less than it had been, say, in 1920 and '21, when she was a very wealthy country, as a result of the prosperity of World War I.

The opponents of the so-called "fleet faction", such as Admiral Takarabi, who was the Navy minister at that time, replied that it was all very well to emphasize naval strength and if Japan were in danger of attack, they were correct. However, since there was no immediate threat, there were other important places to use

Japan's limited funds, so they were in favor of taking a more moderate approach to building programs. The problems were debated in the Diet and in the press, so that it was comparatively easy to follow them. The difficulty that we in the Embassy had was to know how the Japanese people felt about the Navy. Of course, as we all know now, the fleet faction took matters into their own hands later, with the result that several of the prime ministers and other senior officials were assassinated. That, of course, was a danger that any Japanese official ran in going against the programs of the nationalistic younger officers.

It is a pity that events took this turn, but that is the Japanese way of doing things, and curiously enough, although the assassinated officials were very able and had done remarkable things for their country, it was the young hot heads who shot them who had the shrines dedicated to them.

Q: Thank you very much, Captain. This concludes the session on 24 January 1974.

Interview with Captain Smith-Hutton

Date: 31 January 1974

By: Captain Paul Ryan, USN (Ret.)

Q: Captain, in our last session, you were in your last year in Japan as a language student. This would be 1928-29. Are there any significant events in that year you would care to touch on?

Captain Smith-Hutton: Perhaps I should mention that in May '28, I took my examinations for promotion to lieutenant. I went to the USS Pittsburgh, the fleet flagship, which was in Yokahama on a visit to Japan. When that was finished, I spent the summer, as usual, in Karuizawa.

At the end of the summer, the Naval Attache sent me to Nagasaki to pick up some officer-messenger mail which was on the USS Marblehead, which had come into Nagasaki from Shanghai. The only interesting thing about this that I recall was that having gone to Nagasaki in civilian clothes and boarded the Marblehead, I apparently attracted the attention of the Japanese security services. When I left the ship to go back to Tokyo, I saw that for the first three or four hundred miles of my trip on the train, I was shadowed by a security official. He kept his eye on me to see what I was doing. He watched me carefully. I thought I was clever to have noted that I was being followed.

While I was in Nagasaki I met Lieutenant Commander Ellis Zacharias for the first time. He was one of the older language officers, and had completed the course of study in 1923, which was before I arrived. He was on board the Marblehead as a passenger. He impressed me as being a very energetic officer, with many unusual ideas; perhaps slightly eccentric, but talkative and good company.

He said that he would be in Tokyo for a short period at the end of the month, since he was going to leave the ship in Kobe. Actually, he was ordered as Assistant Naval Attache in September '28 and was there until the end of November. It was during this period that the Naval Attache, Commander Courts, became quite ill, and was incapacited for duty. Lieutenant Commander Zacharias acted as the Naval Attache while he was there officially as assistant.

When I returned to the United States the following year, I learned that while he was on duty in the Far East, Lieutenant Commander Zacharias had made the first steps in establishing radio intercept stations in Guam, the Philippines and Shanghai, for the purpose of intercepting Japanese radio traffic. I didn't realize this at the time and he had made no mention of it either. The Marblehead also had special radio personnel on board, who had been qualified to intercept Japanese radio traffic. It was during a Japanese fleet problem that the traffic was intercepted.

Looking ahead the stations in Guam and the Philippines operated for a long time. The Philippine station was not closed until after World War II started, when the personnel were evacuated from Corregidor by submarine. Also, the one in Guam operated for several years, but the Shanghai station lasted only until the Secretary of State, who was then Mr. Henry Stimson, decided that the State Department would have no part in "reading the mail of friends of our country." So that station, which was in the Consulate General in Shanghai, was closed. Actually, a station was re-established in Shanghai when the 4th Marines came in 1932. A communications center including the intercept station was part of the headquarters command of the Marine regiment.

Q: Excuse me, Captain, does that mean that the Navy continued to intercept Japanese radio traffic?

Smith-Hutton: Yes. We had stations on our West Coast, and the station in Cavite later moved to Corregidor continued for years to intercept Japanese radio traffic. At first there was no attempt made to use the stations for operational purposes since there were not enough personnel to use intercepts on a daily basis. However, material was used for research and we did learn which were Foreign Office, Navy and Army codes. Gradually, we were able to read them.

My last year as a language officer passed very quickly. In August 1929, I took my final examination in Japanese, and a few days later was detached with orders to report to the Office of Intelligence. I was given two months delay in reporting, went back to South Dakota to see my family, arriving in Washington and reporting to ONI on 6 November 1929.

Q: At the end of your language training, were you required to take an examination, and did you receive a diploma?

Smith-Hutton: I was examined by the regular examining board. The senior member of the board was Mr. Dooman, the Counsellor of the embassy. Lieutenant McCollum, the Assistant Naval Attache, who had completed the language course in 1925, and the senior member of the Japanese instructing staff, Professor Naganuma. The report, which was made part of my official record by the Naval Attache, in a letter to the Director of Intelligence dated the 6th of September 1929, reads as follows:

"1) Upon completion of the prescribed course of study in Japanese covering a period of three years, Lieutenant Smith-Hutton was examined with the following results: oral, one, conversation, excellent; two, interpreting, very good; three, five minute after dinner speech, excellent. Written translation into English of a well written article on military matters and policy, excellent; two, letter in colloquial Japanese style, excellent. Lieutenant Smith-Hutton has during his three years study perfected himself in all phases of the Japanese language to a remarkable degree. His general knowledge and ability in all branches of the language impressed the examining board as being far above the average. The attainment of this high degree of proficiency in the language and in things Japanese in a period of three years reflects the highest credit on Lieutenant Smith-Hutton and he is worthy of the highest commendation for the very exceptional manner in which he has carried out the duties assigned him. Signed J. V. Ogan, Naval Attache."

Q: Well, that is a very glowing commendation and one I'm sure you merited.

Captain, when you requested duty as a language student, this practically guaranteed that your future career would be devoted in large part to intelligence work. Did you understand this when you returned to the States and when you were ordered to

ONI?

Smith-Hutton: Yes, I realized that. I also realized that few of the language officers had had duty in Washington. So, one of the reasons I was ordered to ONI was for familiarization and training, as well as to have me contribute anything that I had learned to the operations of ONI. It was not supposed to be a regular tour of duty, however, and was for approximately six months. ONI was a very small section of the Navy department at that time, with perhaps 15 officers in all. Lieutenant Commander Zacharias and one Marine officer were in the Far Eastern section. There was one officer in the British desk, one officer had the European desk, and one officer had the Latin American desk. There were three or four officers in domestic intelligence, that is, in security, and they had very good relations with the district intelligence officers and with the Federal Bureau of Investigation. It is possible that the domestic intelligence security section was the most efficient of all.

Q: Another term for security would be counter-intelligence, would it not?

Smith-Hutton: Yes, counter-intelligence is exactly what it was.
Captain A. W. Johnson was the Director of Intelligence when I reported and he was swamped with work. He attended long conferences in the State and War Departments, and there was considerable work in connection with the preparation for the London

Naval Conference which was to open in 1930. He talked to me at considerable length about the Japanese attitude toward the coming conference and about the Japanese political situation.

In addition to the London Conference, which of course, was uppermost in his mind, he felt it was very significant, that the Japanese had in 1928, stopped the northward movement of General Chiang Kai-chek's troops at Tsiwan in Shantung. Shortly thereafter, they had blown up the train on which the warlord of Manchuria, that is, Marshal Chang Tso-Lin, was killed.

He asked many questions about that and was correct in placing great significance on what the Japanese Army might do in connection with North China and Manchuria.

I worked for Captain Johnson for about three weeks, and found that he was very pleasant to work for. Again I got the impression that the prestige of ONI was not high in the Department. It's possible this was because some of the officers who sought assignments to duty in Europe were more interested in social life in foreign capitals than in intelligence, but the officers in ONI had much work to do, and were very busy.

I also noted that there was a tendency on the part of the War Plans Section to insist that the Office of Naval Intelligence was just a collection office, and that War Plans had the evaluation function. This seemed absurd to me, but I was a very young officer at that time. The Far Eastern section had a very good filing system and information that was needed was quickly available but they did not have enough personnel to prepare special reports.

Q: Captain, you and I know today that Naval Attaches depend upon specific requests for information (SRI's) which are sent to them by ONI and then they develop their collection programs abroad. But as I understand you, there was no formal program for developing SRI's within ONI.

Smith-Hutton: That is correct. There weren't enough personnel to do that, so the questions that were asked of the Attache were invariably questions that came from other sections in the Department, or perhaps from the State Department, asking the Office of Naval Intelligence to supply information to them.

Q: Captain, could you describe any of the counter-intelligence operations that took place while you were there?

Smith-Hutton: ONI had collected masses of material which came from the wastepaper baskets of various Japanese officers throughout the country, including the consulates, the naval inspector's office in New York, and other places where the Japanese were careless enough to not burn their papers. Unfortunately, these were mostly handwritten letters, and difficult to read.

I could read them and most of them were personal letters of little intelligence value. We did get some information.

I do remember that the offices of the Japanese Naval Inspector in New York were entered and the codes were photographed. I believe that Lieutenant Commander Zacharias and Lieutenant Commander Foster, who was then on duty in New York, did this.

Q: Captain, after World War I, I understand that the Navy instituted a crytography unit within the Office of Chief of Naval Operations. Could you tell us something about that?

Smith-Hutton: A section in the Office of Naval Communications, called Op-20G, was started about the time that the State Department and the War Department started an office in New York under Mr. Herbert Yardley. The Navy, I believe, was invited to take part in this operation, but since Yardley was concentrating on diplomatic codes, with perhaps some Japanese Army codes, the Navy felt they should concentrate on naval codes. So they declined to join the New York group and there was a certain amount of ill feeling. But by the end of the 1920's, the Navy was really the only department that was active because Mr. Stimson, the Secretary of State, had directed the War and State efforts be stopped. He also wanted the Navy to stop, but the Navy effort was only research. There was a very small group in two rooms in the Department. When I was ordered to ONI, I was informed that I was to spend some time in Op-20G.

The head of the office was Lieutenant Commander Laurence Safford, who was helped by Lieutenant Commander Struble, Lieutenant Thomas Lewis and Lieutenant Gardner. It was a research office, specializing in codes. They had examples of Army and foreign office codes. The Foreign Office traffic was obtained from Western Union Telegraph Company, which gave copies of messages to ONI.

In 1929, it was said that Mr. Yardley, who later wrote the book "The Black Chamber", had a very low opinion of Navy cryptographers. All the specialists in Op-20G were pleased that the Navy had this reputation, because there was no need to boast of their accomplishments.

Q: Captain, perhaps you can tell me why the Japanese language officers were so necessary to this Op-20G?

Smith-Hutton: The reason is that the cryptographers never know what they are producing. The messages they decode were originally written in Japanese, then put in code. They are trying to decode the message and rewrite it in Japanese again, so only a person who knows the language can say that the decoding was correct. Therefore, the cryptographers and the language officers have to work closely together, to see that the decoding is accurate and the final product really Japanese.

It so happened that the Navy sent one officer, who was one of our best cryptographers, to Japan to study language. He continued with cryptographic work throughout World War II.

Q: What was his name, Captain?

Smith-Hutton: That was Lieutenant Commander Joseph Rochefort, who was in charge of Radio Intelligence in Pearl Harbor. He worked very closely with Lieutenant Commander Layton, who was Admiral Nimitz's intelligence officer during most of World War II. He came into the Navy as a reserve officer, he specialized in cryptography and became an accomplished language officer.

Q: Thank you, Captain. I think we'll discuss Lieutenant Commander Rochefort's career possibly later in your narrative. You recall about this time the London Naval Conference was being scheduled. In ONI, did you people pay any attention to that event?

Smith-Hutton: The Japanese delegation to the London Conference passed through Washington, and while they were there, they were received at the White House by the President. Lieutenant Commander Zacharias and I were ordered to be in full dress uniform and to go to the White House, so we could stand by in case we were needed to act as escorts or interpreters. We had dinner at the Army-Navy Club and were taken to the White House in White House automobiles. But when we got there, there was apparently no need for us. We waited in the reception hall, but didn't see any of the Japanese delegation.

I recall now that Lieutenant Commander Zacharias was annoyed because ONI wasn't called upon to furnish Far Eastern specialists for the conference. He said that it was because Colonel Stimson, who was Secretary of State and head of our delegation, was not fond of Naval officers. Whether that was so, I can't say, but Mr. Stimson did take Colonel Burnett, who had been Military Attache in Tokyo, as his principal advisor to the conference. Zacharias was quite annoyed at this.

Q: It certainly was short sighted of the White House group not to have used two Japanese interpreters to talk to the Japanese delegation. Who knows what information you might have gleaned.

Smith-Hutton: That is very true. As a matter of fact, at London, the Japanese insisted on increasing their ratio of cruisers and destroyers, to about 10-8 instead of the 5-3 ratio, and they would not accept a limitation on submarines. However, the French and Italians were equally difficult although the London Treaty extended the Washington ratios for five years, the Japanese naval delegation decided that the ratio system would end in 1936, when the treaty ended.

Q: What did you do after your ONI tour, Captain?

Smith-Hutton: Early in April, although I was still attached to ONI, I asked to be sent to a naval air station to get what was then called "elimination flight training." So about the middle of April in 1930, I was ordered to report to the Naval Air Station, Hampton Roads. I left Washington and drove down to Hampton Roads. At that time, Captain E. J. King was in command of the air station, and I saw the captain very briefly when I reported.

I was there for about three weeks, and during this time I got in ten hours of dual instruction in seaplanes. It turned out that I couldn't pass the eye examination because of faulty depth perception. The instructors said that I was erratic in leveling off the plane above the water, and that this fault would result in a crash. I did learn a great deal about naval aviation, and had a little first hand experience that I might never have had otherwise.

I returned to the Office of Intelligence on about 9 May, and had another month in Op-20G before I was detached on 6 June 1930 to report to Newport News, where the Houston was being completed and was going to be commissioned.

Q: Captain, the Houston was one of the first of the new treaty cruisers, 10,000 tonners, eight-inch guns, coming into the U.S. Navy, the Pensacola and Salt Lake City being the predecessors of the Houston.

We had built no new cruisers since the end of World War I. In 1930, I think we actually had something like 19 cruisers in the whole Navy and these were light cruisers. Would you describe your first few months in the Houston?

Smith-Hutton: As you say, the Houston was a new type of ship in our Navy. She was a comfortable and beautiful ship. We went in commission on 17 June, with Captain J. B. Gay commanding. I was the communications officer, the signal officer, the radio officer, and the senior watch officer. We had many officers on board but I was the only one assigned to the Communication Department.

We left Newport News shortly after the 17th, and went to Long Island Sound, where we spent most of the summer, exercising in seamanship and ship handling and drilling the crews. Toward the end of the summer, we crossed the Atlantic and visited Southampton in England and LeHavre in France. On our return home in November, we went south to Houston, Texas to receive a silver service for the wardroom which was presented to the ship by the city of Houston. Houston was very proud of the cruiser. The recently completed canal between Galveston and Houston in theory made Houston a seaport, and while we were not the first large ship to go up that canal to Houston, we were the first large warship.

So when we arrived in Houston, we were given a very warm reception in real Texas style and they made a great deal of the officers and crew. And the guest of honor at the presentation was the Assistant Secretary of the Navy, Mr. Ernest Jahncke. He was there, and the ceremony was successfully completed. On our way from Houston back to New York for overhaul before the final acceptance trials, we learned that our captain, who had neglected to meet Mr. Jahncke at the airport when he arrived from Washington, was to be relieved. He was relieved two or three weeks later by Captain R. A. Dawes. It was Captain Dawes who took the ship to China.

The Houston was scheduled to become the flagship of the Asiatic Fleet so we were all looking forward to completing our overhaul, running full power runs and final acceptance trials, and getting under way for the Far East.

Q: Captain, in 1930 the Navy had something on the order of 80,000 enlisted men and 5500 line officers. The Navy was shorthanded. The country was in a Depression and the Navy was being cut back slowly. I see that you were communication officer, radio officer, senior watch officer and signal officer. Were you the only officer in your department?

Smith-Hutton: Yes, I was the only officer in the department, and I remember that I was discouraged when I tackled the job of correcting all of the registered publications which I received from the naval station at Newport News. They had never been corrected and I didn't have anybody to assist me, so frequently I would work until late at night trying to bring these publications up to date.

We had perhaps 40 officers, but the captain felt that they should be assigned to the gunnery and to the engineering departments, because the ship did have to move, and we weren't going to be operating with other ships until we arrived in the Far East. I agreed with that, but did feel that perhaps I had a fairly heavy burden to bear.

There were radiomen and signalmen, and we got along.

Q: I hope that situation improved a bit when you got out to the Far East.

Smith-Hutton: Yes, it did.

Q: You preceded in the Houston to the Far East, I gather, without any significant events occurring. And when you arrived in Manila, the Houston took aboard the Commander-in-Chief, Asiatic Fleet and his staff. Do you want to comment on that?

Smith-Hutton: We arrived in Manila early in March 1931, after an uneventful trip across the Pacific via Honolulu and Guam. Within ten days of our arrival, the flag lieutenant of the Commander-in-Chief, Admiral Charles McVay, who was Lieutenant Felix Johnson in the class of 1920, asked me whether I would like to be ordered as his relief on the staff. Of course I had not known Admiral McVay, but I did know his son, Charles McVay III, who was a classmate of Felix Johnson. After some hesitation, I said yes, so about 13 March I was detached as a ship's officer and ordered to the staff. Two or three weeks later, Lieutenant Johnson was detached to return to the United States, and I reported and took over his duties as flag lieutenant.

Admiral McVay, who had been Commander of the Yangtze Patrol Force in the middle Twenties, knew China very well. He was an excellent officer and very easy to serve with. I enjoyed my duty as flag lieutenant very much and I also learned a great deal.

It so happened that Admiral McVay had been in the Far East for two years, and he left about the 27th of August 1931 to return to the United States. He was relieved by Admiral M. M. Taylor, and I was ordered as the Fleet Intelligence Officer on Admiral Taylor's staff.

Interview with Captain Smith-Hutton

Date: February 8, 1974

By: Captain Paul Ryan, USN (Ret.)

Q: Captain, last week we were discussing your new assignment as Fleet Intelligence Officer of the Asiatic Fleet under the new commander, Admiral Montgomery Taylor. As it seems to me, prior to World War I there was no such thing as a fleet intelligence officer and even, I believe, in the U.S. Fleet in 1931 there was no fleet intelligence officer, why was there a fleet intelligence officer in the Asiatic Fleet?

Captain Smith-Hutton: The Commander-in-Chief in China had many contacts with military and diplomatic officers, and received a great many reports in regard to political and military matters. So the billet of fleet intelligence officer was started with the idea having a staff officer charged with collecting information for the use of the Commander-in-Chief and his staff. We received numerous reports; many of them were long and complicated. Admiral Montgomery Taylor was a great reader and he read all of them very carefully. I had to summarize them for the chief of staff, Captain F. J. Fletcher. Most of the reports were destroyed after a year or two or, if they were no longer pertinent, because of the limited storage space on board ship in the office of the Commander-in-Chief.

It would be more exact to say that the duties of the Fleet Intelligence Officer were those of a confidential secretary to the Commander-in-Chief because all classified correspondence except registered publications was handled by the intelligence officer and his yeoman. The yeoman was a very efficient Chief Yeoman who had the job for many years, so he knew exactly what was in the files.

The duties of the intelligence officer, of course, depended on the Commander-in-Chief. For instance, I recall that shortly after Admiral Taylor came, he said that he wasn't as much interested in what happened yesterday, as in what would happen tomorrow. He hoped I would, as intelligence officer, concentrate on tomorrow. The admiral read the papers but he liked to discuss events with somebody. The intelligence officer was the logical staff officer for this. We spent much time discussing what was going to happen tomorrow, so that the admiral would be better prepared.

Since my duty was that of a confidential secretary, I saw the admiral every day. He signed many confidential letters. And during that time he frequently asked me my view of events in the Philippines, in China, in Japan. Very soon, we established a friendship. I admired Admiral Taylor very much.

We passed on few reports to units of the fleet or to ONI unless the admiral wished to add to a report that we had received.

The admiral also expected me to keep in close touch with diplomatic officials and with the officers of foreign navies.

We had particularly close relations with the British and the British Commander-in-Chief whenever we were together. But it did depend, as I say, on the Commander-in-Chief.

Q: Captain, you explained the interest of the Admiral in intelligence. What were the main concerns which faced him, which caused him to ask for all this intelligence from the consuls and ambassadors and foreign liaison officers?

Smith-Hutton: The area under the Commander-in-Chief of the Asiatic Fleet extended from the International Date Line in the middle of the Pacific to the Persian Gulf, which is a large section of the globe. Of course in that area, his primary concern was China, which was the place where there was the most unrest. There were problems of all kinds in China. Shortly after he took command, that is, on 18 September, there was the beginning of the so-called Manchurian Incident, where the Japanese Kwantung Army took over the whole administration of Manchuria. There were frequent disasters in China. The Yangtze frequently flooded. There were American citizens' lives endangered. And there were the overall political problems caused by the actions of the Japanese armed forces. It was a very extensive command and the Admiral had a relatively small force to handle problems.

There was the fleet flagship; three divisions of destroyers, two divisions of submarines, a small number of mine sweepers and mine layers. In the Yangtze River was the Yangtze Patrol Force of nine gunboats. In South China there was another small patrol force, usually two gunboats. So the Admiral, who was interested in a large section of the globe, felt that the more he knew about events, the better he would be able to carry out his duties of protecting American interests and even extending them, if possible.

One point I might make here is that at this time, we had no communication intelligence collection organization. We did have an officer attached to the staff who came directly from Op-20G. This officer, who later became Rear Admiral Joseph Wenger, was a distinguished officer especially competent in communication intelligence.

His duty was to prepare plans for an expanded intercept network. This was largely research; Wenger and I worked together since we'd known each other for years and had worked together in Op-20G.

We had no agents ashore, no covert collection, and the overt collection was more than filled by our reports from diplomatic and consular officials who were really efficient. Sometimes fleet units were directed to photograph and describe the harbor facilities of the ports they visited, but most of these had been well covered, and except for new construction, it was not necessary to make duplicate reports.

We tried to maintain the very closest relations with State Department officials so that they would let us know what their problems were. If they needed assistance, they were to inform the Admiral as soon as possible.

Q: Captain, would you tell me if any of this intelligence which you collected was used operationally by the Admiral?

Smith-Hutton: Only as necessary. The reports from the consuls and from our ships which were received on the flagship were also available in Washington either in the State Department or the Navy Department. So the information was not just for the operational use of the Commander-in-Chief.

Frequently, when ships were sent on missions, the Admiral

would brief the commanding officer or the senior officer of the unit personally or through a written communication or operation order. He did that personally or designated the chief of staff or the operations officer to do so. I can't recall that I ever assisted in the preparation of operation orders, and I believe the Admiral gave verbal briefings where necessary.

Q: Captain, with regard to the tenuous situation in China, I remember when I was a high school student that the 4th Marines left San Diego for Shanghai, and I think there was even a song written about it. Were you out there at the time? What was it like?

Smith-Hutton: Yes. This happened in the early winter of 1932, We were in Manila engaged in exercises and training, as usual. As a result of the Japanese seizure of a large portion of Manchuria and their obvious aggressive intentions in North China, the Central Chinese government decided to create a diversion in the Shanghai area. So they attacked a small Japanese naval unit near the golf course in the outskirts of Shanghai. Several Japanese bluejackets were killed. Of course, that brought this whole Japanese force in the Shanghai area into action, and within a few days, fighting in the area became general. General Chiang Kai-chek ordered the 19th Route Army to defend the area. This army consisted of three German trained divisions. There was much anti-Japanese feeling because of Japanese actions in Manchuria. The troops all hated the Japanese. Within a short time, the fighting became severe and the international settlements became endangered, so the Consul General recommended that our forces in Shanghai be increased. The admiral felt that under the circumstances he must take general command of the protection of the settlement and of American interests in the area himself.

So we left Manila on very brief notice. On the way to Shanghai we received other reports, indicating the need for an increased landing force. Since the British had ordered a regiment of troops from Hong Kong, the Admiral decided that our forces should be strengtened by Marines. He asked the Navy Department to send a regiment of Marines, and this was done in the way you recall. The 4th Marines left San Diego, and within three weeks were landed in Shanghai. The new Japanese naval commander was Admiral Nomura, who had been Naval Attache in Washington about 12 years before. He was friendly toward the United States, and he liked Americans. Shortly after we got to Shanghai he and Admiral Taylor, in a series of conferences, arrived at agreements and understanding. Admiral Taylor recognized that the fighting in Shanghai in this instance had not been brought on by the local actions of the Japanese, and he also realized that the Japanese were anxious to settle problems in the Shanghai area.

The fighting lasted for about three months, and the affair was not settled by the Japanese navy. Actually the Japanese Army had to send in approximately three divisions of troops before they drove the Chinese troops away from the international settlement and the Shanghai area was swept clear of the 19th Route Army. The fighting was heavy and the Chinese, although they were no match for the Japanese, did as well as any Chinese troops could have done at that time. They were helped by German officers and advisors who had trained them.

Q: Captain, I recall you told us that in 1925 when you were aboard the destroyer Peary that you had been in a landing force which went ashore in Shanghai to establish order. How did you compare the 1932 landings with your 1925 experience?

Smith-Hutton: In 1925 the Chinese were threatening to take over the international settlement, so our forces were on the defensive. There were no battles, just actions against mobs. But in 1932 the Chinese Army was actively engaged against the Japanese. Of course, the international forces had many of the same problems. For instance, in both actions our landing forces spent considerable time on the Shanghai race course, which was in the heart of the International Settlement. When our Marines came into Shanghai from the transport anchored in the river, they marched up Nanking Road which went through the heart of the settlement, with literally thousands of Chinese and foreigners watching them. They marched to the racetrack where they were billeted in tents for the first few days. Shortly after that, they took positions assigned to them under an international agreement, that is, they took over the control of what became known as the American sector. Shortly afterward they moved into billets. It was always obvious that they knew what they were doing and the Marines were, as usual, a very colorful outfit. They created a feeling of security among the American residents in the city, because there was no doubt that the defense forces were increased.

I remember that Colonel Hooker, who commanded the regiment, called several times on Admiral Taylor and conferred with him at length. The colonel was a typical Marine officer who knew his business, and the admiral had great confidence in him.

Q: Captain, do you recall how many men were in the 4th Marine Regiment?

Smith-Hutton: Yes, there were about 1200 men in the regiment, and I can add in parenthesis that they remained in Shanghai until 1941. They were sent to the Philippines just before the outbreak of World War II. The 4th Marines have a long history of service in the Shanghai area.

By the outbreak of World War II, I mean until Pearl Harbor when we became involved in the war.

Q: In this Shanghai incident, were there any particular affairs that stand out in your mind?

Smith-Hutton: Perhaps my own personal experience which happened after the fighting was over, that is, the middle of April. The Chinese had fought well, but were finally driven away from the settlement by an overwhelming force of Japanese under the command of General Shirakawa. The Japanese command was, of course, anxious to make an impression not only on the Chinese populace but on the other inhabitants of Shanghai, the great cosmopolitan center. So they decided to have their forces celebrate the victory by a parade. This was held in Hongkew Park which is at the end of the settlement, the sector where the Japanese were concentrated. About 5000 elite troops -- I believe they were from the Imperial Guard division -- paraded, in battle dress, in front of a large reviewing stand which was erected for the occasion. General Shirakawa took the review.

On the reviewing stand were many Japanese dignitaries, including Admiral Nomura, who was in command of the China Fleet and Ambassador Shigemitsu, who was the representative of the Japanese government; (Shigemitsu later became prime minister and foreign minister.) and many other dignitaries. I was there unofficially but in uniform representing Admiral Taylor, and was standing about 100 away from the reviewing stand, when in the middle of the ceremonies, a bomb exploded.

It developed that a Korean revolutionary had walked up to the reviewing stand and while everybody's attention was directed toward the troops passing in review, had pushed a bomb close to the center of the group which was taking the review.

When the bomb exploded, General Shirakawa was killed, and several Japanese who were close to him were badly wounded. Admiral Nomura got a splinter of the bomb in his eye and was blinded in that eye. Mr. Shigemitsu had his right leg blown off, and several others received more or less serious wounds.

Of course, the Japanese military police immediately took charge, cleared the area, and started searching all Japanese and Chinese . . . .

I returned to the flagship as soon as possible to report to Admiral Taylor what had happened. He instructed me to proceed immediately to the Idzuro, the Japanese flagship, to express to Admiral Nomura Admiral Taylor's wishes for a speedy recovery and his regrets that this had taken place.

I was informed then that Admiral Nomura would probably lose the sight of his eye, but that the wound was not otherwise serious. I was also informed about Mr. Shigemitsu.

Q: Captain, did you encounter either of these two gentlemen, Admiral Nomura and Mr. Shigemitsu, in later years?

Q: Captain, did you encounter either of these two gentlemen, Admiral Nomura and Mr. Shigemitsu, in later years?

Smith-Hutton: In later years I saw both of them from time to time in Tokyo. Admiral Nomura returned to Japan, and although he was retired from the Navy, served in the Cabinet as Foreign Minister, and was the Japanese Ambassador sent to Washington just before the Pearl Harbor attack.

Mr. Shigemitsu was sent to Great Britain as ambassador. He also served in a number of posts, including Foreign Minister at least twice. One of his last duties was to represent the Emperor at the surrender ceremony on the Missouri in 1945. I did not know them well but both knew who I was and I did see them, as I say, from time to time.

In 1945 I was one of the officers who took the Japanese delegation from the dock in Yokahama to the Missouri in the destroyer

Landsdowne. It was obvious that Mr. Shigemitsu with a wooden leg would have difficulty getting into a small boat to go to the Missouri. So the captain of the Landsdowne at my request made available a bos'n's chair and we lowered Mr. Shigemitsu from the deck into the boat without any difficulty. When he returned to the Landsdowne after the ceremony, he was picked up with the bos'n's chair and landed on deck.

Q: This concludes the interview on 8 February. Thank you very much, Captain, for your fascinating account.

Interview with Captain Smith-Hutton
Date: 14 February 1974
By: Captain Paul Ryan, USN (Ret.)

Q: Captain, in the last session we were discussing China in 1932. That spring there occurred the Shanghai Incident, wherein the foreign fleets had gathered there, the British, the French, the U.S., the Italian and the Japanese, because of the lawlessness raging in China. As the fleet intelligence officer you were Admiral Taylor's right hand man. May I ask you to describe your activities?

Captain Smith-Hutton: During the early part of 1932, Admiral Taylor decided he was needed in Shanghai because of the serious fighting between the Japanese and the Chinese armies in the Shanghai International Settlement area.

The settlement was neutral. The Chinese area was defended by regulars who had come from South China and who forced the fighting. The Japanese feared for the safety of their part of the settlement and counter attacked to drive the Chinese armies away.

The fighting lasted until April. The operation was a peculiar one, in that it was possible to visit the Chinese headquarters in the morning, this being in an area just north of the settlement, and then by coming through the settlement and traveling to the eastward in the direction of Hongkew, one could visit the Japanese headquarters in the afternoon. In that way if one had the proper passes and knew who to talk to, it was possible to follow the course of the fighting with great ease.

Of course, I also kept in touch with the British and the French because they had excellent sources of information.

The fighting ended when the Chinese were driven away by a superior force of Japanese troops.

Q: In your relationship with the French Navy, was the French naval intelligence officer of any value to you, Captain?

Smith-Hutton: Yes, the French were very well informed in regard to China, particularly since France was responsible for the Catholic missions. The heads of the Catholic missions, many of whom were Jesuits, were extremely well-informed and had many sources of information which were usually denied to the other foreigners. Therefore, the French intelligence officers, both on the flagship and at the French consulate general, had information as to what the Chinese were thinking and doing. So we kept in close touch with them.

Q: Captain, during this period of several months, I suppose that with the vast investments of foreigners in Shanghai, that there was a tendency to carry on business as usual. Is this true?

Smith-Hutton: Yes, it was. Shipping, particularly coastal shipping, continued, keeping clear of the zones where hostilities were in progress, but small ships ran in and out of port without complications, and below Shanghai, there were small docks that were in constant use by British, French and American ships. The

Chinese and the Japanese were both anxious not to damage American, British or French property because they wanted to remain on good terms with the powers that were involved in commerce in Shanghai. In this instance both sides did their best to avoid damage to us.

Q: In the event that worst came to worst, Captain, did the U.S. Navy, Admiral Taylor, that is, have an evacuation plan for U.S. citizens?

Smith-Hutton: Yes. The admiral and the operational staff working with the consular officers made a constant review of the situation. The consuls assured Americans that if there were changes for the worst, the Navy would attempt to evacuate all that wanted to leave, using both naval ships and the merchant ships which were in the area. Actually, the plan was kept current and up to date as much as possible. Fortunately, there was no need to put it into effect.

Q: After viewing this situation for several months, how did you and Admiral Taylor view the Chinese war with special regard to the future of China?

Smith-Hutton: Both of us were very disappointed that the 19th Route Army had to bear the brunt of the fighting with the Japanese, because, as I've mentioned, there were additional central Army divisions near Shanghai. They did nothing and it seemed to us as though the Central Government, headed by Chiang Kai-chek, wanted to liquidate the 19th Route Army but otherwise remain neutral. That showed that China was not really unified, and that the Central Government had no intention of forming a national army. It was a disappointing development. Of course, the same policy continued on to the 1930's.

Q: When you say policy, Captain, you're referring to this policy of Chiang Kai-chek, are you not?

Smith-Hutton: Exactly.

Q: With the situation becoming tranquil in Shanghai, did the Admiral decide to depart the city?

Smith-Hutton: Yes. His presence in Shanghai was no longer necessary. The Japanese were sending men and equipment back to Japan and our Consul General could see no objection to his leaving. The emergency was finished. So the Admiral decided to go up the Yangtze River as far as Hankow, making stops at Nanking and Kiukiang. The Admiral was very much interested in the situation in China and although he had been in the Far East for only a few months, (he had arrived in August 1931) had read extensively about the Far East. I was always amazed at the extent of his knowledge. He received many callers who were anxious to talk to him, and he listened carefully; asked far reaching questions, and he liked to discuss Far Eastern problems with any one who could be considered an expert.

Q: Captain, you had a unique experience which people would no longer have, at least Westerners, of going up the Yangtze River for 600 miles. Could you describe the trip?

Smith-Hutton: Yes. Actually, the trip was uneventful but the Yangtze is a mighty river as shown by the fact that the Houston, a 10,000 ton treaty cruiser, could go up as far as Hankow. The pilot who came on board was Chinese, and he brought two Chinese steersmen with him. It was interesting to see how they worked together, because they never exchanged words. They used hand signals. The pilot would make a slight motion with his right index finger, and the steermen would follow until he held up his hand, which was apparently the signal for "steady as you go."

The trip up was slow because in many areas the ship could make only 12 knots against the current without creating a large wake, and we anchored at night.

Ours was a very competent pilot, to be able to navigate a river where there are almost no navigational marks for several hundred miles.

The first stop was at Nanking, which was then the capital of China, and the Admiral exchanged calls with various officials. He had hoped to see the President, Chiang Kai-chek, but Chiang was away from Nanking. Our next stop was Anking, then Kiukiang. Nothing important happened in either of these cities but calls were exchanged with local officials.

At Hankow we anchored off the Bund, that is, the main part of the city, which at one time had been one of the most important cities of China, with a large foreign colony. The city had been taken over by the Chinese in 1928 when they occupied all of the concessions, which were then returned to Chinese control. In the years that followed, the city had greatly deteriorated and lost much of its importance.

When we were in Hankow, Admiral Taylor decided to visit the upper river, and since the Houston could not go he decided to fly to Chungking.

There was a weekly plane service on the river from Shanghai to Chungking, with 8 or 9 stops. We found that he could get passage from Hankow to Chungking and in the course of the flight, the plane followed the river through the gorges.

Q: This must have been a rather exciting form of transportation for the Admiral, who had not flown too much, I'm sure, in those days. Could you tell us what type of aircraft, something of the pilot and the trip in general?

Smith-Hutton: The aircraft was a Loening amphibian. It had eight seats and carried a small amount of mail and cargo. The pilot was an American who had been an Army air corps pilot, and was an Army reserve officer. He was a capable young fellow. We took off from Hankow early in the morning, the Admiral and I and Lieutenant Commander Warren, the Flag Secretary.

The first stop was Ichang, which is just below the gorges. We let one or two passengers disembark, took on some mail, and refueled to capacity. Then he took off on one of the most spectacular flights that you could imagine, the Gorges of the Yangtze River, where the churning river was in sight below the plane and the banks rise perpendicular from the river for about 1200 feet. We could see the lush fields in the distance and it was a beautiful and interesting landscape.

We arrived at Chungking late in the afternoon, were met by the captain of the gunboat Tutuila, which was then station ship.

Q: Captain, you and Admiral Taylor having arrived in Chungking, did you get a understanding for the situation under which U.S. citizens lived, and the conditions in which U.S. property rights prevailed?

Smith-Hutton: Yes, we did. We spent three days in Chungking. The captain of the Tutuila and the head of the Standard Oil Company office acted as hosts. They were very solicitous of our well being and anxious that we see everything and do everything that we wanted to do. I remember the Standard Oil manager, in particular, as a very able man. He was born in China, spoke Chinese perfectly, had been graduated from an American university and engaged by Standard Oil to go back to China. He had excellent contacts and was familiar with the political and economic situation in the big province. He provided an interpreter when we called on the local governor, who was General Chen, an impressive figure. He received us courteously in his large residence and invited us to a banquet. The Admiral, who had a slightly upset stomach, asked to be excused, and the governor said that he understood because frequently in his travels he had to be careful. He suggested that the Admiral drink only the finest liquor since this would hasten his recovery.

We enjoyed our trip. Chungking is a spectacular city, not well known at that time, but very well known ten years later when it became the capital and seat of the central government during the war with the Japanese.

We saw almost all of the American colony, which wasn't large, but the missionaries and the Dollar Line representatives and the Standard Oil manager and his staff were most courteous. We left Chungking after a stay of three days, and we rather regretted to be going down river on the Tutuila.

Q: Captain, where did you and the Admiral stay during this three day visit to Chungking? Were you impressed with the surroundings?

Smith-Hutton: We slept on the Tutuila. We used the state rooms of two of the officers. The officers that gave up their rooms for us just moved to a barge which was moored alongside where they had a small supply of liquor which they kept in lockers. It was on this barge that the officers entertained when guests came to the ship, because, of course, it is against regulations to have liquor on board ship. The officers put up cots on the barge, which was roomy. Part of it was made into an enlisted men's club where the men could play games or cards and have beer, and so life on board the Tutuila as we observed, was comfortable and easy going.

The servants, that is, the mess boys were Chinese, as they were for the ships in the Yangtze and the South China patrols, and the fleet flagship. These boys were men who had been in service for years and were hard working and competent. It goes without saying, that the officers in the Asiatic fleet, particularly the Yangtze Patrol and the flagship, were better cared for than any ships in the Navy.

The trip down the river on the Tutuila was also spectacular. It was another experience with a competent Chinese pilot and helmsman. It was beautiful to see how he took the ship through the rapids missing rocks by three or four feet in water which was churning six to eight knots. The trip up the river, of course, would be much more tedious but going down river we seemed to be shooting the rapids on a gunboat more than a hundred feet long, and moving at a very fast pace.

The pilot never lost control for a moment, and we made it down the river to Ichang in quick time.

There were two merchant ships that had been wrecked a few days before. They were being salvaged and were hauled up on the rocks on the river bank, but they didn't need our assistance. It showed what could happen to cargo ships and gunboats in that dangerous stretch of water through the gorges.

Q: After the Yangtze trip, what did the employment schedule call for next, Captain?

Smith-Hutton: The Admiral, never having been in North China, planned to visit the usual summer fleet operating areas, so we went north to Tsingtao. Tsingtao was the normal operating base for the fleet flagship, and the submarine squadron with the tender Canopus.

In Tsingtao in 1932, the governor was Vice Admiral Shen, Chinese Navy. He had two small cruisers, the Hi Chi and the Chow Fu. They were sister ships, built in England before World War I. They were obsolete but they were without doubt the cleanest war ships I've even seen. I made boarding calls several times on them because they were meticulous in sending boarding officers to us and when I returned the call, they invited me to the wardroom. Everything on board was spotless, all the bright work was polished, and it was really a pleasure to see what the Chinese could do as far as ship keeping was concerned. We had no way of knowing how good they were in the use of their guns, but they looked beautiful -- it was a pleasure to visit them.

Admiral Shen was very courteous. He spoke some English, and he liked to have the American Navy in port, as did all the Chinese and Japanese residents. The submarine officers and the flagship officers spent a great deal of money in the three months they were in the Tsingtao area which made the city very prosperous, even though there were also a great many other summer residents. Tsingtao, of course, had a long history, but the modern city had been built by the Germans in 1900. It looked like a German city with beautifully laid out gardens and streets. The houses themselves were usually painted white with tile roofs, so the city looked like a European city.

The Japanese had captured Tsingtao from the Germans in 1914 and had stayed until 1922. They left as a result of the Washington treaty agreements but they had also added to the city, since they hoped to make their occupation a permanent one. They had spent much effort, thought and time building it up, and the industries, including spinning mills and factories, flourished even after the Japanese left.

I remember the German influence included Tsingtao beer which was a very delicious brew, exactly like German beer.

Interview with Captain Smith-Hutton

Date: 22 February 1974

By: Captain Paul Ryan, USN (Ret.)

Q: Good afternoon, Captain. We start this session recognizing that in November of 1932, you were on the staff of Admiral Taylor anchored in Shanghai aboard his flagship, when you received dispatch orders. Would you tell us about that?

Captain Smith-Hutton: In early November 1932, I received orders to proceed to Tokyo upon being relieved as the fleet intelligence officer by Lieutenant David Wells Roberts, who was the class ahead of me at the Naval Academy. He was assistant naval attache in Tokyo, and he was ordered to the staff of Admiral Taylor, as my relief.

I received these orders, and was detached from the staff on 9 November. I proceeded on the steamship President Jackson from Shanghai to Yokohama. Again the transportation was furnished by the naval purchasing officer, Shanghai. I arrived in Yokohama and reported to the Naval Attache in Tokyo on 15 November. The naval attache at that time was Captain I.C. Johnson, class of 1904.

Q: Captain, speaking of Lieutenant Wells Roberts, I recall that he was a fellow language student with you in Japan. Whatever happened to him?

Smith-Hutton: He and I studied Japanese together and we lived together in both Tokyo and Karuizawa. His mother was kind enough to keep house for several language officers. We were all close friends. He was executive officer of the cruiser Houston, which was sunk in early February 1942, in the action off Java, and lost his life then. This was a great loss to the service.

Q: Captain, it had been three years since you left Tokyo. Did you notice any changes in the embassy and the city?

Smith-Hutton: Yes, indeed. In the three years since I left, almost all traces of the 1923 earthquake had been removed. Tokyo and Yokohama had been rebuilt. There were many new buildings and the suburbs were greatly extended. Japan had a prosperous busy air, but much of this prosperity was only on the surface. While trade with Manchuria was flourishing and there was little unemployment, prices were high and the country and farmers were having difficulties making a living.

Q: In 1929 the embassy had been located in a downtown office building in Tokyo. Was this still the case?

Smith-Hutton: No. The new embassy buildings had been completed in those three years and were well suited for their purpose. The embassy is located in the Keinanzaka section of Tokyo on a small hill about 75 feet high. The ambassadors residence is well suited for an embassy residence with reception rooms, dining rooms and studies, and with quarters for the ambassador and his servants.

The entrance hall is impressive. There is a white circular staircase to the upper stories and in all respects a beautiful embassy. It was little damaged during World War II and was used later by General MacArthur during his long stay in Tokyo as Supreme Commander. It is used today as the ambassador's residence.

Below this hill on a lower level is a pretty garden with a large swimming pool, and a pond with lotus flowers. On this same lower level are two apartment houses, each with approximately six small apartments, for the clerks and secretaries. Between the apartments and the street is a three story office building where the embassy offices are. The naval attache was assigned three good-sized offices on the second floor.

Q: Well, that sounds as if your office conditions had improved a lot in three years, by going to new buildings. What about your own housing, Captain? Did you benefit there, too?

Smith-Hutton: Yes, I was lucky because Lieutenant Roberts and his wife had a large Japanese style house in the western suburbs. They had furnished it, and since he was going to sea, had left their furniture in the house for me to use as long as I wanted it. The house had a beautiful garden.

So I moved into it knowing that I would be comfortable and that I could do the necessary entertaining. I engaged the same cook that had worked for me when I had been a language officer, so I was well taken care of.

Q: Captain, your ambassador in Tokyo at that time was Joseph Grew. He was an East Coast aristocrat who has written his memoirs, which are widely published. What was your impression of him?

Smith-Hutton: Ambassador Grew, who had been appointed earlier that same year, and had arrived in early June 1932, was an experienced diplomat who had long service in Europe. He had joined the foreign service in 1904, and his last post had been as ambassador to Turkey. Although he was new to the Far East, he soon had a wide circle of friends in Tokyo and became familiar with Japanese problems. He worked easily with his staff, and made it a practice to consult with the staff frequently. He wrote very well and soon long and detailed reports on all phases of the situation in Japan began to go from the embassy to the State Department. He was interested in everything.

Q: Captain, Joseph Grew obviously was an experienced diplomat. But he knew nothing about the Far East. Why did President Roosevelt appoint him to this post? In your opinion.

Smith-Hutton: I believe the President, who knew Mr. Grew personally, since they had been in Groton and Harvard about the same time, felt that the situation in the Far East and our relations with Japan required an experienced diplomat. The previous ambassador had been Mr. Cameron Forbes, a political appointee from Massachusetts, a very distinguished man, but also with no previous experience in the diplomatic service, whereas Mr. Grew had had long experience. He was one of the last of the old line diplomats. He was tall and distinguished looking, inclined to be formal and proper, but that really helped him in his work with the Japanese officials, who are somewhat formal themselves. This certainly did not hinder his relations with other representatives in Japan. He soon became one of the outstanding figures in the diplomatic corps in Tokyo.

His work was facilitated by the fact that he had a considerable income in addition to his salary, and Mrs. Grew was a charming hostess. The embassy entertained frequently and well. I might mention that Mrs. Grew was also well liked by the Japanese. Soon all important Japanese knew that she liked Japan and the Japanese people, and was proud of the fact that Commodore Perry, who had opened Japan to foreign trade in 1854, was her great-uncle.

Q: Ambassador Grew's memoirs are apparently based upon a voluminous diary which he kept, and in the diary he mentions occasionally that he types and he taught himself to type. Did he actually type these daily dairy reports himself, or did he have enough secretarial help to do it?

Smith-Hutton: While the ambassador did type many of the rough drafts of reports himself, he had very competent help. For instance, he himself hired a young secretary, always a young man who had been recommended by the rector of Groton School who had graduated from either Harvard or Yale. He paid these young men their salaries. I can remember three of them. The first was

Graham Parsons. The second was Marshall Green, and the third was Robert Fearey. All of them have had distinguished careers and eventually became Assistant Secretaries of the State. They worked for the ambassador and frequently typed his diaries and reports.

In addition, he had a faithful secretary, Mrs. Marian Arnold, who was a State Department employee. She was cleared for secret work, and typed final copies of the diaries and his reports.

Q: In 1932, the policy of the Navy Department on intelligence collection was rather fundamental, and I don't think it's changed since then. And as I understand it, naval attaches were required to collect political, military, naval, economic and industrial information on their particular country. Was your office organized to do this? And how did you find the task?

Smith-Hutton: The naval attache to whom I reported was Captain I.C. Johnson, who had been in Tokyo more than two years. He had another year to serve before returning to the United States, because it was usually a three year assignment. Although Captain Johnson didn't speak Japanese, he had made many friends in Japan and was well liked by Japanese officers. He was a bachelor, and since Japanese ladies play little part in social life, that made no difference.

Captain Johnson was a thoughtful keen officer whose judgment of events was sound, and he had a wide circle of acquaintances among American businessmen and the Japanese. He played good golf and poker, was popular, and had many contacts.

The Navy department gave us additional money which was called "maintenance allowance" in those days. The naval attache had a maintenance allowance of $300 a month, and I had a maintenance allowance of $200 a month. This was for the purpose of entertaining because in getting information, it is necessary to have officials and friends to whom you can turn who will speak frankly to you. These extra funds enabled us to widen our circle of acquaintances, friends and contacts, and improve the intelligence reporting of the office.

In addition to that, we had a small amount of money, about $300 a year, which we could use for the purchase of information. I mention this but in fact we seldom used any of these funds.

Q: There were two officers in the Tokyo post, Captain. What sort of staff did you have to help you organize your work?

Smith-Hutton: Of course we paid great attention to the newspapers, magazines and all official publications issued by the Japanese Navy Department and the government. Any mention of the Navy was noted and discussed between us. One valuable member of the staff was a retired chief yeoman named Leonard Wagner. He had been in the naval attache's office since 1920, and had learned to speak and read Japanese. He was a very sound, and a reliable, sober man. He kept the fiscal accounts, including the pay records, and he typed up the final reports which we sent to our Navy Department. Thus all our reports were prepared by security minded Americans. In the course of the years, Wagner had become an expert on the Japanese budget, among other things, and each year he prepared a detailed breakdown of the naval budget as it appeared in the "Official Gazette", which corresponds to our "Congressional Record", and of course, the "Official Gazette" carried much valuable information. For instance, the naval debates in the Diet, that is, in the Japanese Parliament, where the building programs and naval policies were discussed openly and in great detail.

Q: Did you have any translator help in the office, Captain?

Smith-Hutton: Yes. We could call on the language officers for translation work if necessary, as I had translated the Japanese Coast Pilot when I was a language officer. In addition, we had two Japanese members of the staff. One was a Japanese translator named Iwamoto. He was in his early forties, of a good family, who had been sent to the United States to school and graduated from Harvard University. He was married to an American lady. He translated all communications to and from the Japanese Navy Department; the notices to mariners and, of course, anything else that was given to him.

We had a young messenger. In Tokyo many things had to be delivered by hand, and our messenger was the one who did deliveries.

Q: Do you recall what the salaries were of the two Japanese?

Smith-Hutton: I think the salary of Mr. Iwamoto was about $200 a month, and the salary of the messenger was about $100 a month.

Q: Obviously, you were conscious of a security problem in the office. How did you cope with it, Captain?

Smith-Hutton: We took great care to keep the two Japanese in the office from knowing anything about the reports, and information sent to Washington, because while we had no reason to suspect either of them, we realized that both were probably questioned by the secret police from time to time. There were never any suspicions in regard to either of them, and of course they realized that our sources included the "Official Gazette", newspapers and magazines, because they helped translate them, but there could be no objection to this on the part of the Japanese authorities.

Q: Just about the time you arrived in Tokyo, the world was at the peak of a world-wide depression, where trade was stifled between countries, and with Japan enmeshed in Manchuria and China, economic conditions must have been poor. I mention, at the same time, in the U.S. Navy we were feeling the pinch, with not much ship building going on. How did you find the economic conditions in Tokyo?

Smith-Hutton: Actually there was considerably inflation, because there was a shortage of goods, and articles which had to be imported became more and more expensive. But while the exchange rate between the yen and the dollar was controlled in Tokyo, the control wasn't complete, and in China it was possible to get twice the official exchange rate in Tokyo. The official rate was 3 yen for 1 dollar, in 1932, in Tokyo, and it remained that throughout the thirties. However, in Shanghai and even unofficially in Tokyo, the rate was as high as 4 or 5 yen for the dollar. Before the end of that decade, it even went to 10 or higher, showing how badly the yen was deteriorating on the international market.

That, of course, was an advantageous exchange rate, and at 5 yen for 1 dollar, it wasn't expensive to live in Tokyo.

Q: In 1933 I'm sure you recall, the Navy sustained a 15 percent pay cut across the board. Did this affect your allowances in Japan?

Smith-Hutton: Yes, it did. As a matter of fact, our maintenance allowances were cut approximately 25 percent. Captain Johnson's allowance was reduced from $300 a month to $225, and mine was reduced from $200 a month to $150. That reduction was in effect all the rest of my stay in Tokyo as assistant attache.

Q: Captain Johnson, the naval attache had been in Tokyo for some time. Did he remain there long after your arrival?

Smith-Hutton: He was there approximately a year, but in September 1933, he was relieved by Captain F. F. Rogers, who had been the first language officer ever sent to Tokyo. Captain Rogers was in the class of 1906 at the Naval Academy, and in 1910 he was sent to Tokyo to study Japanese. There was another officer with him, a Lieutenant Lake, but Lake retired very shortly after he completed the course. Captain Rogers arrived in September 1933 and he and Mrs. Rogers soon became very popular in the diplomatic corps. Although he'd forgotten much of his Japanese, the Japanese liked him and he was a successful naval attache. He died about 10 years ago, after the war, but Mrs. Rogers still lives in Newport and although she's 90, is a very active lady. She takes great interests in things Japanese and in the Navy.

Q: I recall that Captain Rogers was the officer who inspired Zacharias to become a Japanese language student. I believe Admiral Zacharias points that out in his book Secret Missions. Also Captain Rogers, after he left Japan, at least subsequently to that, became commanding officer of the Naval Training Station at Newport, and during World War II was very successful in administering the training of the SeaBees there.

Captain, in the early Thirties, diplomatic relations between the U.S. and Japan were not good. Secretary Stimson was unhappy with their Manchuria adventure and was not exactly their friend. Did this situation affect your social relations with the Japanese Navy?

Smith-Hutton: Not too much. Our relations with Japanese officials, including the Japanese Navy, continued to be good during my entire period of duty. Without exception, the naval officers with whom we dealt showed no signs of personal unfriendliness, nor did they appear to show any resentment of the critical attitude of our press toward the Japanese actions in China. On one or two occasions, some senior officers at large gatherings, who had had too much to drink, wanted to argue with me. They were always stopped by their friends before the discussions became heated. I found that almost without exception, the Japanese officers were familiar with the official government policy lines, and were quite frank about discussing them. However, this was not personal and they assumed that I was their friend and they were my friends.

Q: How did the Japanese naval officers see their country's policy?

Smith-Hutton: The unofficial arguments ran something like this, "Japan is a small island country with few natural resources and with a large population. She is in reality exploding, and must have room to expand. America has excluded Japanese citizens, so the excess population cannot go to the United States. Japanese decline to go to a country where the level of living is lower than it is in Japan. Next door to Japan is Manchuria, which has many resources and is sparsely populated and badly governed. Actually that was the land of the Manchus and China's only claim to it is from the fact that the Manchus conquered and ruled China for several hundred years. While the Chinese did overthrow the Manchu emperor, Manchuria is now governed by half a dozen war lords. Now Japan has restored the former Manchu emperor to his kingdom and proposes to assist him to rebuild it."

"And if Japan doesn't do it, the Chinese or Russians are probably going to try, and we don't think they have any more right to Manchuria than Japan does. If United States would like to help, there is no reason why our trade cannot increase. America's trade with Japan is already three times that with China. Japan plans to go ahead with the program. Japan is building up an army so that she can defend herself against possible attack by Russia, and is building up a navy against possible attack by the United States. In our view the Japanese way of life is the best in the world and other nations would do well to copy our system."

"So if the United States is really interested in keeping the peace, why don't they come to some kind of an agreement or compromise with us?"

"It is true that we had treaties about limitations of navies but when they expire, we will not renew them. We don't plan to agree unless the civilian government forces us to."

That was, in brief, the gist of their arguments.

Q: Captain, prior to your arrival in Tokyo, there were two sensational murders, assassinations, the first one done by a military group and the second by a naval group. The apparent intent of these assassinations was to obtain a greater role for the military and possibly higher military and naval budgets. Can you tell us about that?

Smith-Hutton: Although these two assassinations happened shortly before I returned to Japan, the repercussions continued. The first was the assassination in 1930 of Prime Minister Hamaguchi. Hamaguchi was a liberal statesman and a very wise one. He was an experienced politician and he objected to the Army policy in Manchuria and to Army control of policy. As a result, a group of young army officers determined to eliminate him and his influence from the government. They thought that if Hamaguchi were killed, the remaining politicians would agree to larger appropriations for the army, and would agree to army plans on the continent.

As you know, the Japanese Army did shortly thereafter start the Manchurian adventure and began to build a new state called Manchukuo

The second assassination in May 1932, was that of Prime Minister Inakai. This was inspired by a group of young naval officers who resented the fact that Mr. Inakai and his naval advisors had agreed to the extension of the London Naval Treaty. These young officers felt that the restrictions placed on the Japanese Naval building program was very much to Japan's disadvantage. They felt that the only way in which the country could prosper was to build up the Navy to the point where it could control the Western Pacific which was the duty of the Navy. So they killed the Prime Minister and demanded a bigger budget.

Q: In your conversations with Japanese naval officers, did you have occasion to comment on these assassinations, and what were their reactions?

Smith-Hutton: Japanese naval officers were reluctant to discuss them in detail. However, I was able to meet my friends, and if there were no other Japanese present they talked quite freely. The senior officers, that is, the captains or above, almost always said they thought that the officers who took part in the assassination of the prime minister were patriotic but completely unbalanced, and had done a great disservice to the Navy and to the country. The younger officers were trying in a sensational way to influence public opinion through the assassination.

Q: Was there a tradition in Japanese history that would lead you to think that these political assassinations were proper?

Smith-Hutton: That is a peculiar fact of Japanese political life. The Japanese, for some curious reason, have felt that if someone is serious enough to attack and kill a political enemy, he is showing what they call "great sincerity," and his ideas merit considerable attention. The result is that many officials have in the past been assassinated, although the assassin was a misguided or even mentally deranged young person, without any merit whatever, and the official who had been assassinated was a fine able man. The peculiar result of this attitude has been that shrines have been erected to these worthless young assassins, and the official who was assassinated, in spite of his great merit, is sometimes completely forgotten.

It's difficult to understand how this could be, but nevertheless, it's true, and of course the two cases we have just discussed of the assassinations of the two prime ministers are perfect examples of this.

Q: Perhaps we can note, Captain, that political terrorism is not alone related to Japan, and we have ample evidence today with the skyjackings and political murders and even the Hearst kidnapping which we are reading about even today.

Interview with Captain Smith-Hutton

Date: 28 February 1974

By: Captain Paul Ryan, USN (Ret.)

Q: In the period 1932-1933 when you were settling down in your job as assistant naval attache, Japan was becoming increasingly isolated in the international community, by virtue of adventures in Manchuria and China, and also its stand on the treaty system, where Japan thought it was being wronged. As a result, there was a lot of anti-U.S. feeling in Japan. How did this affect your personal relationships with the Japanese Navy?

Captain Smith-Hutton: Curiously enough, these affected us very little. One result of the visit to the Far East of the Lytton Commission of the League of Nations, when the Commission was in Japan in the summer of 1932, was that they decided that Japan's actions in Manchuria were based on false premises, that is, Japan did not act in self defense, and there was no self-determination in Manchuria.

Of course, these decisions didn't change the Japanese attitude. The Japanese were very bitter against the League of Nations, against the Lytton Commission, and much of their bitterness was directed toward the United States.

Their dislike of Mr. Stimson too was very strong. He was a main target of their animosity.

This, however, did not affect their attitude, at least on the surface, toward us in the embassy. My naval officer friends continu to be my friends and there was no change in their attitude.

Many Japanese, of course, were reluctant to see their former American friends, because they felt they would be criticized, so perhaps contacts were harder to maintain. But personal and individual friends generally kept the same attitudes. They had hostile feelings for the United States, rather than for individual Americans.

Q: Did Ambassador Grew find the same situation true?

Smith-Hutton: Ambassador Grew found exactly the same situation. And he went on record as saying that in his reports to the State Department.

Q: How did this affect your official visits to Japanese naval installations?

Smith-Hutton: It had practically no effect. Captain Johnson and I made the usual inspection trips. It's true that perhaps we were not shown as much as we might otherwise have been shown, but as far as we could see, there was no change officially or unofficially. Our visits to yards and bases continued as in previous years.

Q: What about being shadowed or followed, Captain?

Smith-Hutton: As far as I know, there was no attempt to follow us or shadow us either in Tokyo, or while we were on trips. Of course, an American or non-Japanese is easily noticed in a Japanese crowd or in a Japanese area. But as far as we knew, we were not followed.

Q: Captain, I have here a report to the U.S. Navy's General Board, made in 1934, and this report stated, "Regarding Japanese naval defense plans ... the backbone of this Japanese naval defense plan would be swarms of Japanese submarines based on Mandate Islands and backed up by a powerful naval air force based on shore ..." What is the justification for this statement? I suspect that your office was reporting this to Washington, and it popped up before the Navy's General Board.

Smith-Hutton: As a matter of fact, that was the classic solution that Japanese naval writers gave to the problem of defense of the Western Pacific. They planned to form a perimeter of defense, which the United States Navy must come up against since the only direct approach to the Western Pacific from Hawaii and our West Coast is through the Mandate Islands.

So they wrote about using the Mandate Islands as unsinkable aircraft carriers, and about the use of their submarine force. They boasted that they considered their submarines to be the elite arm of the service. This they planned to use this combination of aircraft and submarines to reduce the superiority of the United States Navy, which was larger than the Japanese Navy, so that by the time the U.S. Fleet reached the Western Pacific, whether it was in the Philippine area or farther north, it would be reduced in strength to approximately the same as the Japanese Navy.

These ideas were attributed not only to Admiral Suetsugu, but to other officers who wrote for naval publications. There were the publications of the Suikosha which also included the naval clubs which were also subsidized by the Navy. Then there were commercial publications, which were for youngsters of high school and secondary school age. The Navy made great efforts to popularize the service, and many articles appeared, all using the same theme. It is interesting to note that the Japanese submarines, the crews of which as I say were very carefully selected, were used ineffectively during the war, much to the astonishment of all of us. We could arrive at only one conclusion, and that was that the Commander-in-Chief of the fleet, Admiral Yamamoto, who was a very able, dedicated and aggressive officer, was entirely oriented toward aircraft and the use of aircraft in naval warfare, and paid very little attention to the possibilities of using submarines. At the same time, the anti-submarine warfare arm of the Japanese Navy was also almost entirely neglected, which helped our submarines greatly when they were able to attack convoys and other surface craft.

Q: Captain, you mention these naval journals which talked about the power of the Japanese destroyer force and Japanese naval air arm. Were some of these journals published by nationalistic societies?

Smith-Hutton: Oh yes, they were, and most of their readers were members of nationalistic pro-Navy or large Navy patriotic societies.

Q: That's very illuminating and it certainly confirms what Admiral

Suetsugu said, regarding his plan against the U.S. Navy for the placing of Japanese naval aircraft on the mandated islands, and that Japanese destroyers and submarines would be used to wear down the U.S. Fleet when it crossed the Pacific to the defense of the Philippines.

Smith-Hutton: Right.

Q: Captain, in 1933, the U.S. Navy under FDR started a large building program, and some time in the mid-Thirties Japan started a Navy buildup. Were you aware of this buildup and did you get any details on the type ships?

Smith-Hutton: We knew about the building programs, because the debates in the Japanese parliament showed the size of the budgets allocated for Naval building. We knew the details of the Japanese programs whether it was the large Yamato class battleships, or the cruisers or the destroyers. We knew the names and numbers of the ships being built because they were mentioned in the debates in the Diet.

However, the security in regard to the building programs was effective, in that the debates never showed the exact characteristics of the ships. The characteristics were made public but almost without exception the ships were larger and more heavily armed than the published figures would indicate. The liberals and businessmen in the Diet were against large military expenditures since they felt that the military were going to bankrupt the country. These so called liberals included many men who were close to the Emperor and who were moderates in their views.

Q: Captain, in the period 1933-34, Admiral Saito was the Prime Minister. He obviously had opposition in the Diet with liberals who were opposing large naval budgets. Did you note any large effort in the Japanese media to try to educate the Japanese public toward the need for a big Navy?

Smith-Hutton: Oh yes, the publicity effort which the Navy gave to strengthening the fleet was a continuous effort, and there was almost no outspoken opposition. The Navy and the strong Navy advocates were able to get the support of the most important and influential newspapers for a reasonable article, advocating increases in the Navy. There were numerous writers who favored a strong Navy. Strong naval forces and strong army forces had so many advocates among the Japanese that there was no difficulty in finding very capable men to put forth their views. The only limiting factor was how to finance the military programs.

Interview with Captain Smith-Hutton

Date: 28 February 1974

By: Captain Paul Ryan, USN (Ret.)

Q: Captain, in 1933 the Japanese Navy was divided into various factions and one of them was known as the fleet faction -- the Big Navy faction. In 1933 Admiral Fushimi was named head of the Naval general staff. Do you recall him?

Captain Smith-Hutton: Yes, I recall him very well. Admiral Prince Fushimi was a cousin of the Emperor, a member of the Imperial Family, as is done in England and in the British Royal Family. The Prince had graduated from the Naval Academy at Etajima, had had sea duty, and was a well qualified officer. In 1933, although he was not as old as some of the other admirals, he was in his early fifties when he was promoted to Admiral.

Of course, the Japanese cannot criticize except in moderate terms anything that is done by a member of the Imperial Family. So having an Imperial Prince as Chief of the Naval General Staff automatically stored most of the criticism. The Navy and the General Staff were still criticized, but in much more reasoned and moderate terms than might otherwise have been the case.

This was a very clever move on the part of the naval leaders to have Prince Fushimi promoted, and made Chief of the General Staff.

He was also named Chief of the Naval General Staff just before Pearl Harbor although the real Chief of Staff was Admiral Nogano.

The Prince had a large estate near the center of Tokyo not

far from the Imperial Palace, he was a great fancier of orchids, and had a number of hothouses for them. He gave garden parties and guests were usually shown through the hothouses. It was said that he had 1400 different kinds, many of them exotic orchids from the South Pacific, the Netherlands, East Indies and the Malay Peninsula. They were beautiful, and flower fanciers got much pleasure in visiting his gardens and hot houses.

In some of our future discussions, in talking about the years just before Pearl Harbor, I will have other things to say about the Prince, who was a very good man.

Q: Captain, in 1933 the aggressive people in the Navy evidently forced the Naval Minister to give up his power to determine the strength of the Navy and to dispatch ships abroad. These powers reportedly went to the Chief of the Naval General Staff. Was there anything to this?

Smith-Hutton: Yes, as you say, that was done. I think we can over-emphasize the reasons behind this. The Minister of the Navy was a Cabinet officer, of course, and as such was expected to maintain good relations with the other Cabinet officers. The Chief of the Naval General Staff was not subject to any civilian influence. However, I'm sure that the Navy Minister could and did work closely with the Chief of the General Staff, because that is the Japanese way of doing things. The Navy Minister being close to the fiscal authorities knew what could be spent on the Navy. Civilian control over the Navy was weakened and at the same time the Navy minister could excuse himself to his cabinet colleagues.

Q: Captain, can you discuss the role of the Japanese military and Navy in the government? This recent ascendency, was it something new in Japanese history, or was this the way it always had been?

Smith-Hutton: The Japanese constitution as originally drafted stated that the Minister of the Navy and the Minister of the Army must be active duty officers. No civilians were ever appointed to these positions. In practice, this meant that the Cabinet was unable to carry out policies or programs which met with the opposition of the armed services. The Japanese are experts at compromises and for doing things in a way that does not hurt others or step on many toes. However, in cases where the Navy or of the Army refused to compromise, the minister resigned which caused the whole cabinet to resign. No active duty officer would accept the cabinet post until the prime minister agreed to do what the service wanted. It is difficult to say exactly how many times this happened and I'm sure that the Navy or the Army did not always have their way in cabinet disagreements but they did often force the government to accept their programs simply by refusing to serve with the Prime Minister. Sometimes the whole cabinet resigned and a new government was formed.

Q: Captain, in this era of anti-U.S. feeling in Japan, the time evidently was not conducive to visits by U.S. naval ships. Were there any such visits?

Smith-Hutton: Yes. As a matter of fact, in the summer of 1933, Admiral M. M. Taylor, who was at that time Commander-in-Chief of the Asiatic Fleet, visited Japan in his flagship, the cruiser Houston. You would have thought that since relations between the two countries were not cordial, such a visit wouldn't have been welcomed. It was, however, a very successful visit from all points of view. Mr. Grew received Admiral Taylor in Tokyo and then Mr. Grew went to Yokohama to return the visit. Admiral Nomura, who had worked closely with Admiral Taylor during the 1932 Shanghai trouble, was in Japan and his presence helped.

I remember that some of the state department officers in the embassy remarked that their friends who had been reluctant to see Americans in public, changed completely as a result of the visit. I know that the ambassador felt that this visit was an unqualified success.

From Admiral Taylor's point of view it was also a success because he played golf on several excellent golf courses, not only in the Tokyo-Yokohama area but near Kobe. Since he was an enthusiastic golfer, he enjoyed himself to the fullest.

Q: Captain, we've talked of official matters quite a lot. Let me ask you about your beautiful house in Tokyo and your outside activities.

Smith-Hutton: My social life in Tokyo was very much like that of a bachelor in any part of the Far East. After office hours, particularly if the weather was good, we would make up a game of tennis or golf. I played tennis much more frequently than golf because I found that golf required a lot of time, although not as much in Tokyo as in other places. Still it was 20 minutes to the nearest golf course, whereas the tennis courts were five minutes walk from the embassy. The Tokyo Tennis Club had about 150 members and by the club rules half were Japanese and half were non-Japanese. The club had been built by a wealthy Japanese to provide a place where young Japanese could meet young Americans, British, French and other nationals. There were never that many non-Japanese tennis players but the club was popular and we played every day that weather permitted.

In the evening, we gathered there or at the Tokyo Club, which was just across the street, or at a Japanese restaurant down town.

Some of my particular friends were Morris Hughes, a third secretary, Cecil Lyon, also third secretary, and Frederick Munson, a Captain in the Army. My house was large and so when Cecil Lyon complained that he could not find a place to live, I suggested that he come to live with me. I had a Japanese house with a beautiful garden, also three servants, including the cook that I'd had as a language officer. He accepted with pleasure, particularly when Elsie Grew, the ambassador's daughter, seconded my suggestion, since she and Mrs. Roberts, the wife of my predecessor, had chosen the house.

Cecil lived with me for six months. The last three months, he was very busy courting Elsie. They were married in the spring of 1934, and then were sent to our embassy in Peking.

I was a member of the wedding party, which was one of the social events of the season in Tokyo since Elsie and Cecil were both very popular not only among the Japanese but among the young

American and British residents.

Munson and I played tennis frequently, and Morris Hughes, who later became consul general in Paris, also played with us. It was a pleasant life even with long hours of work at the office.

Q: Captain, you obviously played more tennis than golf, and I note that Captain Fred Rogers, the naval attache, was a golfer, as was Mr. Grew. What kind of hours did they observe as golfers?

Smith-Hutton: It would depend, of course, but frequently the ambassador, who was an early riser, was up at 6:30 and in his office in the chancery by 7:30. He used the morning hours for reading, writing reports, tending to business. He would leave the embassy after lunch, have a round of golf and be back in the office by 5 o'clock. Then he would work late into the night if the situation demanded it.

Also I know that he was called many times in the middle of the night. That is, he would be called by the duty office in the chancery with a priority dispatch which needed attention right away.

The fact that the ambassador played golf did not reduce the efficiency of his office or the amount of work that he did, in fact he worked better because of it.

He was very keen on having personal contact with prominent persons; Japanese or foreign, who came to Tokyo. He asked diplomats and businessmen to join him at lunch at the embassy, and they almost invariably accepted. The reputation that the embassy had of serving delicious food was well deserved. He saw and talked to almost every important person who came to Tokyo. This helped him in carrying out his mission.

Q: Did Mr. Grew speak Japanese?

Smith-Hutton: Unfortunately he didn't, so it was difficult for him to converse with Japanese officials who did not speak English, but he spoke good French and German, and almost all Japanese diplomats are able to speak English, French or German.

The ambassador made no effort to learn Japanese because by the time he arrived in Tokyo, he was partially deaf, and he knew that it would be almost impossible for him to learn to speak Japanese with that handicap. However, this did not prevent him from having excellent relations with the Japanese.

Q: Captain, we know today that the Japanese people as a whole are avid golfers and there are hundreds of golf courses in Japan. Was it like this in the 1930's?

Smith-Hutton: No, it wasn't. There weren't many golf courses, but there were a few good ones, and even then they were very keen on playing golf. The difficulty was that there were so few courses and it was so expensive to become a member of a club that only well-to-do people played. However, there were matches between the diplomatic corps and the Japanese Foreign Office or between the embassy and the Foreign Office.

The ambassador was one of the most prominent members of the Tokyo Golf Club, and he gave a number of cups to be played for in competition. He was made an honorary life member of the club, after the war.

Q: That was the Tokyo Golf Club, was it not?

Smith-Hutton: That was the Tokyo Golf Club at Asaka, near Tokyo.

Interview with Captain Smith-Hutton

Date: 7 March 1974

By: Captain Paul Ryan, USN (Ret.)

Q: Captain, on our last session you described Ambassador Grew. At the same time, you had acquired a new superior in the person of Captain Fred Rogers who relieved Captain Isaac Johnson in 1933. Could you describe Captain Rogers?

Captain Smith-Hutton: Captain Rogers, who had graduated from the Naval Academy in the class of 1906, was one of the first naval language officers in Japan. With a classmate, Ensign Lake, he was sent to Japan in 1910 and studied there till 1913. He was a very quiet, excellent officer, hard-working and efficient. The Japanese liked him because he wasn't demonstrative and didn't lose his temper or become excited. He entertained a great deal, since he and Mrs. Rogers were wealthy. They had many Japanese and American friends, both official and unofficial. He'd forgotten much of his Japanese in the years that he'd been away, but he started to study when he returned and soon had no difficulty in ordinary conversations with the Japanese.

They had a very pleasant house near the embassy. It was the same house that was occupied later by Captain Bemis and then by me, when we were attaches.

The garden was adjacent to that of the embassy.

It was a very successful tour of duty for Captain and Mrs. Rogers. Mrs. Rogers was a fine hostess. She was especially fond of the language officers. She gave excellent parties for them. I would say that Captain Rogers was one of the more successful naval attaches from a diplomatic-social point of view that we ever had in Tokyo.

Q: Could you discuss their physical appearance and their personalities? I know Mrs. Rogers is still alive.

Smith-Hutton: Captain Rogers was of medium height, dark complexioned. He was about five feet seven, weighed about 160 pounds, squarely built and was always dressed elegantly.

Mrs. Rogers is smaller. As a matter of fact, she is rather a small lady, and has rather a birdlike appearance. She is now in her nineties and is still active and alert. She is really a remarkable person.

Q: Captain, did Captain Rogers enjoy the same good working relations with Ambassador Grew as did his predecessor, Captain Johnson?

Smith-Hutton: Curiously enough, he did not. I can't explain why but there was some personality clash. They were always, of course, very correct with each other, and there were no outward antagonisms. Perhaps the ambassador did not have as much confidence in Captain Rogers as he had had in Captain Johnson or as he'd had in Lieutenant Colonel Crane, the military attache. I'm sure that the ambassador did not consult with Captain Rogers to the same extent that he had with his predecessor.

Q: Captain, in the early Thirties, the era we're talking of, I sense from Ambassador Grew's memoirs that he was not entirely happy with the policy guidance or lack of it that he was getting from the State Department. Did you have that feeling? As a second question, did you yourself get proper guidance and sufficient guidance from ONI?

Smith-Hutton: I'm sure that your impression is correct. I recall that he voiced that opinion at staff meetings and it was a continuing complaint.

I very rarely got special instructions from the Office of Intelligence or from the Navy Department, but I exchanged letters frequently with the officers in the Far Eastern Section, particularly with Lieutenant A. H. McCollum in the class of '21. While these letters were not the same as official word from the director or official instructions, they were very helpful, and I never had the feeling that I was working in the dark.

Q: Captain, one of the tools of the naval attache is the camera, and in some countries there's no restriction on its use. How was it in Japan?

Smith-Hutton: The Japanese were always on the alert for anyone trying to spy on the secrets of their country. Any non-Japanese who was carrying photographic equipment was immediately suspect. Sometimes they were held temporarily by the police and made to give up the film that was in the camera.

I remember that in 1934, the First National City Bank branch in Osaka got into difficulty with the military police. They had been instructed by New York to take pictures showing various companies that they serviced in Osaka. So they took pictures of some of the larger buildings that had been recently constructed. They planned to use them with a text saying that the First National City Bank has this company in this impressive building as a customer. Some of the buildings were so beautiful that they had the staff of the bank photographed in front of the building.

This aroused the suspicions of the senior military police in Osaka, who first confiscated the film, and then started a virulent anti-American campaign, claiming that the American bank was an agent of the government. According to the story, the pictures were part of a bombing plot. This news was carried in all seriousness in the press.

Actually, it was absurd but the ambassador felt he must make representations to the Foreign Office. The Foreign Minister, admitting that it was absurd, said that there was nothing he could do about it. Since the military police had jurisdiction, we just had to accept it.

However, shortly before I left Tokyo, after I'd been in Japan for six years, I decided that there were many famous places that I had never visited. One Sunday morning, I parked my car near the bus station where sightseeing buses left, and got on the bus with some 40 other people. They were all Japanese except me. I had my camera strapped to my shoulder, and lots of film. We drove around Tokyo for seven hours, had lunch together, laughed and talked and there wasn't the slightest suspicion of me. They could see I wasn't Japanese and that I lived in Tokyo but I was accepted as one of the group. So there's a great deal of luck in how these things work out. How did they know I was not on an intelligence mission?

Q: Captain, I see that you have here a handsome silver cigarette box with engraved signatures from the Naval Attache club in Tokyo. What is the significance of that?

Smith-Hutton: The Naval Attaches met periodically for luncheon. We discussed the Japanese or news or anything that was of interest.

The French naval attache, Commander De La Noe was the doyen during my time as assistant attache. That box was given me by the attaches at a luncheon in March of 1935, before I left Tokyo. Some of the names on there are rather interesting. The Russian Attache was a Captain A. Kovaleff, who is said to have killed the captain of his ship during the Revolution in Leningrad in 1919. He returned to Russia after he left Japan, and was never heard of again.

Captain Ghe, the Italian, was killed in World War II. He was captain of the <u>Trieste</u>, a cruiser sunk at Taranto. Ghe was a very cheery fellow and liked to laugh and to drink. He is said to have wasted no time on finding out about the Japanese Navy, because he felt that the Italians did not need to have any information about Japan. But he was a very pleasant companion.

The British attache was Captain Guy Vivian, who became a rear admiral and distinguished himself in destroyer actions in the Norwegian campaign. Vivian was a typical British officer, tall and formal, but easy to get along with and very friendly toward us.

His assistant was Commander A. C. Ross, an engineering commander who was a most intelligent fellow. He gave me good information in regard to the Japanese machinery in their Navy yards, since many of the Japanese yards had technical relations with British ship yards. He was a very capable officer. After the war when he retired, he held an important position in the shipbuilding industry in Great Britain.

The Chinese naval attache was Rear Admiral T. U. Lin, who was a native of Foochow. He was tall, handsome, spoke excellent English, and had been in both the United States and Great Britain. Although the Japanese and Chinese had not declared war, they were fighting. However, Admiral Lin was well received and well liked by the Japanese.

The last member of our group was Captain G. W. Wenneker, the German attache. He was a typical German naval officer, blond and good looking. He looked as though he could be a cavalry officer. He was well liked by the Japanese. When war broke out he had command of the pocket cruiser Deuteschland, the well known raider in the North Atlantic. He captured many British ships, sank them and sent the crews into Norwegian ports.

After he was relieved, he came again to Japan as naval attache and spent the rest of the war. He's given credit for organizing the exchange of commodities and technical information by submarine between Japan and Germany that was carried out all during the war.

We sank a number of these submarines carrying materials back to Germany, in the Bay of Biscay, since we knew their itineraries and were able to plot their positions.

Rear Admiral Wenneker was interrogated at length by Rear Admiral Ofstie of the strategic bombing survey when the war ended. He also gave Admiral Ofstie considerable information in regard to the Japanese Naval operations.

Q: We'll come back to your experience in Tokyo right after the surrender. You were there. Did you happen to see Admiral Wenneker under these vastly changed circumstances?

Smith-Hutton: Yes, I saw Admiral Wenneker after the war. He had changed very little and looked as though the war hadn't affected him. I knew that Admiral Ofstie was questioning him so I made no effort to duplicate the interrogation.

Q: Captain, ever since World War II the U.S. Navy has been strong on public relations, with our Chief of Information sitting right in the Pentagon as a rear admiral. The purpose of our public relations, of course, is to gain support for the Navy, to explain the Navy to the people, and to mold public opinion in favor of the Navy. In the 1930's, did the Japanese Navy have a similar organization at headquarters?

Smith-Hutton: Yes, they had a public information bureau, which was a section of the Naval Affairs Bureau. That is the general administrative section in the Navy Department. One public affairs group was called the Japan Current Club. In Japanese this would be the Kuro Shio Sha or Duro Shio Kaurabu. The Japanese Current flows along the eastern coast of Japan and continues north to Alaska then down our West Coast, in much the same way as the Gulf Stream flows in the Atlantic. This name has a rather romantic connotation for the Japanese. The public relation groups had no difficulties since the Japanese liked their Navy. They liked the way in which the sailors behaved when they were ashore, they took great pride in the fleet, even in the years before they began to rival the United States and Great Britain.

So the Kuro Shio, which prepared interesting articles about the fleet and the Navy and got them published in the great Japanese newspapers such as the <u>Asahi</u> or the <u>Mainichi</u> or those published in the provinces had a very easy job. Many articles describing the services were published and they were usually well received, not only by young people and children, but by the general public. I would say that the Japanese Navy had very good public relations and was well thought of by all classes.

Interview with Captain Smith-Hutton

Date: 14 March 1974

By: Paul Ryan

Q: Captain, we were discussing your last few months of your three year tour in Tokyo as assistant attache, and perhaps this is the time for me to ask, how did the U.S. embassy and the naval attaches view the political atmosphere of Japan vis-a-vis Manchuria, China, Russia and the United States?

Captain Smith-Hutton: During 1934-35, the embassy felt that the situation in Manchuria was fairly stable, but reports from North China were more disquieting. They showed that Japan was keeping up a relentless steady pressure to consolidate her economic control in the area south of the Great Wall, and that there was a great deal of smuggling. Trucks of cigarettes, kerosene, sugar, rayon, and cotton goods, almost all of Japanese manufacture, were smuggled into China from Manchuria, and the Japanese bribed Chinese officials to ignore this trade. There were reliable reports that there was a very lucrative heroin and morphine trade growing up in the Japanese concession in Tientsin. It showed that the Japanese planned to expand south of the Great Wall. Since there were no clashes, the situation appeared more calm than it really was.

The Japanese policy on the continent did seem to fluctuate at that time, and sometimes those who favored aggressive action against Russia seemed to be in control, and at other times those favoring a southward advance in China seemed to be in control.

Looking at it now, I felt that one reason for this apparent difference was that the high command in Tokyo and Manchuria hadn't decided which way they should go.

We also noted that the Russians were apprehensive, and also seemed to try to incite anti-Japanese feeling in China, perhaps with the idea that this might induce the Chinese to resist the Japanese more strongly which might turn Japanese attention more toward China and relieve some of the pressure on them.

Relations with Russia also appeared strained from time to time because negotiations for the purchase of the Chinese Eastern Railway were taking place. These were difficult although the Russians knew that the Japanese were going to take over the railway whether the negotiations were successful or not.

Please remember that as early as 1932 the embassy informed the State Department that the Japanese Army was going to carry out their program in Manchuria unless prevented by superior physical force, and that liberal Japanese statesmen carried little weight and could do nothing to prevent this.

They made no secret of their plans. In the fall of 1934, the spokesman for the Japanese Foreign Office, Mr. Amau, said quite frankly that Japan had the sole responsibility for the preservation of peace in the Far East, and no interference from foreign countries would be tolerated.

Of course, Secretary of State Hull, answered promptly that we had certain treaty rights, that these could not be abrogated unilaterally and that we expected them to be observed.

At that time Hirota was foreign minister and our ambassador, who saw him frequently felt that he was a clever diplomat, he worked hard to create a basis for dealing with China, Russia, Great Britain and the United States and considering the problems he had with the military, he was reasonably successful.

Q: Captain, Ambassador Grew in his memoirs has a passage that's interesting to read. During a round of farewell dinners for Lieutenant Henri Smith-Hutton, the younger Japanese naval officers were freely outspoken in stating that war with the U.S. was regarded as a foregone conclusion, because the U.S. was bound to oppose certain definite policies of Japan in China, and that an inevitable conflict would result. I imagine that the ambassador is quoting your memorandum to him on this farewell dinner, isn't that so?

Smith-Hutton: Yes, that's quite correct. The young Japanese officers that he referred to were the officers who were the followers of Admiral Kangi Kato, and Admiral Suetsugu, both of whom had been Commander-in-Chief of the Fleet. These were the same officers who stated that in case of a war the United States would have to take the offensive and move westward from Hawaii. In this event, the Japanese plant was to attack our forces and carry on a war of attrition, using destroyers and submarines as well as aircraft.

Interview with Captain Smith-Hutton

Date: 14 March 1974

By: Captain Paul Ryan, USN (Ret.)

Q: Captain, you were discussing the attitude of the young Japanese officers, in a possible war with the U.S., when we ended our last session.

Captain Smith-Hutton: To continue, some younger Japanese made the assumption, that war was inevitable, but I think that this is a difficult conclusion to reach in view of the situation that existed at that time. While we opposed Japanese domination and control of the Far East, Mr. Hull made no threats of war and most of the American people were against war.

It is true that we had differences with Japan, but American public opinion was against going to war with Japan over these differences.

One of the reasons the Japanese younger officers took such a belligerent attitude was that they wanted an excuse for the expansion of the Japanese Navy. They had to have a potential enemy, and the obvious enemy was the United States.

At the same time, the Japanese Army frequently pointed to Russia as a potential enemy, so that the appropriations for the Army would be increased.

Q: That's a very interesting thought, and certainly it may be true of our country and our Navy in the sense that we look upon Russia today as the enemy, and possibly rightly so. It's a reason for asking for higher appropriations.

I have a new question, Captain. At the time you were assistant naval attache, 1932-35, there was quite a number of U.S. naval language officers in Japan. Do you remember them, and could you comment upon their capabilities, both as language officers and possibly as collectors of intelligence?

Smith-Hutton: There were 12 language officers on duty in Tokyo during the three years I was there as assistant attache, and, of course, I knew them very well, because one of my duties was to be a member of the examining board on their yearly and final examinations in Japanese, to measure their progress in the language.

There was Lieutenant (jg) Redfield Mason, who was in the class of '25. Mason was an excellent officer and a fine language officer. He became one of our best communication intelligence officers and during the war he commanded several stations in the United States, in Hawaii and in Australia. He was very competent in the language.

Another officer was Lieutenant (jg) Daniel J. McCallum in the class of '24, a quiet, skillful officer. He spoke very little in either English or Japanese, although he could speak clearly and well in both of them. He was an excellent translator. He was on Guadalcanal for eight months during the height of the campaign in the Southwest Pacific, as part of Commander South Pacific's intelligence group. One of his assignments was to listen to the voice communications of the Japanese Army and Navy in the area, and report to our commanders what was being said.

Another was Lieutenant (jg) Henri DeB Claiborne, class of '26. Claiborne, although a good companion and a good officer in general was not as good in the Japanese language as most of the others.

Another was a Lieutenant (jg) A. D. Kramer. Kramer, as you recall, was the officer who was attached to Op-20-G and who made the rounds of the President's office, the Chief of Naval Operations' office and the Secretary of State's office, with the translations of the Japanese messages received just before Pearl Harbor. He was an intelligent, able officer.

Q: That was the famous Fourteen Parts message, was it not, Captain?

Smith-Hutton: That is the one Kramer worked on/in Op-20-G for a long time. He was an excellent officer and was in charge of the translation section in Op-20-G at the time.

First Lieutenant K. H. Cornell, a Marine officer, was another student and was also a competent officer. I believe he was attached to Marine units in the South Pacific. I must say I haven't heard of Cornell and have lost touch with him.

Lieutenant (jg) J. A. Carlson, also in the class of '26, was assigned duties with Op-20-G and the cryptographic sections in Hawaii and in the Australian areas, as was Lieutenant (jg) Ransom Fullinwider.

Another officer was Lieutenant (jg) M. M. Ricker. Unfortunately, although he tried hard, was unsuccessful. I had to recommend that he be detached since he was not suited to learn the language.

This did not reflect on his worth as an officer.

Lieutenant (jg) M. R. Stone was another good language officer. Stone worked not only in cryptographic sections in Hawaii and Australia but he later joined General MacArthur's headquarters in Tokyo after the war.

The same could be said in regard to Lieutenant (jg) Joseph Finnigan, although Finnigan spent most of his time in Hawaii.

Lieutenant (jg) H. E. Karrer, in the class of '29 and Lieutenant (jg) F. D. Jordan also in the class of '29, complete the 12 officers. I think that there were more officers in that period, than at any other time in the history of the language course. It was too bad that there weren't more of them.

Q: Captain, in the three years that these students were in Japan, did you, as naval attache, ever assign them any intelligence collection duties?

Smith-Hutton: No. I felt that their primary job was to learn the language. They were not trained and could get into trouble. On the other hand, all of them were informed that if they learned anything of naval interest they were to report it to me.

Q: Thank you for the evaluation of that large list of officers. It's quite clear that the fact that the U.S. Navy sent them to Japan for this training paid off in World War II.

I have a question here, Captain, regarding the round of farewell dinners which were tended to you on your departure. Could you describe where they took place and who attended?

Smith-Hutton: Several dinners were given by my friends in the Japanese Navy. Invariably, they followed the same pattern, and held in one of the large and elaborate establishments called geisha houses. These were bachelor parties. The guests sit on the large straw mats that the Japanese use as a floor, and are served on low tables by the geishas. During the course of the dinner, the geisha perform dances, sing and play Japanese musical instruments. They are professional entertainers, and some of them are very attrative. Their mission is to make the men in the party enjoy themselves, and after a fashion they are successful.

Also there is a considerable amount of sake (a warm Japanese rice wine) served, and the food is always Japanese food. This traditional entertaining of the Japanese is well known and it is pleasant after you have become accustomed to it. Japanese men enjoy it, to put it mildly.

I remember one reception which was given for me at the Navy Department which was a departure from this traditional style. It was an afternoon tea party, held in the reception rooms of the Navy Ministry. The unusual thing was that many young Japanese women, the wives and daughters of younger naval officers, were invited. This was the first time such a party was ever given. The hosts were the admirals who had been naval attaches in the United States. One of them was Vice Admiral Yamamoto who later became Commander-in-Chief, and Admiral Nagano. I felt that they were preparing younger officers and their wives to take part in

American and European style receptions and parties, which were unusual in Japan, and therefore that this party was in the nature of a training exercise. I felt honored to be included in that sort of exercise.

Q: I'm sure you're right in your assumption, because I recall in the summer of 1936, when as a new ensign I reported to the Navy Yard at Bremerton and we had a reception for the Japanese training ship that had just arrived, I'll never forget how shy and introverted the Japanese midshipmen seemed and how reluctant they were to go through the receiving line.

Captain, having spent three years in Japan, did Ambassador Grew take any official recognition of your departure?

Smith-Hutton: Shortly after I got back to the United States, I received a letter from the Chief of Operations, signed by the Director of Intelligence, saying what Ambassador Grew had told him when they met in Washington shortly after I returned.

Q: You seem to have a letter there, Captain. Do you mind reading it into the record?

Smith-Hutton: This letter, dated 7 February 1936, is from the Chief of Naval Operations to Chief of the Bureau of Navigation, and the subject is Lieutenant H. H. Smith-Hutton, USN, commendation of, "1) In a recent conversation with the Director of Naval Intelligence, the American Ambassador to Japan, Mr. Joseph C. Grew, volunteered the following comments on Lieutenant H. H. Smith-Hutton, who completed the tour of duty at the American Embassy, Tokyo, in the capacity of assistant naval attache."

"A. that Lieutenant Smith-Hutton has the reputation of being the most accomplished language officer to have studied in Japan."

"B. that this officer possesses intelligence and judgment to an outstanding degree;"

"And C. that he is most desirous of having this officer with him again at the earliest possible time."

"2. It is requested that this be placed on his record.

Signed, W. D. Puleston, by direction."

Q: Perhaps we should identify W. D. Puleston.

Smith-Hutton: Captain Puleston was, at that time, the Director of Naval Intelligence.

Q: Thank you, sir. Captain, when were you relieved, who relieved you, and when did you finally depart Japan?

Smith-Hutton: My relief was Lieutenant Ethelbert Watts, Naval Academy class of 1924. He had been a language officer, had arrived in Japan two years after I came, and he relieved me in April 1935. I was detached on the 6th with orders to report to Washington. I sailed on the Dollar Line steamship, President Grant, going to Seattle by the Northern route. There were only about 30 passengers on board, since most people crossing the Pacific preferred the

Southern route, via Honolulu, where they spent several days. It was better weather and the break in the voyage at Honolulu was usually a pleasant one.

Although it was spring, the Northern route was cold and foggy. Fortunately, there were no storms and I spent most of my time sitting on deck, well wrapped up, or down in my stateroom reading, because there was little else to do on the ship. Many of the other passengers were from the Philippines and from China, American businessmen and their families traveling by the quickest route, returning after periods of duty in the Far East. They were very good companions, but I was exhausted after the round of parties in Tokyo, so I decided to rest.

On arrival in Seattle, I was furnished rail transportation to Washington, was allowed a month's delay in reporting, the delay acting as leave, so I went home to the Black Hills in South Dakota. Unfortunately, it was a sad trip, since my mother, who'd been ill with cancer, died about ten days after I got there. It was a blow because I had expected to spend my leave with her.

I went on to Washington and reported there on the 20th of May, 1935.

Smith-Hutton #18 - 180

Interview with Captain Smith-Hutton

Date: March 21, 1974

By: Captain Paul Ryan, USN (Ret.)

Q: Captain, as I understand the setting for this session, we are now in Washington in the spring of 1935, you're reporting in to the Director of Naval Intelligence who is Captain William Puleston. What did you think of Captain Puleston when you were briefing him on your stay in Japan?

Captain Smith-Hutton: I thought that Captain Puleston was a very able officer, and that he had done a great deal to build up the character ability and number of personnnel in the Office of Intelligence. He was very aggressive. He asked many questions about Japan. He had read a great deal. He read Ambassador Grew's cables and reports and he also read many of the embassy and consular reports from China and it seemed to me that he and his officers paid a great deal of attention to Far Eastern problems.

The head of the Far Eastern Section was Lieutenant McCollum. The head of the Intelligence Section was Captain Heard, and I think Commander Van Hook was head of Security.

In the Far Eastern Section, officers who had proper clearance followed the program to break the Japanese code, MAGIC very closely, and it seemed to me that they were making every effort to improve the sources of information and the accuracy of data. I thought that the Far Eastern Section was a hard-working, alert section and very well-informed. Actually I had no way of judging the efficiency of the other sections because I was there such a short time, but I was very much impressed by the office.

As far as my reports were concerned, no one asked my views about general strategic questions of the Far East. Our conversations were in regard to technical matters, such as details of the budget, the cost of materials, the expansion of plants, new aircraft and the merchant ships that I had seen. ONI officers were anxious to have me elaborate on our reports, if I was able to do so. In some cases I could and they were pleased.

Q: Captain Puleston was not only a very fine naval officer but an author of note. Was he bound and determined to upgrade the status of ONI within the Navy Department?

Smith-Hutton: Yes, and it was my impression that there was great rivalry in the Chief of Naval Operations' office, particularly with the War Plans Division. It seemed to me that Captain Puleston, who was an aggressive officer and interested in getting superior personnel in Intelligence, was doing a fine job. He seemed to want to make ONI one of the outstanding offices in the Department.

Q: Captain, Lieutenant McCollum as the Far Eastern Desk officer was your liaison between ONI and Tokyo when you were there. What was the background that gave Lieutenant McCollum such a fine understanding of Japan?

Smith-Hutton: Lieutenant McCollum had been in Japan as a child.

His parents were teachers in a missionary college, and he had returned to Japan in 1922, just a year after he graduated, to study Japanese for three years. That is, he was there from 1922 to '25. Then from October 1928 to June of 1930, he was assistant naval attache, and was promoted to Lieutenant Commander while he was there. He returned to the Office of Intelligence several times, always in the Far Eastern Section. So he knew Japan thoroughly. He not only spoke Japanese well, he read it, and he understood the Japanese people.

Q: Yes, I recall Rear Admiral McCollum when I was serving in Washington in 1969-72, and I believe he's still active.

Captain, while you were at ONI during your debriefing in 1935, you must have sensed the attitude of ONI and naval officers in general to Japanese aggression in Manchuria and China. Could you discuss that?

Smith-Hutton: It seemed to me that Naval officers in Washington in general took a very realistic view of China, perhaps much more realistic than other Americans because many of them had served in the Asiatic Fleet, had seen how inefficient, divided, poverty-stricken and poor the Chinese were. They had also seen how selfish and dishonest the warlords were, including the very highest officials in China. Most of our officers felt that it was about time China put her own house in order, that we could not do more than we were doing to help them. They felt that we didn't have to fight Chinas' battles for her, that since the Japanese action was concentrated in Manchuria, the Chinese should be able to handle that themselves; that the Japanese had had an interest in Manchuria from the late 19th century and that there was serious rivalry there between China and Russia.

I felt that there was little anti-Japanese feeling or pro-Chinese feeling among our officers at that time.

At the same time, they realized that our fleet was concentrated in the Pacific, on the orders of the President, with the idea of trying to curb Japanese expansion. If that was the policy of our country, it was a decision made at the highest echelon, and of course the Navy carried out orders without questioning them.

The Office of Naval Intelligence wanted complete and accurate information to assist in preparing war plans, so that whatever mission was assigned, the Navy could carry it out properly. One of our big regrets was incomplete intelligence especially in regard to the mandated islands where our information was very sketchy.

Q: Well, Captain, where did you stay during your debriefing period? At the Army-Navy Club?

Smith-Hutton: No. During this short stay in Washington, I spent the first part of it with an old friend, Lieutenant Jay Pierrepont, in my class, who had a house on R Street in Georgetown. He and his wife wanted me to spend my entire period in Washington with them, but after about ten days I moved to a small hotel not far from the Navy Department, the Roger Smith.

Q: You'll be glad to know, Captain, that the Roger Smith is still in operation.

Smith-Hutton: It's a nice hotel.

Q: Captain, how did you receive orders for your next tour of duty?

Smith-Hutton: My original orders, which detached me from the Office of the Naval Attache, were as executive officer of the Jacob Jones, an East Coast destroyer. As I was on my way home, these orders were modified, and on my arrival in Washington, I found that new orders ordered me as executive office of the destroyer Lawrence.

On 9 July 1935, I was detached from ONI to report to the Lawrence, then in San Diego. I went by train and reported on 13 July.

Q: To put the picture in perspective, one might mention here that the Secretary of the Navy's report for 1935 mentions that there were 117 destroyer-type ships in operation, of which the Lawrence was one. We also had 15 battleships, four carriers, 26 cruisers, 53 submarines and 89 auxiliaries.

Captain, was the Lawrence a World War I type destroyer?

Smith-Hutton: Yes. The Lawrence was Destroyer 250. She was one of the flush deck, four stack destroyers that were built at the end of World War I. Some of them saw action in World War I. They were excellent destroyers of approximately 1190 tons, 27,000 horsepower with an overall length of 314 feet, 31 foot beam and nine foot draft. They made 35 knots, carried four 4-inch guns, one 3-inch gun and 12 torpedoes in four triple tube mounts. The crew was usually six officers and 122 men. They were good seaboats, and were as successful as any destroyer that had been constructed up to that time.

Since they were designed to combat German submarines, they carried depth charges, and were good convoy escort vessels. The Lawrence was named for Captain James Lawrence of the frigate Chesapeake who was killed in action with the British Frigate Shannon in the War of 1812.

Q: Were these World War I vintage destroyers still in action in World War II?

Smith-Hutton: Yes, they were, and they continued to give good service until they were replaced by more modern ships. In 1940, we gave 50 of these ships to the British in exchange for base rights in the Caribbean and in the Western Atlantic. They served the British well, even though they were, many of them, more than 25 years old.

Q: In 1935, Captain, we had a Navy of approximately 82,000 men. We were building up the Navy under the Vinson-Trammel Act, so although we had more ships, we didn't have more men to man them, so most of the ships were under-manned. Did you find this the case? And what kind of enlisted men did you have?

Smith-Hutton: While the crew of the Lawrence was certainly not large, it was sufficient for normal operations during peacetime. One of the things that struck me was that the young men enlisting in the Navy at that time, were higher type men than you might have expected. That was because of the depression and the fact that young men wanted to work. At any rate, many of the crew had been in high school and some were high school graduates, so training them was much easier than it would have been with a crew with less education. The discipline was good, and we had few personnel problems in the ships operating out of San Diego at that time.

Q: The skipper of Lawrence was Lieutenant Commander R. A. Dierdorff. What kind of officer was he, Captain?

Smith-Hutton: Lieutenant Commander Dierdorff was a first class officer. He was in the Naval Academy class of 1919. He had been in destroyers during World War I since his class had been graduated from the Naval Academy in 1918. He had served in the destroyer squadron operating out of Queenstown, Ireland. He was an experienced officer, and was an excellent ship handler. His skill at maneuvers, handling the ship in and out of harbor and around docks, was so expert that all hands were very proud of him. He was a very human officer, well liked by the crew, a real gentleman, which made the Lawrence a happy ship.

Q: Did Lieutenant Commander Dierdorff speak of his World War I service?

Smith-Hutton: He had been in a destroyer in 1918. His ship, whose name I cannot recall, was one that had been cut in two in a collision with a large transport. The bow was sheered off. The commanding officer was Commander William Glassford who became a Vice Admiral. They eventually got the ship into Queenstown, and put a new bow on her. For his conduct he was given the Navy Cross. He really was an experienced destroyer officer.

Q: Did he take the opportunity as captain to train his deck officers in ship handling?

Smith-Hutton: We spent many mornings drilling, taking the ship alongside other ships, simulating picking up a buoy, or doing standard ship handling exercises that are necessary to train a good officer of the deck.

Q: What was the makeup of the wardroom officers? Were they all Academy graduates? Did you have any staff officers aboard such as supply officer?

Smith-Hutton: There was no supply officer except the division supply officer who was not in the Lawrence and there was no medical officer either. We had an experienced pharmacist's mate, and an experienced chief storekeeper, so we were well taken care of.

Q: And all the officers were from the Naval Academy?

Smith-Hutton: All the officers were Naval Academy graduates.

Q: Captain, the goal of the fleet was to exercise and train the fleet to the highest state of efficiency, according to the Secretary of the Navy's report. Can you comment on that?

Smith-Hutton: I can say that we spent many hours under way and we spent hours in drills and exercises which are important for destroyers, especially with submarines. I remember that Commander Charles Lockwood, who commanded a submarine squadron, came aboard for exercises during an entire month period. We alternated in training the ships in his submarine squadron and the destroyers in our squadron. The submarines actually fired torpedoes at us and then these torpedoes were recovered, and then we would take turns in trying to locate the submarines, using our rather primitive sound gear.

The submarines were more efficient in attacking us than we were in locating them, but we tried hard to train personnel and to get good anti-submarine warfare training which is one of the most important things that destroyer officers have to learn.

Other exercises included division tactical exercises. A fleet exercise was also held. One afternoon about 1 o'clock, we received a message addressed to all ships present from the Commander-in Chief, to get under way as soon as possible and sortie from San Diego Harbor, to have no communication with the shore, and to hoist no general recall.

The Lawrence was under way in about 30 minutes and we stood

out with the other destroyers of the Scouting Force. We steamed in fleet formation for approximately 48 hours, conducting simulated torpedo attacks on the Scouting Force main body, and then returned to port. There had been no word sent ashore as to the purpose of the exercise, so the Commandant of the District informed the newspapers that it was a training exercise. This quieted rumors which started to circulate as soon as people ashore saw that the ships were leaving port. The Admiral considered the exercise a success, and he was much pleased at the alertness of the ships and the speed with which most of them got under way having had no previous notice.

Q: Captain, the Fleet Commander as I recall was Admiral Joseph Reeves, who was an aviation enthusiast and probably the father of the carrier task force. In the spring and summer of 1935, you participated in Fleet Problem 17. Can you describe that exercise?

Smith-Hutton: The fleet problem had several phases. The first part consisted in tactical drills, on the way south to the latitude of the Panama Canal. Then the scouting force was formed into a force to attack the Canal. The carriers, Saratoga and Lexington were in the attacking force. In the course of these exercises, the scouting force destroyers took part in several simulated night actions. We made simulated night torpedo attacks on the battleships. After these exercises were completed, we anchored in Panama before transiting the Canal. The critique of the exercise was conducted ashore by the Commander-in-Chief. Then the scouting force, including destroyers, transited the Canal and went north to East Coast ports.

Q: Lieutenant Commander Dierdorff undoubtedly attended the critique of this exercise in Panama. Did you receive any comment from his on the success or failure of it?

Smith-Hutton: He came back and gave us an account of the briefing, and indicated that the Commander-in-Chief, Admiral Reeves and his staff considered that the exercise had been a very useful one. It had shown that the Canal was very vulnerable to air attack from carriers; he recommended that this kind of exercise be repeated since we had learned many lessons from it.

Q: Captain, with regard to torpedoes in the destroyer navy, I recall that as midshipmen we had to learn that torpedoes were 21 inches in diameter and had a weight of 2100 pounds and cost $21,000. Also, we later learned in World War II that the warheads of our submarine torpedoes were in many cases non-explosive. We'd fire, hit the target, and nothing would happen. As a destroyer officer in the mid-Thirties, did you have any opportunity to observe the performance of our torpedoes?

Smith-Hutton: We fired many torpedoes of course, not only in the Asiatic Fleet, but also in the Scouting Force, so we knew that our torpedomen could adjust them so that they ran normally, that is, hot and straight. However, torpedoes were not exploded and there were no exercises which called for the use of warheads because in the Navy in those days $21,000 was not expended for exercise purposes. However, the exploder mechanisms should have been tested by ships. And I don't know why this was not done.

Q: Yes, I agree that it's too bad that somebody in the Bureau of Ordnance didn't schedule some explosive tests before we ran into that World War II problem.

Captain, could you describe the recreation program that you as executive officer ran aboard the ship?

Smith-Hutton: The recreation program centered around the baseball teams, and the baseball games with the other destroyers in the squadron.

The crew of the Lawrence had ships parties, the baseball schedule and the movies. They seemed contented and we spent much time in port. There were recreation facilities at the destroyer base, so there was no lack of recreation for the crew of the ship.

Q: Thank you, Captain. I gather that the morale aboard the USS Lawrence was very high quality, due to the leadership on board. With regard to Lieutenant Commander Dierdorff, do you know what ever happened to him?

Smith-Hutton: Lieutenant Commander Dierdorff stayed in the ship until 1937, and then to shore duty in Washington. During the early part of the war, he had command of a large transport which took part in the landings in North Africa and in the Mediterranean. Then he took his ship to the Pacific. Toward the end of the war he commanded a transport division, with much success, and with credit.

Q: I believe he made flag rank also, Captain?

Smith-Hutton: Yes, that is correct.

Q: And I believe he passed away several years ago.

Smith-Hutton: Yes, he did. He was a very fine officer.

Q: This concludes the session on 21 March, and thank you very much for a fine session, Captain.

Interview with Captain Smith-Hutton

Date: 28 March 1974

By: Captain Paul Ryan, USN (Ret.)

Q: Captain, we're reaching the end of your tour of duty as executive officer of the destroyer Lawrence, and the time now is in the spring of 1936, and the ship was engaged in annual maneuvers in the Panama area. Could you pick up your narrative from there?

Captain Smith-Hutton: After the completion of Fleet Problem 17 and the critique in Panama, the Scouting Force went through the Panama Canal enroute to East Coast ports, we sailed with the squadron through the Caribbean. The Lawrence arrived in Norfolk, Virginia on 10 June 1936.

Q: Was that a permanent transfer to the Atlantic, Captain?

Captain Smith-Hutton: No, it was only temporary. On completion of summer exercises on the East Coast and visits to various ports, some ships had overhaul periods in Navy yards. The Scouting Force returned to the West Coast in late summer of '36. They had been on the East Coast long enough to give the crews a chance to visit their families, many of whom were still on the East Coast.

Q: That certainly was a hardship that people probably accepted but they never would accept today.

Smith-Hutton: That's very true.

Q: I note from your record that you were detached from the ship shortly after your arrival in Norfolk. Was this a surprise?

Smith-Hutton: No. I knew that my orders were coming. I had learned that I was to be detached on 12 June to proceed across the Continent by rail in time to arrive in San Francisco before 10 July. The orders specified that I was to board the SS President Hoover sailing for Manila on the 10th. The delay was to count as leave, and it was given to me so that I could get married.

My future wife, whose father was an Army officer on duty in Sioux City, Iowa, was to give his daughter to me on 26 June.

Q: Could you tell us the names of your future wife and her father?

Smith-Hutton: He was Lieutenant Colonel M.A.S. Ming, U.S. Army, and my wife's name is Jane. She is his older daughter. The orders specified that in case I did not want to accept them and pay for the transportation across the Continent, I could return them to the Bureau of Navigation, for re-issue.

Q: Was this part of our economy campaign?

Smith-Hutton: This was still part of our economy campaign.

An incident which is worth mentioning took place on my way from Washington to Sioux City. I planned to spend the night in

Omaha, Nebraska, in order to arrive at Sioux City at a convenient hour, and I'd been sitting in the parlor car such as was then was attached to passenger trains. I'd been reading an article from a Japanese magazine and making notes from it and I saw that several people were regarding me curiously.

Before arrival in Omaha, I put all of my papers, including my orders and these Japanese articles, in my briefcase. When I left the train I went to the hotel where my father was staying. He was coming to attend our wedding.

I went to the hotel, and then to his room with my luggage. My father was there and we decided to have dinner, so we locked the room and went to the dining room. When we returned, the room was in great disorder with our clothing scattered about showing that someone had made a hurried search. However, the only articles missing were my briefcase and a suit of clothing belonging to my father. It did not appear to be an ordinary burglary because on the commode in our room, I'd left a valuable Leica Camera and a gold pocket watch which were not taken. There were no papers of value in my briefcase and the Japanese material was of no importance, but the burglar must have thought they were. There wasn't anything in the briefcase that anyone could possibly want.

The hotel reimbursed us for the value of the briefcase and the clothing, and I got a certified copy of my orders from the Bureau of Navigation, but we never did find out who took them. Some of my friends in ONI were convinced that it must have been a Japanese agent, but if it were, he wasn't a clever one.

Q: On the other hand, Captain, it might have been an over-zealous American counter-intelligence agent who was convinced that you were an Oriental spy and that he was going to be a hero.

Smith-Hutton: That could be, yes.

Q: Captain, I think before we proceed, it might be wise at this point to have you give us a resume of your orders.

Smith-Hutton: The orders read to proceed by rail to San Francisco, to report to the Commandant 12th Naval District for passage to Manila. I was authorized to delay until 10 July 1936, to take passage on the SS President Hoover, and on arrival to report to the Commandant 16th Naval District and to the Commander-in-Chief, Asiatic Fleet for such duty as might be assigned to me.

We proceeded in accordance with these orders and went first to San Diego, where my wife had been going to college when I met her. Then to San Francisco, and on 10 July we sailed on the President Hoover for Honolulu, after stopping at Yokohama and Kobe, the ship continued on to Shanghai.

On arrival in Shanghai, I received orders from the Commander-in-Chief modifying my original orders instructing me to disembark at Shanghai and proceed by the first available commercial conveyance flying a foreign flag to Tsingtao, to report to the commanding officer of the Augusta for duty.

There were no governmental or U.S. commercial ships available, so I proceeded on the Japanese steamer SS Tsingtao Maru, and arrived in Tsingtao on 30 July 1936.

Q: Let me ask, Captain, was life in the Far East new to Mrs. Smith-Hutton?

Smith-Hutton: No, she had been in the Far East for several years and had visited China and the Philippines as a young woman, so this was not her first visit.

Q: Captain, when an officer goes to a sensitive billet such as you were going to, it's usual to bring them to Washington for some instructions and briefing. I forgot to ask you, did you go through Washington before proceeding to Shanghai?

Smith-Hutton: Yes, I spent a week in Washington being briefed on the Far East and my probable assignment. I was told that I would be assigned as communications officer of the USS Augusta, the flagship, and I also learned that Lieutenant Joseph Wenger, a close friend who was a radio intelligence specialist, was to be assigned to the Commander-in-Chief's staff, and would arrive in the Far East shortly after I got there. It was also known that Admiral H. E. Yarnell was to relieve Admiral Murfin toward the end of October, and it was our understanding that the Admiral was already selecting his staff. Lieutenant Wenger was to be assistant communication officer, according to the word in Washington.

Q: As I understand it, you received this information from officers such as Lieutenant Commander McCollum and others.

Smith-Hutton: That's correct.

Q: At this time did they refer to our program to break the Japanese code as "Magic"?

Smith: Yes, and later the normal designation became Ultra.

Q: I imagine that your trip in the Tsingtao Maru was a safe passage, and you arrived in this North China port to find quite a contingent of the U.S. Asiatic Fleet there.

Smith-Hutton: Yes, Japanese steamers running between Shanghai and northern Chinese ports were comfortable and well run. We got to Tsingtao on the 30th, and went right to a small house that we had arranged to get through the kindness of a friend, Lieutenant Commander Sabalot who was the navigator of the Augusta.

We had a small house which was in a pleasant garden, my wife being very fond of gardening, and we settled down to an enjoyable summer. The ships operating in Tsingtao were the submarine squadron, the submarine tender, the fleet flagship, and the minesweeping group. The destroyer squadron and the destroyer tender were in Chefoo which is on the north side of the Shantung Peninsula, not far from Tsingtao.

Summer is pleasant in North China and we carried out routine gunnery training and ship handling drills. The political situation was quiet, ships usually spent the weekends in port, and the crews got regular shore leave and liberty.

Q: Captain, could you describe who the skipper of the flagship was and something of his personality?

Smith-Hutton: The captain of the Augusta was Captain Felix Gygax. Captain Gygax was of Swiss origin, a very fine officer with great intelligence and force of character. He was an excellent ship handler, competent in every way. He'd had intelligence duty in Germany before World War I. He spoke German fluently. He became Admiral and would have made a name for himself in World War II if he had been in better health. His health failed and although he was not retired, he was restricted to shore duty and became the Commandant of the First Naval District. He was one of the finest officers that I've served with.

Q: Could you compare him with any other officer that we know of?

Smith-Hutton: In my view, he was as able and as competent as Admiral Spruance.

Q: What I deduce from this, and I think we all know it, is that luck plays an important part in a senior officer's career.

Smith-Hutton: It does indeed.

Q: I recall from our conversations that when you were communication officer of the Houston some years back, you had very little staff help. Did you find the same situation prevailing this time?

Smith-Hutton: No, indeed. The communication organization of the
Augusta was excellent. I had two fine radio officers, a radio
warrant officer and an excellent signal officer. The ship's
organization was in reality a part of the communications organization of the Commander-in-Chief. The captain gave every assistance
to the communication department, since it was of very great importance. It was quite different from the situation that I had in
the Houston when she went in commission in 1930. I was very happy
to be communication officer. We got everything we needed to do a
good job.

Q: From your description of the communication department, it was
quite efficient. Did the department receive any official recognition during the time you were there?

Smith-Hutton: Yes. At the end of the competition year, that is
in 1937, the captain of the Augusta, who was then Captain H. V.
McKittrick, received the following letter from the Acting Chief
of Naval Operations.

"The USS Augusta under your command from 16 March 1937 to
30 June 1937 during the competition year '36-'37 attained in communication the highest score obtained by any ship of the cruiser tender
class, in competition group 1 of the Asiatic Fleet. The Chief of
Naval Operations congratulates you on the success obtained by the
Augusta and on the efficiency evidenced thereby. You are authorized
to attach copies of this letter to the records of such officers of
the communication department of the Augusta by you to have been

responsible for the score attained. The Chief of Naval Operations has requested the Bureau of Navigation to attach a copy of this letter to your record. The USS Augusta has been authorized to display the White "C" and the commanding officer to pay $830 in prize money and award White "E's" in accordance with the communication competition rules for '36-'37."

The captain of the Augusta sent me a letter via the Commander-in-Chief saying that my service in capacity as a communication officer had contributed toward the attainment of the score, and I deserved a share of the credit. That is the reason a copy of this letter is attached to my record.

Q: That's a very interesting letter and I'm noting also that $830 in prize money was awarded, and I presume that was to the enlisted members of the department.

Smith-Hutton: Yes, the money was divided among the enlisted personnel.

Q: We don't do that any more, Captain, which may be regrettable for our enlisted men.

Captain, you mentioned that Lieutenant Joe Wenger was going to the Augusta, I gather as a communication intelligence officer. Could you describe how his operation worked?

Smith-Hutton: There were about six radiomen in his group. Their assignment was experimental radio intelligence. Lieutenant Wenger had them copy not only Japanese communications, but the communications of other nations with radio stations, including the French, the British, and the Russians. They were too few to keep regular intercept watches as was done in Cavite and in Shanghai. However, since the Augusta was a mobile station, they could supplement the work of the other stations.

Lieutenant Wenger was detached after a short time for an urgent assignment at home and his place was taken by Lieutenant Jack Holtwick who stayed on the Commander-in-Chief's staff for several years.

Q: Captain, that's very interesting, and I think that Lieutenant Wenger's activities show the increased sensitivity in the U.S. Navy as to need of gaining foreign communication intelligence. Can you tell us, what shore activities was Lieutenant Wenger interested in in addition to the sea-based Augusta station?

Smith-Hutton: Our major station in the Far East was in Cavite. There was a small group of Marine radiomen, with a Marine Corps officer in charge attached to the Fourth Marine Regiment in Shanghai, which was a very important station, from both a local and an experimental standpoint. At one time there was an intercept station on Guam, but it was found that this duplicated Cavite and Shanghai so Guam was phased out before World War II started. Lieutenant Wenger continued in this very important work during his entire career. During World War II he was the communication trouble shooter for all areas including the Mediterranean and United Kingdom.

He became an Admiral as a communication specialist and was one of our experts in that field.

Q: Captain, the new Commander-in-Chief of the Asiatic Fleet is Admiral Harry E. Yarnell, and he was relieving Admiral Orin Murfin. Would you describe what took place with the arrival of Admiral Yarnell in October?

Smith-Hutton: Admiral Murfin had prepared a schedule for the remainder of 1936, and had submitted it to Admiral Yarnell, who was still in the United States, for his approval. About the middle of September, we received word that Admiral Yarnell had approved the plans for a Southern cruise.

On 30 October Admiral Yarnell relieved Admiral Murfin, but about 15 days before that, the Augusta had gone to Shanghai. The change in command took place in Shanghai. Shortly afterwards the ship sailed for Hong Kong for a ten day visit. During that period, the Admiral and his staff conferred with the British Far Eastern Commander-in-Chief and made a brief visit to Canton.

After 10 days in Hong Kong, we left for Singapore. Six destroyers accompanied the Augusta on this cruise, so in between ports it was possible to exercise attacks and gunnery exercises. There were no actual target practices.

At Singapore, we were very well received, and the Admiral conferred with the British officers and with the governor. He was very much interested in this area, and I know that he asked many questions and discussed frankly with the British common Far Eastern problems. Although I did not know it at the time, I learned later that in both Hong Kong and in Singapore, he sounded out the British officers on joint defense problems and he was appalled to learn that there were no real understandings on operations between our Navy and the British Navy, in case of war in the Far East.

I found out later too that he recommended to the Chief of Naval Operations that conversations which would lead to joint understandings be started. Unfortunately, there were difficulties of a political nature which prevented an agreement until a few days before the outbreak of war.

The Admiral was shown the military installations in Singapore and was very much interested in them. After five days in Singapore we went to Batavia, where we got a warm reception from the authorities of the Dutch East Indies. In Batavia after the usual exchange of courtesies there was time for sightseeing and travel. There were about 15 wives of the staff and ships' officers who were in Java at the same time the ships were. They were much interested in the country and much impressed by the beauty of the Dutch East Indies, which are lovely.

After ten days in Batavia, we went East to Bali, where we spent four days, much to the amusement of all of us because in 1936, the women in Bali dressed just as they do now -- topless.

The four days in Bali were enjoyable as were the two days we spent in Macassar, in the Celebes Islands.

This visit to Macassar was our farewell to the Netherlands Indies, and after a quick visit to Tawi-Tawi in the Philippines, the ships returned to Manila, arriving on 20 December just in time for the Christmas holidays. It was an enjoyable cruise and we were all delighted with our experiences.

Q: How did Admiral Yarnell strike you as a Commander-in-Chief?

Smith-Hutton: Admiral Yarnell was certainly a splendid officer and a great Commander-in-Chief. He was extremely intelligent. He made no attempt to impose his ideas on others, and I noted that invariably he began conversations by asking many questions. During the course of the conversation he gradually injected his own opinions in a modest cautious way. The result was that he got along equally well with governors, admirals and newspapermen. You always had the feeling that you were talking to somebody who was an extraordinarily good listener. He was a simple man with no "side", and he impressed everybody as being a genuine, fine gentleman.

Q: Captain, I appreciate that when you're a ship's communication officer and you have the Admiral's flag allowance come aboard, that things can get a little tense sometimes in communications. What was your relationship with the flag?

Smith-Hutton: The relations between the ships' communication division and the flag communication division were excellent. The fleet communication officer at that time was Lieutenant Commander Tex Settle, who later became a vice admiral. He was also a distinguished lighter-than-air man. Settle had been in command of a gunboat on the Upper Yangtze River and was ordered as a fleet communication officer, since he also had much communication duty. He was a fine man to work with. There was never any real conflict between ship's personnel and staff personnel. When the staff was on board, the combined staff and ship's complements supplemented each other's work. Of course, we kept the two separate organizations because there was always the possibility that the staff would be suddenly transferred to another ship.

The ship's communication volume was small in comparison with the staff's, so the organization had to provide for the requirements of the Commander-in-Chief.

Q: Did the Admiral ever transfer his flag to another ship?

Smith-Hutton: Yes. There was a trim, beautiful yacht, the Isabel, that was the relief flagship. The Isabel had been taken over by the Navy in World War I, and used as a patrol vessel. She had powerful engines and was built like a destroyer and could make 27 knots. She had been sent to the Far East after World War I and for approximately 20 years was the flagship of the Rear Admiral who commanded the Yangtze Patrol Force. About 1932, we built six modern gunboats especially designed for the Yangtze River and the USS Luzon became the force flagship.

At that time, the Isabel was made the relief flagship of the Asiatic fleet. Frequently the regular flagship was at sea engaged in gunnery exercises and maneuvers, in the Philippine area and in China ports so the admiral could shift to the Isabel which remained in port.

During the winter of 1937-1938 the admiral desired to stay in Shanghai because of the tense situation in China and at that time he sent the Augusta to Manila keeping only his flag lieutenant and the fleet intelligence officer with him, on the Isabel. In this way he remained in touch with our ambassador in China, with the authorities in Shanghai and the commanding officer of our Marine forces.

Q: As a large cruiser, how did the Augusta receive major alterations and repairs?

Smith-Hutton: Most of the work was done at Cavite Navy Yard. For instance, early in 1937, on completion of the cruise to Singapore and the Netherlands Indes, the ship went to Cavite for overhaul which lasted approximately two months. The ship anchored off Cavite and the workmen were sent out from the yard. Almost all the word that was required was for the engineering department. The capacity of the yard to do hull overhaul was limited, but the Augusta was a new ship, and no hull work was required.

In the course of the overhaul, the ship's force was able to make the minor gunnery changes that had been authorized and make the routine inspections and do upkeep. Thus the overhaul was accomplished with the ships force assisting the yard force.

When the ship required docking, she was put in the famous Dewey Drydock at Olongapo which was about 50 miles north of Manila on Lingayen Gulf on the west coast of Luzon.

Q: This concludes the 28 March session, thank you very much, Captain, for a most interesting talk.

Interview with Captain Smith-Hutton

Date: 4 April 1974

By: Captain Paul Ryan

Q: Captain, we left our last session where you were serving in the USS Augusta in China as a communication officer. About this time, you received orders to report to the staff of the Commander-in-Chief Asiatic Fleet as Intelligence officer. This would be in February 1937, would it not?

Captain Smith-Hutton: Yes. The Commander-in-Chief's orders of 5 February 1937, ordered me detached from the Augusta on 8 February to report to him for duty on his staff as Fleet Intelligence Officer. I relieved Lieutenant Commander L. P. Lovette, who had served as intelligence officer for Admiral Murfin, and had stayed on for three months with Admiral Yarnell but who was now due to return to the United States.

I reported to the staff on 8 February, while the Augusta was in Cavite.

I had served with Lieutenant Lovett on the first ship, that I reported to after graduation; that is, the Huron which was then the flagship of the Asiatic Fleet. He was the senior watch officer and was in charge of the instruction of the junior officers. He inspected our journals, and helped us keep them. He had been Fleet Intelligence Officer for about a year and a half. He was a fine officer and was easy to work with.

Q: Captain, we might say that a Lovett-trained man then relieved him.

Smith-Hutton: Yes, that's exactly right.

Q: Captain, would you tell me, what were the sources of the intelligence reports which you received, and upon which you based your intelligence analyses for the Admiral?

Smith-Hutton: The consuls in all the ports in China, the various military commanders ashore, the embassies in Peking, Nanking and Tokyo, and the naval and military attache, sent us copies of their periodic situation reports. Most of them were Confidential or Secret. In fact, the intelligence officer was the confidential secretary to the Commander-in-Chief and handled not only intelligence reports, but all classified and confidential materials that came to him.

The Flag Secretary handled non-classified correspondence.

The specific duties of the intelligence officer depended entirely on the Commander-in-Chief. He frequently asked me to get information for him and I used the best sources I had presenting it to him in the way in which he wanted it. With Admiral Yarnell as with Admiral Taylor, most of the time I gave him the information orally and we discussed it.

In addition, we had radio intelligence intercepts. They were brought to me by the assistant communication officer, Lieutenant Holtwick. I translated items of interest for the Chief of Staff and the Admiral.

Q: Captain, Admiral Yarnell was recognized in 1936-37 as one of the top strategic planners of the U.S. Navy, and had come from the Navy Department. He had not been out in the Far East for a number of years. What did he do to acquaint himself with the Far Eastern situation as far as orientation goes?

Smith-Hutton: One of the first things that the Admiral did on arriving in the Far East in October 1937 was to confer with British Commander-in-Chief Admiral Little during a visit to Hong Kong. He talked to the senior officers during his visit in Singapore, and to the Dutch officers while in the Netherlands East Indies.

Thus, during the first three months in the Far East, he had visited many of the important ports south of the Philippines, and conferred with the senior naval officers.

Then he returned to China, in the Augusta, leaving Manila for Hong Kong in late March. We arrived in Hong Kong about 3 April, and again, the Admiral spent considerable time talking to Admiral Little. He made a short trip to Canton in the river gunboat Mindanao which was the flagship of the South China Patrol.

He was impressed with Mr. Ballantyne, who was the American Consul-General in Canton. Mr. Ballantyne had served for many years in the Far East. He was a Japanese service officer, spoke Japanese well, and had a clear grasp of the situation in South China, in Japan and the Far East in general. He talked very well, and the Admiral enjoyed discussing the situation with him.

After that brief stay in South China, the flagship continued north and spent four days in Amoy, where the Admiral talked with the American consul and then on to Shanghai arriving toward the end of April.

After about a week in Shanghai, the flagship left to go up the Yangtze River, the first stop being at Nanking. Ambassador Johnson was there and the Admiral saw him and then called on the President and Madame Chiang Kai-shek.

Q: Captain, we interrupted your talk here. You were going up the Yangtze River with the Admiral, with Chiang Kai-shek and Madame Chiang Kai-shek. What was the Admiral's impression?

Smith-Hutton: The Admiral remarked that Chiang Kai-shek, who was the acknowledged leader among the Chinese, was too distant and stiff to be a good leader of men. He acknowledged that he was the outstanding Chinese personality, but he did not believe, from his talks and his observations, that the training or the morale of the Chinese forces would improve under the leadership of General Chiang Kai-shek. He felt that Madame Chiang Kai-shek, who was a beautiful charming lady who spoke English, was of great assistance to him in relations with the Western world. He wasn't sure that the Chinese were impressed in the same way. The Admiral had no fixed ideas and further meetings might make him change his opinions, but I felt that he was depressed by the lack of unity in China and was disillusioned with the Chinese leaders who appeared unable to make China help herself.

Q: You returned to Shanghai down the river, I'm assume, Captain. I see by your record that you were a lieutenant commander by this time. Would you describe the examination that you sat for?

Smith-Hutton: I spent the last ten days of the trip on the Yangtze River undergoing an examination for Lieutenant Commander. This was a long and fairly difficult examination, and I had spent many hours studying marine engineering, navigation, international law, and gunnery. I had begun to prepare for the examinations at least eight months before I actually took them. When they were over, I was very very happy to have them behind me.

We returned to Shanghai and after a brief stay the Admiral announced another trip for us.

Q: After this ten days of examinations you were glad to proceed on the Admiral's orientation tour of the area, were you not?

Smith-Hutton: I was indeed. We left Shanghai about 7 June for North China, and arrived in Chinwangtao on 9 June. The Admiral inspected our Marine guards in Tientsin and in Peking, and several members of the staff including me were ordered to accompany him on this inspection trip. We traveled by rail from Chinwangtao to Tientsin and from Tientsin to Peking.

After the completion of the inspections in Peking, we were allowed to take a short holiday in Peking. I stayed in Peking for about ten days.

Q: You were fortunate to see this city of Peking; maybe more Americans will in the future. Where did you stay, and did anything out of the ordinary happen?

Smith-Hutton: The senior American diplomat in Peking. The charge-d'affaires was Lawrence Salisbury, who had been in Tokyo. He was a Japanese language specialist. He was unmarried but his mother was there, and we spent an enjoyable ten days with them. Also in Peking at that time were Ambassador Grew's daughter, Elsie, and her husband, Cecil Lyon who was then second secretary. It was pleasant to meet old friends of Japan days in Peking.

During this stay we saw the countryside by plane, the first such ride that my wife had ever made. The plane was a small sight-seeing craft flown by an American pilot, who took us for a two hour flight along the Great Wall as far as Kalgan, then back to the coast in a really spectacular flight. My wife was thrilled, although at first she was a bit nervous.

Q: This account of your visit to Peking is very interesting, in view of the fact that as fleet intelligence officer, you were permitted to fly in an aircraft over an area which must have been viewed as strategic to the Japanese military forces who were in Peking. Did you or any of the other American diplomats sense any feeling of tenseness, because in one month the Marco Polo Bridge incident was about to take place?

Smith-Hutton: I must say that during our visit to Peking, there were no indications that the Japanese were about to make another important move south of the Great Wall. The situation in North China was unchanged with the Japanese penetrating gradually into the area, expanding their trade and doing a great deal of smuggling. This had been going on for a long time but there was nothing to indicate that the Chinese were increasing their resistance or were even taking special steps to defend themselves against possible Japanese moves. They did of course have German advisors in the Army and there were paper plans to build up an Army of 60 or 80 divisions, however, they were making little real progress in that direction. Our Marine commandant in Peking and the commandant of the Japanese embassy guard were on good terms. These guards were there as a result of the agreement which ended the Boxer Rebellion. There was no indication that the Japanese had alerted these guards. It is very probable that the only persons in the Japanese High Command who had knowledge of the plans which were set in motion on 7 July, were the senior commanders in Manchuria and North China and possibly their chiefs of staff.

The Marco Polo Bridge Incident was expressly staged by the Japanese, and was all arranged.

Q: After you returned from Peking by train to Tsingtao, what was the reaction to the Marco Polo Bridge Incident, as far as protection of U.S. lives and property in Tsingtao goes?

Smith-Hutton: The situation in Tsingtao became tense, there was a great deal of publicity and Japanese moves were followed closely.

When the Japanese reinforced their troops south of the Great Wall and occupied Peking and Tientsin, there was about 10,000 Japanese residents, and about 300 U.S. Navy dependents, wives and children of the fleet personnel.

One of the first considerations was for the safety of these dependents, and the usual evacuation plan was prepared. All of the wives were notified of the signal for the evacuation. In this particular instance, it was repeated blasts on the whistles of the ships in the harbor. On this signal, the wives were to proceed to the large dock in Tsingtao with their children, not attempting to take any of their belongings except their valuables. Boats would be there to take them to the ships. If the situation became quiet again, they would be escorted back to their homes and they could collect their more important belongings, so that they would not have to abandon them.

This was a standard plan, and was the plan in effect in Tsingtao.

Q: Fortunately, the evacuation plan never had to be used. As a Japanese linguist, with 10,000 Japanese residents in Tsingtao, did you establish any sort of liaison with important Japanese?

Smith-Hutton: Yes. Mr. Otaka, the Japanese consul general in Tsingtao had been in Canada and he and his wife spoke quite good English. He was very popular among the Japanese residents and was also well liked by Admiral Shen of the Chinese Navy, the mayor of Tsingtao. Due to the fact that there were many Japanese civilians, they had for years cultivated each other. The Chinese wanted

Japanese business to flourish in Tsingtao and wanted relations between China and Japan to remain cordial.

We knew the Otakas well and on a number of occasions we entertained Admiral and Mrs. Yarnell and the Otakas in our small home in Tsingtao.

About this time, the Japanese Navy sent two cruisers to Tsingtao to protect their nationals. There was one incident which took place about one week after the Marco Polo Bridge Incident, in which a Japanese officer was shot and it had been impossible to find out who the culprit was, but this was settled satisfactorily.

The Japanese cruisers were under the command of Rear Admiral Shimomura, who had been naval attache in Washington and whom I'd known for years. Admiral Shimomura and Consul General Otaka came to our house for dinner one evening, and in our talks they made it quite clear that they were most anxious to avoid any trouble locally. They said that there was no reason why the local Chinese and Japanese couldn't weather this latest storm peacefully, and they indicated that they were determined to do everything in their power to prevent trouble.

As a result of these conversations, which agreed with the estimate that Admiral Yarnell had made of the situation, he considered that there was no reason to defer his plan to visit Vladivostok which had been arranged through diplomatic channels. This was the first visit of a U.S. naval vessel to a Siberian port since 1922.

Q: Captain, our last naval interest in Vladivostok had been in after World War I during the Siberian Expedition. You had previously mentioned to me, when we were discussing this, that there had been a small naval radio station there to support the U.S. consul but it had been withdrawn, some time ago. What was Admiral Yarnell's interest in going to Vladivostok?

Smith-Hutton: Admiral Yarnell wanted, before visiting Japan, to pay a brief visit to Vladivostok to show the Chinese and the Japanese that although we had recognized Russia as recently as 1933, our relations were gradually becoming normal. Perhaps we might visit Siberian ports every year. We had long visited Chinese ports, and Japanese ports, and now we were going to start to visit Russian ports.

So the arrangements which had been made to visit Vladivostok went ahead in spite of the tense situation which had developed in North China and which had reached Tsingtao.

Q: What were the dates of this trip to Vladivostok? Did any other ships accompany the Augusta?

Smith-Hutton: The squadron left Tsingtao on 24 July. In addition to the fleet flagship Augusta there was a division of destroyers which joined en route.

We arrived in Vladivostok about 27 July 1937, and remained there until 8 August, so that it was quite a long stay. In most ways it was an enjoyable visit.

Q: Who originated the idea of a squadron visiting Vladivostok?

Smith-Hutton: Admiral Yarnell made the original proposal and there was no opposition in Washington. I think the Russians were pleased because about that time the Japanese, the Germans and the Italians were negotiating the Anti-Comintern Pact. Any friendly gesture from the United States pleased the Russians.

Interview with Captain Smith-Hutton

Date: 11 April 1974

By: Captain Paul Ryan, USN (Ret.)

Q: Captain, we were talking about the visit to Vladivostok in July 1937. Will you describe your impressions of the Russians and their hospitality?

Captain Smith-Hutton: The Russians in Vladivostok were very glad to see us, and they were as hospitable as they could be. In a way, it was old fashioned hospitality, because they thought that we expected large receptions where we would drink as much whiskey and vodka and eat as much as we could, and then go to bed and return for another drinking party.

Vladivostok in late July is a pleasant place. The days are sunny and bright, the harbor and the surrounding hills are beautiful. We were impressed.

The first day of our visit began with the usual exchange of official calls. That evening all of the officers of the Augusta and the six destroyers went to a dinner party at the largest hall in the city called the Red Army Hall. It is decorated in the style of the 1900's. There were about 100 Russian officers and 50 American officers at the party. The dinner was delicious with caviar, lobster and roast beef, and all very well prepared. The drinks were copious. The Russians were obviously trying to make us drink as much as possible. They too drank heavily. It was a jovial occasion, but the Admiral in his quiet way kept most of the officers from drinking considerably more than they might have. He himself drank only small amounts of liquor, and most of us felt that we had to follow his example. However, some of the officers did have too much to drink.

The next night, curiously enough, the Russians invited the petty officers of the squadron to the same kind of dinner. We were told that the Russian officers who attended the second party were the same ones who had attended the dinner for Admiral Yarnell with possible minor exceptions. The Russian Commander-in-Chief, his staff officers, and the senior officers of the submarines, entertained the petty officers of our ships as lavishly as they had entertained the officers.

We felt that this was possibly to show their own enlisted men that there were no class distinctions so petty officers were shown the same courtesies that they extended to the officers.

Q: Captain, did the Russians show you the surrounding countryside of Vladivostok?

Smith-Hutton: Yes. They arranged for us to go on two picnics, one in an easterly direction and one in the foothills to the north of the city. The first picnic when we went toward the Pacific Ocean, was a very successful one. The day was bright and sunny. We rode in old American cars probably salvaged from our expeditionary force that had been in the Vladivostok at the time of our Siberian expedition. They were completely renovated and in good condition. However, we knew that the Russians weren't manufacturing many automobiles.

We drove in the direction of the coast of the Sea of Japan, and the scenery was spectacular. We had a delicious lunch, walked around about an hour and then came back to the city.

The city itself was rather delapidated, obviously in need of repairs. All of the buildings recently constructed were shoddy and even the Russians themselves complained that the plumbing was bad and that the bricks were inferior. They said better construction materials were urgently needed.

The second picnic could have been interesting too because it was in the area where the fortifications had been. Unfortunately, the day was overcast and a few minutes outside the city we ran into a thick fog which lasted for the entire picnic. A damp wet fog makes it impossible to have a very pleasant picnic.

The Russians did their best to be hospitable, but it was not a good day.

Q: I'm sure that the Admiral reciprocated the Russian hospitality. Was there some sort of a gesture?

Smith-Hutton: Yes. Two days before the squadron sailed, Admiral Yarnell invited the Russian officers and their wives to a reception and a tea dance on the Augusta. He wanted to entertain the ladies and to return the official hospitality. It was a beautiful day and it could have been a very enjoyable party. However, the Russians were not easy to entertain. The ladies were very shy and they declined to dance saying they didn't know how. Their clothing was fresh and clean but in the style of the 1890's.

Flowered dresses and large hats. They seemed ill at ease. They were strong, fresh, healthy looking ladies, but obviously not accustomed to going to tea on board ship.

The officers too were also very sturdy and strong looking men who looked like farmers. None could be classed as aristocrats. Only three or four of them spoke English, so unless you were with one of these interpreters, conversation was difficult. Although the interpreters wore naval uniforms, I'm not sure that they really were naval officers. Unfortunately, none of our officers spoke fluent Russian. In spite of this the party went off fairly well, and our guests drank tea and ate quantities of sandwiches and cakes. They strolled around the upper deck, and we showed them everything we could. One of the officers wanted to see the place where we flogged the enlisted. Since there was no such place on the Augusta, we did not understand what he wanted for quite a while and I think he didn't believe us when we denied the existence of a flogging area.

Q: I think flogging went out in the U.S. Navy about 1840 actually, Captain.

Smith-Hutton: Nobody recalled that fact so we just said there wasn't any such place. I think the Russians and their ladies enjoyed the party because there were many things new for them, and it was a different experience. It went off about as well as one could expect.

Q: Did the Admiral and you make any effort to collect intelligence on the Russian ships in the harbor?

Smith-Hutton: Yes. We arranged with the Russians to have them send officers to our destroyers and to come to the Augusta, and in exchange, we arranged to have the executive officer of the Augusta, Commander Braine, who was an experienced submarine officer with several other submarine specialists, visit their ships. We made reports on the Russian submarines which were all old and obsolete types. Commander Braine was impressed by the good upkeep and cleanliness of the submarines. There were several ancient gunboats in the port. Lieutenant Phelan who had recently been ordered as my assistant was a photographer by specialty, and he took many pictures from the Augusta of the harbor and the harbor installations.

We had been informed before our visit that the Office of Intelligence had reports of the Vladivostok area as of 1920 which were prepared during the Siberian Expedition when there were many naval vessels in the port. Unless there was new construction, we were to avoid risking antagonizing the Russians. There were no new ships or installations. From an intelligence point of view we saw nothing new.

Q: Judging from what you say, then, on the lack of strength of the Russian Navy in Valdivostok, they posed no particular threat to the Japanese Navy in that theatre of operations.

Smith-Hutton: Certainly not from the Navy. We knew that since

1935, the Russians had strengthened their forces in the Far East, and that there were strong Army and Air Force units in Mongolia and to the West of Manchuria, but there were none in Vladivostok and there were very few personnel in uniform in the city streets.

Q: Captain, when you returned from the Vladivostok visit to your summer port of Tsingtao, things were heating up in Shanghai with the Japanese and Chinese. Were you and the Admiral concerned as to the escalation of trouble there?

Smith-Hutton: Yes, we were. The Admiral said, when he went ashore on 10 August, that if the situation got worse, it would be necessary for the Augusta to proceed at once. Unfortunately, the situation did get worse. A Japanese military unit was fired on, not far from the race course outside the city and a Japanese sailor was killed. The situation became acute very quickly, and the Admiral decided, on receipt of that information from the commanding officer of the 4th Marines, that he must go to Shanghai. That night, all of the officers who were living ashore were notified to return to the ship early in the morning, because the flagship was sailing at 9 o'clock.

The original plan had been to make a full power run to expedite our arrival, but the weather did not permit. A violent typhoon was headed north along the coast, and the ship had to pass through it en route. There was considerable damage to the ship. One of the whale boats was carried away and some of the ships furniture got adrift and was damaged. We had to steam at slow speed which delayed our arrival until the morning of 12 August.

At first the ship anchored off the Shanghai power plant, instead of the usual berth off the Bund. While at anchor there, in spite of the fact that we had large American flags spread on top of the turrets, two Chinese aircraft dropped bombs. One bomb missed the ship by only about 20 yards, but she was not damaged. During this same attack, another Chinese plane dropped bombs in front of the Cathay Hotel on Nanking Road and another on Nanking Road near the race course. Several hundred Chinese civilians were killed or badly wounded in these attacks. One report said 950 people had been killed but that may have been an exaggeration. The target was the Japanese flagship "Izumo" hundreds of yards away.

Q: To sketch in the background of the situation in Shanghai as I understand it, we had about 4000 U.S. civilians there, and we had 1500 U.S. troops including a small detachment from the Augusta. What were your operational intelligence duties with regard to the U.S. forces there?

Smith-Hutton: Since the 4th Marines were part of the defense force, and had excellent relations with all elements of that force, Admiral Yarnell decided that I could follow the action best if I were in the 4th Marine headquarters. About 18 August I was ordered to report to the commanding officer of the 4th Marines. I spent the night ashore, studied the reports and situation maps and made visits in the forenoon. After lunch I returned to the Augusta to report to the Admiral and to answer any questions he might have.

Almost every morning, Admiral Yarnell went to the office of the Consul General, Mr. Gauss, and conferred with him and unless Colonel Price, the commanding officer of the 4th Marines, was detained by urgent duties, he attended these conferences.

The conference lasted from half an hour to two or three hours, depending on what there was to discuss, but every forenoon our senior officials got a complete review of the situation. The Admiral had great confidence in and liking and respect for Mr. Gauss and Colonel Price. These were important conferences. In the afternoon, he sometimes had other visitors and in the late afternoon, I made my reports to him.

Q: Captain, on the 20th of August, shrapnel fell on the well deck of the Augusta and killed one man and wounded 17 people. I suppose that the Japanese were immediately suspect. What was the Admiral's and your reaction?

Smith-Hutton: Fortunately, I have a copy of a memorandum I wrote to Admiral Yarnell on that date, and I might read it, as an example of the reports to him. This is date, "Shanghai, China, 20 August 1937, Memorandum for the Commander-in-Chief. In accordance with your verbal instructions I proceeded to HIJMS Izumo at 1900, 20 August 1937, to deliver your message to Vice Admiral Hasegawa. Vice Admiral Hasegawa had retired a few minutes previous to my arrival, and therefore your message was delivered to the Chief of Staff, 3rd Fleet, Rear Admiral Sugiyama. I informed Rear Admiral

Sugiyama that several shells had passed over the foreign men of war at the naval buoys, that some had struck the French Bund, that two had burst in the river below the Augusta, that one shell had burst on the deck of the Augusta, killing one man and wounding several others. I informed him that I had been instructed by my Commander-in-Chief to request him to use every possible effort to keep Japanese vessels from firing in the direction of the foreign men of war at the naval buoys. Rear Admiral Sugiyama replied that he regretted to learn of these incidents and that while he felt sure that the shells in question did not come from Japanese ships or shore batteries, he would repeat the instructions which had already been given to his forces, to exercise great care to avoid firing in the direction of neutral vessels. He brought out a chart which showed that the Japanese vessels were firing in only two directions, one in the Yangtze-Poo area and the other at a Chinese battery in the PooTung area about one mile south of the Asiatic Petroleum Company installation. He stated positively that no other areas were being shelled by his ships. In view of this, it was his opinion that those shells were coming from the Chinese battery in PooTung or from the Chinese in Chapei, both of whom had been firing at the Japanese ships below Garden Bend for some time. I repeated the request that he give strict instructions to his ships. The Izumo was under fire from snipers in Yangtze-Poo at the time of my visit, but Rear Admiral Sugiyama stated that although the ship had been hit many times, none of the crew had been wounded. Respectfully, Smith-Hutton."

Q: How did Admiral Yarnell react to this Japanese response?

Smith-Hutton: The Admiral agreed that Rear Admiral Sugiyama was correct, that certainly the Japanese ships were not firing in the direction of the buoys, and that as Admiral Sugiyama pointed out, the Chinese who had been firing intermittently for several days in the direction of the Izumo were responsible for this particular mortar shell.

Q: Captain, in this autumn of 1937, we have an undeclared war between China and Japan, and with Japan becoming more and more entangled. What was Admiral Yarnell's conception of his mission in this murky situation?

Smith-Hutton: The Admiral felt that it was his mission to afford all possible protection to Americans, to their lives and property and to American interests in China. That the Japanese had no right to close off any area, such as the Yangtze or any other area in China, which would prevent us from carrying out our duties of protecting our citizens and their interests. But at the same time, the Admiral realized that there were practical considerations and that the Japanese in certain areas had closed off some of the Yangtze River by mines for their own defense and that to expect them to sweep the mines or clear the mines for our convenience was being unreasonable.

Therefore he was willing to cooperate with the Japanese commanders on a professional and naval level, but without relinquishing any of our rights to free navigation or to free passage or intercourse in any area in China.

It was sometimes a difficult task, but in general, Admiral Yarnell worked carefully and well with the various Japanese commanders he dealt with.

Q: In September of 1937 and thenceforth, Admiral Yarnell was lightly admonished by Secretary of State Hull, because of the Admiral's statement that he was going to protect U.S. citizens. Evidently there were some "Nervous Nellies" in the State Department. What was the Admiral's reaction to this?

Smith-Hutton: The Admiral took a realistic attitude toward these statements. He realized that the President and Mr. Hull were being bombarded by protests from U.S. pacifists who even went as far as to say that all U.S. citizens, U.S. forces and U.S. interests should be withdrawn from China. He knew that the State Department did not approve of his threat to return the fire if fired upon, because the pacifists and isolationists would protest more loudly and write more letters.

However, the Admiral did feel that our Navy must not give in to threats, or if fired upon should turn and run, because that was not inthe traditions of the naval service. Therefore, he made statements and replies to the Japanese, partly in the hope that Americans would remember that we did have rights in China, and a place in the Far East, and that we should not abandon them because of an undeclared war.

He felt that it was proper under the circumstances to make our position clear from time to time and to let Americans in China know that the Navy was going to give all protection possible to them. At the same time, he was not a belligerent fire-eater. He was just being as realistic as possible under difficult circumstances.

Q: Captain, the Asiatic Fleet at this time consisted of one cruiser, 12 destroyers, six submarines, and six river gunboats, plus a few auxiliaries. Did Admiral Yarnell complain about the smallness of this fleet to accomplish the size of the assignment given to him?

Smith-Hutton: Yes. He frequently remarked that the Asiatic Fleet area, which extended from the International Date Line to the African Coast, was much larger than he could possibly take care of. There was no possibility of showing the flag in that large area, with his comparatively small force. He also said that he made recommendations from time to time to the Chief of Operations that additional ships be assigned to the fleet and that he was invariably informed that they were not available. I think that the Admiral realized that the Commander-in-Chiefs of the Atlantic and Pacific Fleets also were asking for more ships. However, he felt that he was not doing his job properly if he didn't inform the Chief of Operations of the difficulties he faced.

Q: There have been some attempts by certain historians to cast

Admiral Yarnell in the role of a fighter who chafed under Department of State orders. How did you evaluate his personality? Was he a fire-eater?

Smith-Hutton: I was on his staff and closely associated with him for a period of two years during a critical time and I know that Admiral Yarnell was far from being a fire-eater. He was very intelligent and clear-sighted, and he knew exactly what the realities of the situation were. He felt that it was a great mistake not to face up to realities, and that just because others, including the Secretary of State or the President, didn't agree with him was no reason for him to change his mind. On the other hand, he was the first to recognize that the President and the State Department had responsibilities to the nation and to all of the American people. While from time to time he protested that his instructions were in error, he did this in a very quiet forceful way not in an insubordinate manner. When his recommendations were not approved he carried out instructions loyally and to the letter.

Q: Just for the record, Captain, I note that Admiral Yarnell was in the class of 1897. He was born in 1859, and at the time he was Commander-in-Chief of the Asiatic Fleet, his classmate, William Leahy, was the Chief of Naval Operations, which probably made for a happy arrangement, to have a classmate in Washington.

Ordinarily, having the CNO as a classmate would be a fine thing, but I gather from what you said before that there was one occasion when it didn't work out.

Smith-Hutton: Yes, I believe that Admiral and Mrs. Yarnell were very much disappointed when Admiral Leahy and Admiral Hart would not arrange for Admiral Hart to arrive about two weeks before the original date to enable them to return to attend the college graduation ceremony of their only son. They said that sometimes the more you advanced in rank, the more difficult it was to get personal favors.

Q: You've mentioned two of the staff officers, Lieutenant Sylvester, the flag lieutenant, and Lieutenant Commander Settle, but do you recall the other staff officers and what their contributions were?

Smith-Hutton: The Chief of Staff Captain McConnel was a fine competent officer, but in mediocre health. He was a good Chief of Staff and worked very closely with the Admiral. However, he retired and died before World War II was over, showing that he was not strong physically. The Flag Lieutenant, Lieutenant Sylvester, became a vice admiral. Lieutenant Commander Settle became a Vice Admiral, as did Commander Deyo, who was Plans and Operations officer. He was a courtly gentlemen with a distinguished air who contributed greatly to the tone of the staff. Lieutenant Phelan was the photographic specialist and Lieutenant Adolph Oswald the flag secretary, retired as a rear admiral. He how lives in Spain. He became a destroyer officer and distinguished himself during the war.

Q: Captain, the President acceded to Admiral Yarnell's request to send the 6th Marines from San Diego to reinforce U.S. forces in Shanghai. What is your recollection of how Admiral Yarnell reached this decision to make this recommendation?

Smith-Hutton: In August, when the fighting started, the British brought their force up to approximately 4000 men. At that time our strength was approximately 1500 including the 4th Marines and about 230 bluejackets from the Augusta and the Sacramento. The Shanghai Volunteer were about 2000 strong and there were some 2000 French troops. The Admiral felt that our force even with the bluejackets should be about the same as the British and should be able to defend our sector in case it became necessary to do so. He recommended to the Chief of Operations that another Marine regiment be sent. In view of the large numbers of Chinese that had been killed in the early part of the fighting and especially the bombing in the Cathay Hotel area, and in view of the publicity and world interest in the Battle for Shanghai, the recommendation was approved. About 19 September, the 6th Marines arrived on board the transport Chaumont. They were commanded by Brigadier General Beaumont, who became the senior Marine officer taking over from Colonel Price of the 4th Marines. The 6th Marine regiment was integrated quickly and completely into the defense force and joined with the 4th Marines to make a remarkable force. Admiral Yarnell was very pleased to have them. At the same time, he realized that the need for the 6th Marines was temporary and he informed the Chief of Naval Operations that he would recommend that they return to the United States as soon as the situation permitted.

Q: When did the 6th Marines return?

Smith-Hutton: They returned early in January 1938, when the fighting had moved away from Shanghai into the Nanking area and toward Hankow.

Interview with Captain Smith-Hutton

Date: 18 April 1974

By: Captain Paul Ryan, USN (Ret.)

Q: Captain, on our last meeting, we were discussing the situation in China in 1937. At this time Colonel Stilwell, later General Stilwell, was the military attache at our embassy. Did you have any contact with him?

Captain Smith-Hutton: We received Colonel Stilwell's reports from Peking and from Nanking. He visited Shanghai and saw the Admiral. Unfortunately, I wasn't present when he was there, and although I met him later, I didn't talk with him and the Admiral at the same time. His reports were excellent. He said that Chiang Kai-shek was making no real effort to prepare China's defenses against the Japanese, and reported that China lacked leadership, morale, cohesion, munitions and training. His reports were based on months of travel throughout China. Colonel Stilwell was saddened by what he saw, because he liked the Chinese and was hopeful that the Kuomintang and Chiang Kai-shek would be able to strengthen China so that she could defend herself against Japan. And when he had to conclude, on the basis of his observations, that they would not be able to, it made him feel that much effort was being wasted. He reported that Chiang Kai-shek was more interested in crushing his opposition than in fighting Japan. He wanted to be the only leader among the Chinese groups, and to eliminate the other generals who were in opposition.

He also felt that the policy of Chiang Kai-shek was to try to get the Americans, British, French and Russians to fight China's battles for her.

His forecasts were remarkably accurate. He spoke excellent Chinese and liked the Chinese people. He said that properly led, Chinese troops would be as good as any in the world. His criticism was of the Chinese leaders, from the top down to company level.

Q: Captain, another source of your intelligence in addition to Lieutenant Colonel Stilwell was the 4th Marine intelligence officer. Would you describe him?

Smith-Hutton: The 4th Marine intelligence officer was Captain R. A. Boone, Naval Academy class of 1920, who was a Chinese language officer and spoke good Chinese. His assistant was Lieutenant Victor Krulak. They were competent officers and they had a good organization. They had a small group of Marine non-commissioned officers, and their reports were good because they had such fine sources of information. The Shanghai police force, which was well organized and well-informed, the local and the international newsmen and the Chinese authorities, including the military were the main sources and Captain Boone was on good terms with all of them. Colonel Price and the Admiral were very well informed in regard to the local military situation. Captain Boone prepared a daily situation report and they were of very high quality. Boone had been in China a long time and he spent most of his career there. Just before World War II, he returned to the United States. He was assigned to duty in the Aleutian area and while there committed suicide. I have never heard why, but it was a loss to the service.

Lieutenant Krulak advanced through the grades and during World War II became a distinguished battalion then regimental commander. Eventually he commanded all the Marines in the Pacific area and retired as a Lieutenant General.

Q: Captain, you were on temporary additional duty with the 4th Marines. You were a Japanese language officer and Captain Boone was a Chinese language officer. What methods did you two gentlemen use to collect information on both sides, the Chinese and the Japanese?

Smith-Hutton: Captain Boone had good relations with the Shanghai Police Force, about half of whom were Chinese, and with the head of the Police Force, who was a retired British Army Intelligence officer, so he followed the local Chinese situation including their plans. Boone maintained contact with the Chinese military commanders too.

My duty was to keep the Admiral and Colonel Price informed about the Japanese. I made periodic visits to the Japanese headquarters in the Hongkew section of the settlement. They were quite frank with me in regard to their operations and intentions.

In addition to that, the 4th Marines radio intelligence station intercepted Japanese diplomatic traffic, much of which we were able to decode. Captain Zern, who commanded the unit, handed me every day a sheaf of messages which had been intercepted. If there were messages of importance, I would translate them and report them to the Admiral. With all of our sources, we were able to follow the progress of the fighting and even to forecast some of the future operations with reasonable accuracy. The Admiral was pleased with the results and he said so many times. For instance, the situation in Tsingtao could have become critical and Mrs. Yarnell was there with other Navy wives. However, I translated a message from the Japanese consul general saying that all Japanese residents would be evacuated by a given date, which meant that there would be no fighting there.

Q: In decoding these Japanese diplomatic messages, did you use a machine, or did you just use a letter cipher?

Smith-Hutton: The messages that we were reading were not on a machine. They were in a letter cipher which was furnished to Captain Zern by Op-20G in Washington.

Q: The Purple Machine was a year or so in the future then.

Smith-Hutton: Yes. I think that the Purple Machine was used in major stations, not in the smaller stations such as Tsingtao and Shanghai.

Q: Captain, what opinion did General Beaumont and Colonel Price of the Marines form of the efficiency of Chiang Kai-shek's army?

Smith-Hutton: The troops that Chiang Kai-shek sent to defend the Shanghai area consisted of three divisions, and they were among the best divisions in his army. They were trained by German instructors, and the commander, General Chang Fak-kwei, was an officer who had considerable experience both in guerilla warfare and in the field against the Communists. He was one of the outstanding generals in the Chinese Army, a competent leader. The Germans had begun to train Chiang's army about two years previous to the Shanghai Incident, and they had recommended to Chiang Kai-shek that the size of the army be reduced. Chiang Kai-shek had well over a million men under arms, and most of the divisions were incompetent and worthless. The Germans recommended that the armies be reduced to 60 divisions or about 500,000 men, the idea being to weed out the less capable units, to organize and equip the remaining 60 divisions, with the best arms that China could afford, and to train them carefully.

Chiang Kai-shek paid lip service to this plan and said that he would carry it out when possible. Unfortunately for China, he never did. Although the war lasted many years and the Japanese occupied much of China by 1941, he still had many badly trained, badly equipped and incompetent units.

This explanation is preliminary to saying that both General Beaumont and Colonel Price said that the three Chinese divisions which defended Shanghai were competent and well-led troops. Their weakness was that they had little artillery, and no aircraft support. So the Japanese success was due largely to the superiority of Japanese artillery and aircraft as well as the support of the support of the naval vessels firing from Whangpu and the Yangtze Rivers. The Japanese had complete control of the air, their artillery was used effectively and naval gunfire support was good.

Q: With the French and British navies represented by flag officers and flagships in Shanghai, what was Admiral Yarnell's relationship with the foreign flag officers?

Smith-Hutton: The British Commander-in-Chief in the Far East was Admiral Little, and the French Commander-in-Chief was Vice Admiral LeBigot. Both of them were good officers and Admiral Yarnell was on excellent terms with both of them. He saw them from time to time. The naval buoys were laid out so that the British had the buoy farthest downstream. The next was the American and the next was the French thus there were three 10,000 ton cruisers tied up to the buoys off the Shanghai Bund.

The Admirals agreed with each other in coordinating international policy toward the Japanese.

Admiral Yarnell had no problems with our European friends.

Q: On the 12th of December 1937, a Japanese naval aircraft sank the U.S. naval gunboat Panay. Do you recall the circumstances previous to the sinking, and then after the sinking, aboard the flagship Augusta?

Smith-Hutton: The Japanese forces were advancing on Nanking and were bombing and shelling the city, and all of the Chinese craft in the Yangtze River in the vicinity. In order to keep them informed of the location of our ships, that is, the Panay and several Standard Vacuum Oil Company ships, we had been in constant touch with the Japanese command in Shanghai, so that they had accurate reports as to our ships. This same arrangement was used by the British, since there were several British gunboats and river steamers in the area also. The Japanese intelligence reports said that numerous steamers carrying Chinese troops were fleeing from Nanking headed up river, so that their air forces, ground forces, and artillery along the banks were firing at these fleeing craft.

All of our ships had large American flags painted on the awnings and they flew large American flags from the masts.

The first indication that we had on the Augusta that something might have happened to the Panay was when she ceased to communicate with the flagship and all efforts to raise her by radio failed. This happened on the afternoon of 12 December. The communication officer reported the failure to answer radio calls to the staff duty officer who reported to Admiral Yarnell that something might have happened to the Panay.

I recall later that Rear Admiral Sugiyama, Chief of Staff to Vice Admiral Hasegawa, came to the Augusta to say that he feared that the Panay had been damanged, and that the crew had evacuated the ship.

I believe this was the first report that was received of the attack. Rear Admiral Sugiyama also said that they were sending medical supplies to aid the survivors.

This word was received with complete disbelief on board the Augusta. We could not understand how the Japanese who knew where the ships were could have made the mistake of attacking them. That, of course, immediately raised the suspicion that the attack was deliberate.

Shortly after the visit of Rear Admiral Sugiyama, Vice Admiral Hasegawa came on board to express his apologies and his regrets. I was present when he came to the Augusta and was greeted by Admiral Yarnell. He was obviously moved and very nervous. He said that he had submitted his resignation, that he had no way of explaining the attack, but he did want Admiral Yarnell to realize that it was not a deliberate attack, that it was completely a mistake, and that he and all of the officers and men in his command apologized for the incident.

Q: Was he speaking English all this time?

Smith-Hutton: Yes, he spoke English. Admiral Hasegawa had been naval attache in Washington and spoke English with a slight accent but spoke very fluently.

Q: He had enjoyed very good relations with the Americans up to this time.

Smith-Hutton: Vice Admiral Hasegawa was one of the most pro-American officers in the Japanese Navy, and was a genuine friend and admirer of our Navy.

Q: What was Admiral Yarnell's reaction to Hasegawa's statement that he was going to resign as Commander-in-Chief of the fleet?

Smith-Hutton: Admiral Yarnell immediately said that he would regret very much if Hasegawa left and that he hoped that the resignation would not be accepted. I believe that Admiral Yarnell suggested to our Navy Department that we request that Admiral Hasegawa be continued as Japanese CinC. Tokyo did not accept Hasegawa's resignation.

However, Rear Admiral Mitsunami, who commanded the naval air group was relieved, and assigned to another command as a result of the sinking.

Q: Admiral Yarnell then appointed a board of inquiry or board of investigation to investigate the circumstances of the sinking and Captain McKittrick of the Augusta was the head of the board. Do you recall what their feelings were? I know what their conclusions were.

Smith-Hutton: Yes, Captain McKittrick was the head of the board and Commander Deyo, the Fleet Operations officer, who was a member, said that there was no real explanation. They could find no reason for the attack, and could not understand how the Japanese aviators could have made the mistakes they did. In view of the Panay's markings, the fact that it was a bright and clear day, and that they had exact information as to her location. The attack showed great negligence on the part of the Japanese forces. The Japanese should be required to pay for the damages.

Q: Captain, on the 17th of December 1937, the gunboat Oahu brought back the bodies of the Panay dead, with the survivors also. They passed close aboard the flagship. Were you present during this occasion?

Smith-Hutton: Yes. It was a very moving occasion. The dead were in caskets covered with the flag, and some of the wounded had to be carried from the Oahu. At that time the Japanese command sent a flight of aircraft at a low altitude over the ships. They did this in complete good will, with the idea of making a salute to the men who had lost their lives. There were newspaper reporters and photographers present. All who saw the transfer were much moved by the ceremony.

Q: Captain, a New York Times correspondent in Shanghai, Hallett Abend, was on the bridge of the Augusta at the time the Oahu came alongside on the 17th of December. Do you recall what type of reporter was Hallett Abend?

Smith-Hutton: Abend was one of the best known and most capable correspondents. He had been in China for years as the New York Times correspondent, and while, like all aggressive newspapermen, he liked to get exclusive stories, he was competent and able. His nearest competitor, shall we say, was the London Times correspondent and the next one perhaps was Victor Keene, the New York Herald

Tribune correspondent. They were both good friends of ours and excellent sources of information.

Abend was very active, and had many good sources of information. He wrote in a colorful way, and was a first rate newspaperman.

Q: Captain, it's characteristic of some foreigners, many foreigners in fact, who live in a city not native to them to become unduly attached to the place. Was this true of Abend?

Smith-Hutton: Yes, I think you could say that Abend was slightly pro-Chinese. He liked and admired the Chinese and knew a great deal about their history, so many of his articles were pro-Chinese. However, he reported the facts as he saw them.

Q: It's believed by many historians that after the Panay incident. that U.S. public opinion toward Japan toughened and hardened, and that our public opinion toward China became more sympathetic. Regarding the stories that were filed by Hallett Abend to the New York Times, which is read by many Americans, do you think these stories helped to foster this pro-Chinese opinion in the U.S.?

Smith-Hutton: I have no doubt of it. Abend was a capable newspaperman, and he wrote well. But since he was fond of China, and sympathetic to their cause, and since in the Panay case the Japanese were very much at fault, many of these feelings were reflected in his articles. He condemned Japan seriously. Since the influence of the New York Times is great, and perhaps was greater than now, there's no doubt that Abend's comments in regard to Japan had considerable influence on public opinion, making Americans pro-Chinese and anti-Japanese.

Q: To conclude the Panay incident, Captain, we might note that although the Japanese Army was identifying the Panay and other foreign ships as Chinese troop carriers, Admiral Hasegawa's air operations officer later said that one of the worst mistakes of his life, and it was an inadvertent mistake, was his failure to radio the position of the Panay to the Japanese naval air squadrons in the area. If they'd received this report conceivably this tragedy never would have happened.

Smith-Hutton: As a footnote to the sinking of the Panay, I have here a copy of the ship's paper, the Augusta Cracker, which is dated 13 August 1938. The ship was in Tsingtao, and I note that Admiral Yarnell personelly presented Navy Crosses to men who displayed extraordinary heroism and distinguished themselves at the time of the sinking of the Panay. There were seven members of the crew of the Panay who were awarded the Navy Cross by the Admiral on the well deck of the flagship. One, a native of China, was given a letter of commendation from the Secretary of the Navy.

Q: Just to keep the record straight, Captain, will you name those men who received the Navy Cross?

Smith-Hutton: Yes. The first is Walter Cheatham, Coxswain, USN.

The second is Maurice Rider, Coxswain, USN. The third was Edward Cowdin, Coxswain, USN. The fourth was John Bonkowski, gunner's mate third class, USN. The fifth was Andrew Wisler, radioman, USN. The sixth was Robert Hebard, water tender 2nd class, USN, and the seventh was James Timothy Murphy, radioman, 3rd class, USN. The Chinese was mess attendant first class, Yuan Te Erh.

Q: Captain, the commander of the Yangtze Patrol was Rear Admiral David Le Breton. What was your recollection of Admiral Le Breton as an officer?

Smith-Hutton: Admiral Le Breton was a brilliant officer. The reports and dispatches that passed over my desk were well prepared, and he was competent in every way. My only objection to the Admiral was that he demanded a great deal in the way of personal services, in contrast to the simplicity and the ease with which one could serve Admiral Yarnell. I knew that it would be much more difficult to serve with Admiral Le Breton. This would not in any way detract from his professional competence.

Interview with Captain Smith-Hutton

Date: 2 May 1974

By: Paul Ryan

Q: Captain, in looking at, say the lessons learned from Japanese actions and attitudes in China, what were some of the conclusions which you drew, in company with Admiral Yarnell as you were talking around the mess table?

Captain Smith-Hutton: In general, Admiral Yarnell was pessimistic about the future of our position in the Far East. For instance, in connection with the Panay incident, he admitted that Admiral Hasegawa had promptly apologized, and Mr. Hirota had negotiated with Ambassador Grew in a frank and friendly way to settle the incident. However, there was no indication that the high command was able to control the younger officers, or that the younger officers, both Army and Navy had changed their anti-foreign attitudes. The long range policy seemed to be to force foreign influence from China. He pointed out that through the China campaigns, the Japanese government lacked control over their forces in China. In connection with the Panay sinking, the government accepted the responsibility, and made reparations. But were the hot-headed militarists deliberately trying to provoke a clash with the United States? There was no evidence this was so, and it was hard to believe that they could be so short-sighted. He hoped that one result would be to aid the President in his attempts to get a naval building program through Congress, and perhaps to give increased popular support for a stronger Navy. The Admiral realized that the President had problems with the groups who were opposed to strengthening our naval forces.

Q: Captain, U.S. historians have found that, or at least emphasized that, Admiral Yarnell, according to them, was in some cases pressing for an economic strangulation, an economic blockage of Japan in the event of war, and we would do this in concert with our allies, Britain, France, possibly Russia, and possibly the Netherlands. Was this a sudden thought, or was this concept pretty well known among you gentlemen of the staff?

Smith-Hutton: We all knew this. Anyone who makes a study of the Japanese foreign trade, realizes that their economic strength is based on imports.

For instance, 90 percent of their oil, and 50 percent of their steel was imported. Their textile industries before the development of synthetic fibers, was based on imported cotton. So it was no secret that Japan was dependent on foreign trade. We also knew that one reason behind her expansion on the continent was based upon her desire to be more certain of the sources of the raw materials that she required for her industry. Therefore, an economic blockade would be effective.

Q: And in fact, I guess we can say that's the way we won the war against Japan.

Smith-Hutton: Indeed it was.

Q: Captain, was there ever any report that Admiral Yarnell had hoped to get command of say the Scouting Force or the Battle Force in the U.S. Fleet? Second, how was he regarded by the American and foreign civil community in the Far East?

Smith-Hutton: He never discussed a possible desire to get a command in the U.S. Fleet. It's possible that he would have preferred to be Commander-in-Chief of the U.S. Fleet instead of the Asiatic Fleet, but if that were the case, he never mentioned that either. I feel that he was such a capable officer that his service to our country was greater as Commander-in-Chief of the Asiatic Fleet than as Commander-in-Chief of the U.S. Fleet, although many officers might not agree.

As far as his relations with civilians are concerned, after the fighting had ended and the city got back to normal in the spring of 1938, the American community in Shanghai gave **a formal dinner** in his honor. All prominent Americans and dignitaries were invited. It was a most successful affair, the most brilliant occasion in the entire history of the club, showing how the Americans in Shanghai esteemed him and appreciated what he had done to protect them and American interests.

Several months later in Tsingtao, the Japan-America Association, made up of important Japanese and American businessmen and the consuls gave a reception and a Japanese dinner party for him.

The civilians of two great cities thus expressed their

admiration for and thanks to him.

Q: Very impressive gentleman.

Smith-Hutton: He was indeed.

Q: Captain, after 1936 and on through to 1939, Italy, Germany and Japan were becoming more friendly, forming an anti-Communistic Axis. What was Admiral Yarnell's reaction to the wisdom of Japan in joining with these European powers?

Smith-Hutton: Admiral Yarnell thought that the Japanese were going to create difficulties for themselves in becoming allied with Germany and Italy. In his opinion the geographical separation will make it difficult for them all to act in concert except possibly against Russia. He said that while the Russians gave a poor account of themselves in 1904 and in 1914, it was by no means sure that that same situation would hold under the Communists. The officers of the Russian Imperial forces were so incompetent that their magnificent soldiers were not properly used. The Admiral urged great caution in under-estimating the strength of the Russians. He felt that the Japanese were going to be sorry eventually that they tied themselves closely with Italy and Germany.

Q: A true prognosticator?

Smith-Hutton: Yes, in that respect he was certainly correct.

Q: In the Thirties Japan started to fortify the Mandate Islands. I'm speaking about the Marshalls and Carolines, particularly Truk. Was there any particular reaction evidenced by Admiral Yarnell and his staff to this?

Smith-Hutton: Not particularly. We realized, of course, that efforts had been made in Washington and Tokyo to arrange to visit the Mandate islands, which was normal. We thought that the Japanese should have permitted us to make visits. Since they refused there appeared little that we could do in the fleet to get them to change their minds. We regretted this because we were completely in the dark as to what they were doing. However, there was no solution at that time.

Q: And you had no long-range aircraft such as PBY's in the Asiatic Fleet?

Smith-Hutton: Not at that time.

Q: So that let out any aerial photography.

Smith-Hutton: There was no possibility of that.

Q: Captain, regarding one of the forgotten segments of the Navy: the wives and children. Can you describe what life was like for the Navy families out there in China during this late 1930 period?

Smith-Hutton: There were approximately 200 wives and children, dependents of the officers and petty officers of the Augusta, the Conopus, the submarines and minesweepers based on Tsingtao. There were about the same number from ships in Chefoo. In Tsingtao, many senior officers' wives lived at the Edgewater Beach Hotel, which was large, modern and comfortable, but it was expensive. The junior officers and petty officers usually found rooms for their families in the smaller pension and hotels. Since it was clean and unusually comfortable for a Chinese city, having been built by the Germans and kept up by the Japanese, the families were usually able to find pleasant rooms much more easily than in most Chinese cities.

When the political situation in China was quiet, summer was enjoyable, because the weather was good. There was good swimming, bathing, hiking, picnicking, golf and tennis. Usually the crews were allowed to go ashore for the weekends.

The situation changed drastically when there were troubles ashore or when there was fighting in nearby areas. Then the wives and children sometimes had problems. That summer of 1937, when the Augusta left port on a few hours notice to go to Shanghai, and in the middle of the night the officers were notified to return to the ship early the following morning. Many officers had little money to leave their families. There were other ships there but I can remember that my wife had to loan money to some of the other wives so that they could send their children to the Philippines to enter school on time. It was difficult to get cash during times of unrest.

There were many other instances when the ships in China left port with almost no notice so the wives sometimes didn't know what to expect or when they would see their husbands again.

Perhaps the most unfortunate of all were the families of the Yangtze Patrol Force. After operations started in the lower Yangtze area in the summer of 1937, there was no communication with the interior except through the Japanese. Even mail was stopped by and some of the officers and wives were separated for periods of months. That was rather trying and it created difficulties for both the wives and the children.

However, the number of wives that came to China didn't change much. Wives knew that they could buy Chinese objects, rugs, silver, linens and silks, so that I think most of the ladies of our Navy were glad to follow their husbands to China, in spite of uncertainties.

Interview with Captain Smith-Hutton

Date: 9 May 1974

By: Captain Paul Ryan, USN (Ret.)

Q: Captain, in our last session, you were with Admiral Yarnell in Shanghai in the flagship in late 1937, watching the progress of the Japanese Army taking over China. Can you discuss those events?

Captain Smith-Hutton: The Japanese Army captured Nanking in the middle of December in 1937, and the whole world remembers that the capture was a bloody affair. The Japanese soldiers looted and burned and according to our embassy officers and newspapermen who were there, killed some 40,000 Chinese civilians. There was worldwide reaction to these atrocities.

It seemed to us that public opinion in the United States turned less isolationist and less pacifist. It may be too strong to say that opinion became anti-Japanese, but certainly the attitude changed, and the Admiral who followed U.S. public opinion closely was very much interested in this change. It was surprising to note that the attitude of the Japanese military toward prisoners and toward civilians had altered radically since the Russ-Japanese War of 1904-05.

Q: Captain, we're talking about the Battle of Tsushima, and Admiral Rojdestvensky, where the entire Russian fleet was destroyed. You say that the Japanese treated the Russians differently. How was that?

Smith-Hutton: Not only the Battle of Tsushima where the Commander-in-Chief of the Russian fleet was captured on board a patrol boat, and a great many other naval officers were taken, but also after the siege of Port Arthur in southern Manchuria, where some 15,000 Russian Army officers and men were captured. The treatment given them was in accordance with the rules of war. They gave their prisoners proper medical treatment, food and care and there were no reports of mistreatment.

The same correct treatment was given some 8000 German civilians and soldiers who were captured in Tsingtao in 1914 at the opening of World War I.

It is difficult to understand and to explain why between 1914 and 1937, their attitude towards prisoners changed, but it certainly did. Whatever the reason, the Japanese military treated captured Chinese soldiers and civilians in the most brutal fashion throughout the entire war.

Q: --- excuse me, Captain, is it possible that the Chinese were using terroristic methods, I'm talking about guerilla warfare and ambushing Japanese soldiers, which in turn caused a counter-terror? Is this a possibility?

Smith-Hutton: That is possible and some of the Chinese who were fighting the Japanese were irregulars and not professionals. They were really bandits rather than soldiers, so it is possible that the Japanese were getting revenge, but even this is not a real excuse.

Q: Captain, in December of '37 the world was shocked by what is known as the Rape of Nanking. What was Admiral Yarnell's reaction and your reaction to this event?

Smith-Hutton: We were also shocked and disgusted and knew that the struggle between the Japanese and the Chinese was to be even more brutal than was necessary. After the capture of Nanking the Japanese made peace offers to China but no Chinese wanted peace after the treatment that had been given the Chinese there. Although they held both Peking and Nanking and appeared anxious to discuss a settlement, their peace efforts were refused by Chiang Kai-shek and the Central Government.

The Chinese government still hoped to get America, Russia and Great Britain to fight their enemies. Chiang Kai-shek was keeping his best troops intact and declined to use them to fight the Japanese. It is true that China at that time was getting a certain amount of help from us and from the Russians. For instance, early in 1938, the Russians sent four fighter squadrons and two bomber squadrons to the Chungking-Hankow area. We attempted to make contact with them to find out what they proposed to do. They kept very much to themselves but from all we could observe, they were a tough and competent group of fliers, and maintenance men. They were a certain amount of assistance to the Chinese. Our Flying Tigers were also helping.

Q: Captain, you weren't in Hankow. How did you get intelligence reports down to Shanghai?

Smith-Hutton: We got them through officers who were still on duty in the upper Yangtze and in the Hankow area.

Our gunboats were still in the Yangtze and in the embassy so they were instructed to learn all they could about the Russians. Also, Captain Chennault of the Flying Tigers was flying with the Chinese. His group sent reports from time to time.

Q: Captain, in these months of late '37 and early 1938, the Chinese had established their capital at Hankow, and the Japanese were being met with Chinese refusals to make peace. What was Admiral Yarnell's strategy to protect U.S. lives and property on the Yangtze?

Smith-Hutton: Our embassy and consular officials, knew where our properties and nationals were as for example, the Standard Oil installations and they sent the information to us. Admiral Yarnell made it his responsibility to keep the Japanese Navy through Admiral Hasegawa, the Japanese commander in Shanghai, informed. We requested him to give protection to these American properties and citizens.

American properties were still damaged but there was nothing else that we could do. We found that the Japanese Navy was willing to try to avoid damaging them. But the army showed little interest.

As I have said, the situation in Shanghai had gradually returned to normal, and the 6th Marines were returned to the United States. Admiral Yarnell became convinced that many of our problems depended on how successful the Japanese trade efforts in the Yangtze became.

The situation in Tsingtao improved considerably about this

time. At the height of the Shanghai fighting, the Japanese had returned all of their nationals to Japan, leaving their homes and businesses to Chinese caretakers. In the spring of '38 they returned to Tsingtao, and in spite of the fighting elsewhere they were generally welcomed back. A certain amount of damage had been done to some homes and properties, especially to the smaller factories, but this damage was not extensive. The Chinese residents were glad to have them back, because it meant more business for them.

When it became evident that the Chinese and the Japanese were getting along well in Tsingtao, the Admiral decided that the flagship and the submarines could go there for the summer of 1938 as usual.

The Augusta returned to Shanghai in late April 1938, and about a month later left Shanghai for Ching Wan Tao. The Admiral decided to visit Peking and see for himself what was happening in the Peking-Tientsin area. We spent about three weeks there.

Q: Captain, one of the signs of unrest in a country generally is that the railroads stop running, and yet you're describing a railroad tour in China. Can you explain that?

Smith-Hutton: The Chinese and the Japanese outside battle area tried to carry on business as usual. We got ashore in Chingwantao in time to catch an 8 a.m. train and we arrived in Tientsin shortly after lunchtime. The Admiral and staff inspected the Marine guard, and the barracks that afternoon. That night we stayed in the Marine barracks. The rooms for guests were very comfortable.

The next morning, we left on an early train for the 90 mile trip to Peking. The rolling stock on the railroad was in good shape. We were in a parlor car fitted with old fashioned plush seats and mirrors. It was a comfortable trip, the train ran smoothly and was on time.

There was considerable freight traffic on that railroad, too. Especially coal and grains from Manchuria, so the railroad was kept in good condition.

Q: Captain, I appreciate that Admiral Yarnell was in Peking for a rest and to talk with the American colony, to evaluate what was going on but what did he do for relaxation?

Smith-Hutton: Admiral Yarnell loved to walk, and at that time of year Peking is a delightful place. He walked in the parks and in the native sections of the beautiful city. He said it was very relaxing, and apparently he walked for several hours a day.

The staff of the embassy was headed by Mr. Lawrence Salisbury who had spent years in the Far East. He spoke fluent Japanese and Chinese. The Admiral spent a long time with him and found him very well informed. He also talked with other officers in the embassy.

The Admiral was always busy but wasn't interested in being entertained. They used his stay in Peking to very good advantage.

Q: Captain, it's interesting that you mention Admiral Yarnell as a walker of note, because he resembles Admiral Spruance of World War II fame in that respect. Admiral Spruance thought nothing of walking five or ten miles of an afternoon.

Captain, after this vacation in Peking, the Admiral and his party returned to Tsingtao. I'm reminded that in the late 1940's Tsingtao had the air of an international resort, with a large hotel and beautiful beaches and wonderful weather. Was the atmosphere that of an international resort in 1938 in the summer?

Smith-Hutton: Yes, indeed. The weather was good and the usual holiday atmosphere prevailed among the summer residents. In addition to the many American, British and other nationals who came as summer residents, there were the French and the British naval vessels. The mayor of Tsingtao, Vice Admiral Shen, Chinese Navy and his staff, many of whom spoke English, was pro-American, and determined to avoid trouble with the Japanese. The Japanese consul general, Mr. Otaka, who had been there in 1937 and who had arranged for the Japanese residents to be evacuated and then arranged for their return in the spring of '38, was still in Tsingtao. He was a forceful officer, and also friendly with Americans. He was probably responsible for the Japan-America Associations arrangements for the dinner for Admiral Yarnell. Thus, in spike of the conflict and chaotic conditions in other parts of China, Tsingtao was a quiet resort where people could forget international problems.

So the summer of 1938 in Tsingtao was a pleasant one. Unfortunately, there were not to be many more like it for Americans in China.

Q: Captain, as the wife of a senior staff officer, Mrs. Smith-Hutton probably had certain social obligations. Can you describe any of those?

Smith-Hutton: My wife became friendly with the wives of various consular officers. Especially Mrs. Sokobin, our consuls wife and Mrs. Otaka. So she frequently invited Mrs. Yarnell and other wives from the Augusta to luncheon at our home. Afterward they played bridge. These were invariably pleasant luncheons. Fortunately, the wives of many Tsingtao officials spoke enough English to make association with them pleasant. Unless there is a common language, social functions are somewhat difficult. However, in Tsingtao that wasn't the case.

Q: Captain, time is now progressing to the point where you are due for a change of orders, having been at sea at least three years. Did you get any feelers from Washington as to your next tour of duty?

Smith-Hutton: I received word from ONI that in the spring of 1939, I would be relieved by Lieutenant Commander R. Mason, and that I would be ordered to duty in the Office of Naval Intelligence. We prepared to return home and although we didn't have many household effects, I arranged to have all we owned shipped to Washington.

However, much to my surprise, I was asked by ONI if I would like to go to the embassy in Tokyo as Naval Attache. When I answered that I would, my original orders were cancelled.

Q: As a lieutenant commander being appointed naval attache at a major embassy, relieving a senior captain, this must have come as a surprise to you. Did you find out the reason for it?

Smith-Hutton: Yes. The officer considered as the relief of Captain Bemis was Captain E. M. Zacharias, class of 1912, also a Japanese language officer. However, he had been in Tokyo briefly in 1927-1928 and at that time had caused considerable friction among the staff. The ambassador and the counsellor of the Embassy both requested that he not be sent to Tokyo because they were anxious to have officers who would work well with others and they feared that Captain Zacharias, in spite of his abilities might again create problems because of his vanity and his unorthodox behavior. They did not trust his judgement. As a result, I was selected to go much earlier than I had expected to go as Naval Attache.

Q: What was Admiral Yarnell's reaction to your orders to Tokyo, Captain?

Smith-Hutton: Admiral Yarnell congratulated me, and said that of course I should go. He sent a message to the Chief of Naval Operations saying that he thought my selection in spite of my junior rank, was a good one. I was very proud of have his comment.

Q: You realized that you'd been away from the States three years and now you presumably were going to be away another three years, but this didn't shock you?

Smith-Hutton: No, it didn't bother me.

Q: Or Mrs. Smith-Hutton?

Smith-Hutton: No, it didn't bother her at all.

Q: Captain, I have here in front of me a letter of commendation which was awarded you by Admiral Yarnell, dated 10 March 1939. With your permission, I will zerox this and send it forward for inclusion in the oral history. Do you agree?

Smith-Hutton: Yes, please do.

Q: Thank you. I presume that your household goods were limited and that you had no difficulty moving from Shanghai to Tokyo. What was your means of conveyance?

Smith-Hutton: Transportation was furnished by the Naval Purchasing Office in Shanghai. I and my wife and our daughter went from Shanghai to Yokohama on the steamship President Taft of the American President Line. We left Shanghai on 23 April and arrived in Yokohama on 28 April after a stop at Kobe.

Q: You mentioned for the first time your daughter. How old was the baby, and where was she born?

Smith-Hutton: Yes, she was born in Iowa, where my wife's father was on duty. My wife was there to have the baby, who was, when we arrived in Tokyo, two years old.

Q: What is her name?

Smith-Hutton: Cynthia.

Q: One of the first tasks that faces a newly-arrived naval attache is to find a decent home, not only for living but for entertaining. Were you successful?

Smith-Hutton: I was very lucky. The house that we rented was the same house that two previous naval attaches had occupied, that is, Captain Rogers, and Captain Bemis. Mrs. Rogers, who selected the house, had insisted that it be enlarged, so a large dining room had been added. It was really a modest house but comfortable and adequate.

Q: Where was it located?

Smith-Hutton: It was next door to the embassy. One wall of the embassy garden and one wall of the garden around our house were the same wall. Our garden was slightly lower than the embassy garden perhaps 10 feet lower, but the wall served both gardens.

It took me about three minutes to walk from the house to my office which was very convenient.

Q: A Western style house, and how much rent did you pay, Captain?

Smith-Hutton: We paid about $200 a month. It was a Western style house with four bedrooms, a large dining room and two medium-sized sitting rooms. It was adequate in every way, and the rent was moderate.

Q: Did you ever have the feeling that you might have been bugged -- that is, the listening devices had been placed there by Japanese intelligence?

Smith-Hutton: Yes, we did. Of course, we had no way of knowing. We were very careful not to discuss things which shouldn't be discussed at home and we also knew that the telephone might be tapped. In talking over the phone we were always careful not to discuss confidential matters.

Q: In your first meetings with Ambassador Grew, did he brief you on the conditions? Or what happened?

Smith-Hutton: Ambassador Grew was very methodical in keeping diaries, files and records, and he had an efficient staff. His private secretary had been with him for a number of years and had come with him from Turkey. He also had a private secretary, a young man who had been recommended to him by the headmaster at Groton.

The ambassador, after welcoming me, gave me a file of recent dispatches that had been sent and suggested that I read it carefully, and when I returned it to him ask any questions that I might have. He urged me to keep in touch with Mr. Eugene Dooman who was the counsellor of the embassy, who had been in Tokyo for many years and who spoke Japanese perfectly, and with the military attache, Lieutenant Colonel Cresswell. My introduction to this tour of duty in Tokyo was thus normal, and satisfactory. As a matter of fact, my relations with the ambassador had always been very good.

Q: What about Captain Bemis? Did he provide you with any good information or did anybody on his staff?

Smith-Hutton: His reports and files were there for my study. Captain Bemis had a poor opinion of the Japanese and he felt that they had not been friendly or helpful to him. He had a number of friends with whom he played golf. He also played poker with some of them. But he felt that information had been with help from him and that he had not been given the facilities that a naval attache might expect.

In looking over the files, I found that the best information in regard to the recent work of the office was in the reports that had been submitted by Lieutenant Commander Ralph Ofstie who had been the assistant for air. He had inspected the Japanese naval air installations thoroughly and knew a great deal about them. His reports were good and I found them very useful.

Interview No. 24 with Captain Henri Smith-Hutton, U.S. Navy
(Retired)

Place: Stanford, California

Date: May 23, 1974

Subject: Biography

By: Captain Paul B. Ryan

Q: Captain, in our last interview you had just arrived in Tokyo to start your tour as a Naval Attache. This is April, 1939. You had last been there in 1935. Did you notice any change in the attitude of the people or in the general economy or their attitude toward things?

Captain Smith-Hutton: There were a number of changes in the conditions in Japan in the four years that I'd been gone. It seemed to me that the people were more somber and subdued. Certainly their clothing seemed more shabby and made of poorer materials. There were shortages of all kinds of articles, especially metals and construction materials. Imported goods had almost disappeared from the stores, and prices were very high; and while vegetables and rice and fish were available, there was little meat, and people had to line up to buy bread.

There was, of course, constant talk of the war in China. The government urged the people to make sacrifices and to save so that the troops in China would be well supplied; and to help buy foreign currencies, for purchases abroad the Japanese were directed to turn in to the banks all articles made of gold.

And, of course, it was forbidden for them to have foreign currency which had to be exchanged for Japanese yen. We diplomats were not affected by these regulations, but the Japanese did request informally that the staffs of the Embassies comply where possible.

Of course, as regards imported articles, the Embassy arranged for the staff to order supplies, foodstuffs, and other things from home. We used a large San Francisco wholesale house, so that as far as we were concerned there was no great change. But my wife did discover that she had to arrange to take the cook some distance from the house to get some foods which used to be available in the local markets. It was necessary, also, she found, to plan well in advance for meals if you were having guests, because frequently provisions -- meats and other staples -- couldn't be purchased on short notice.

Q: Captain, can you describe the reason for the sad state of the Japanese economy?

Smith-Hutton: Of course, the main reason was the expense in conducting the war in China. Japan had mobilized about a million men, many of them were on duty on the continent and they were engaged in active operations against the Chinese from the northern part of China to the Yangtze. Secondly, the military was preparing for other eventualities. In other words, the Army had plans to stockpile supplies against a possible war with Russia, and the Navy was asking for a large budget to build ships against a possible war with the United States. All of this cost money.

At the same time Japan was importing large quantities of oil and steel which were not used for producing goods, but for war. This was the reason that the economy was badly strained.

Q: Captain, in the summer of 1939 Ambassador Grew was scheduled for his triennial leave which would be three months back in the States. Before he left did anything unusual occur?

Smith-Hutton: We thought it was unusual. Shortly before the Ambassador left on home leave, which as you have indicated was a scheduled home leave, the Japanese members of two golf clubs arranged matches in his honor. One was at the Tokyo Golf Club at Asaka just outside of Tokyo, and the other was at a beautiful new course near Atami on the Izu Peninsula. Lieutenant Commander McCallum and I played in the second one, and while we didn't win any prizes, we didn't exactly disgrace ourselves. The Ambassador was very much pleased by these attentions and the arranging of the matches, since almost two hundred members played in each; and they took part in the cocktail parties afterward. The large clubrooms were decorated with American and Japanese flags, and they made speeches and toasts.

In view of the generally poor relations between the United States and Japan and the fact that for several years most of the Japanese members of the clubs were afraid to be seen sitting with American members, it did appear that these were demonstrations of real friendship for the Ambassador, and he took it that way.

Q: Obviously Ambassador Grew is going to discuss affairs in the State Department and with the President in the White House when he returns to the States. Did he mention to you and to other staff members what he planned to say?

Smith-Hutton: Well, I know that the Ambassador for some time had felt that it would be very important for the Japanese to understand a little more clearly than they apparently did, what American policy in the Far East was, and how we felt about some of the things they were doing in China. He was not fixed in any particular plan or program, but he mentioned that while he was home he thought it would be a good idea to consult with the key members of the State Department and perhaps even with the Secretary of State about making an address when he returned to Japan from home leave. He was scheduled to deliver a speech in October before the America-Japan Society and if there were no objections or if he could get the blessing of authorities at home, he felt that it would be an important time to make such an address and to be as frank as possible and to, as he said, mince no words with the Japanese. He told us that that was in the back of his mind. He didn't know whether it would work out, but he hoped that it would.

Well, events proved that it did, and when he came back to Tokyo in early October, we found that he had done exactly as he proposed; that he had made a rough draft of the speech while he was on leave, that he had shown it to the Secretary and had shown it to the Secretary and had shown it to Mr. Hornbeck, Mr. Balentine, Mr. Salisbury, and Mr. Hamilton who were the key members in the State Department in the Far Eastern Division. Whether he had actually consulted the President I've forgotten. But at any rate he had their approval. He had the draft almost completed. He let us read it. That is, he let the key members of his staff in Tokyo read it and signify any objections or any corrections that they might have. And then at the America-Japan Society luncheon he delivered the address in his formal way.

For instance, he outlined our desire for peace and our respect for the sovereign rights of other peoples and our determination not to let Japan's policies in east Asia deprive us of our long-established rights in China. He added that Americans had not forgotten the long-time friendship between Japan and America, but had been shocked by the widespread bombing, the damage to our property and the menace to American lives in China. He said that Americans believed that real peace and stability could be obtained without doing the things that some Japanese forces were doing and which were very injurious to our rights.

Of course, this was a remarkable speech because of the way the Ambassador delivered it -- and, as I say, he minced no words and he called the speech straight from the horse's mouth -- I always took that to mean that it had the blessing of the President, although he didn't say so. It was widely quoted and it had the effect of telling the Japanese the exact truths, but in such a way that they couldn't really take offense, because it was splendid advice. He reiterated how friendly we were, that he was talking to them as a real friend and that he hoped that the Japanese authorities, governmental and armed force authorities, would heed it. Unfortunately, it created a profound impression in Japan among the Japanese who realized how important it was and who were in general on good terms with us, but it had apparently little effect on the Japanese Armed Forces, because they continued much as before. It's unfortunate, but they couldn't say that they didn't know what Americans were thinking about.

Q: Were you there during the speech?

Smith-Hutton: Yes, I was there at the luncheon, and it was every bit as important as I have indicated. There was only one newspaper man there. He was the United Press man, and he sent a summary of the speech by cable. It wasn't more than two or three hours before the Associated Press, the Hearst papers and the New York Times correspondent were queried from their New York offices to report on this important speech.

The Ambassador was very careful not to give to the Japanese agencies copies of the speech, because that was one of the things we always complained about -- a Japanese official in the United States who after making a speech, gave copies to our press. But it wasn't long -- two or three days in any event -- before the Japanese Foreign Office requested that the Ambassador make available to the Japanese news agency and the papers copies of the speech. Thus, it was available in Japan a few days after the speech was made, but at the express request of the Japanese Foreign Office -- a very nice point.

Q: Who served as the interpreter for the Ambassador during this speech?

Smith-Hutton: He spoke in English, and since it was the Japan-America Society, almost all the Japanese there spoke English well enough to understand it. It wasn't translated into Japanese.

Q: Did you notice any consternation on the face of the Japanese who were there?

Smith-Hutton: No. Intense interest, but not consternation. I think they were sympathetic with what the Ambassador was trying to do. He was well liked and he did it in such a courteous, friendly way that even the Japanese couldn't very well take offense.

Q: Who were the staff members who helped the Ambassador in reviewing his speech? You mention that you yourself were one of them. Who were the others?

Smith-Hutton: Mr. Dooman, who was the Counsellor of the Embassy, Colonel Cresswell, who was the Military Attache, and Mr. Frank Williams, who was the Commercial Attache, and I were among those the Ambassador consulted. I think that is probably all.

Q: Well, thank you for the highlights on this very important speech.

Captain, in 1939 the Japanese Navy and the U.S. Navy were involved in a naval race, and international relations between us were deteriorating. At this time the Japanese Army was getting more entangled in China and was casting covetous eyes at French Indo-China. Do you have any personal theory as to why the Japanese Army and Navy decided to go south into the Netherlands East Indies, Indo-China, and Malaya?

Smith-Hutton: As I've indicated, except for a few fire-eaters in the Navy, most Japanese officers were rather friendly to the United States, and many of the senior officers were quite frank in saying so. Among them, of course, were Admirals Nomura, Hasegawa, Yonai, Toyoda, and Yamamoto. All of these officers considered, I'm sure, that Japan could maintain her predominant position in Asia and even strengthen that position without going to war with the United States.

That was the situation until the autumn of 1940 when an important change apparently took place. I think it was due largely to pressure on the Navy by the Army. The first thing that happened was the fact that after years of fighting in China, the Army was still bogged down and the end of the war wasn't in sight. In this situation the Army planners decided that an advance into Indo-China and then toward Malaya and the Netherlands East Indies might be a solution. It seemed to have small risks, because France, Great Britain and the Netherlands were all at war in Europe and the Far Eastern colonies were helpless. They, I think, were under the impression that the United States, which had remained neutral in Europe, would also remain neutral in Asia. However, when they went into Indo-China, the reaction in the United States to this advance was much stronger than expected. Among other things we terminated the treaty of commerce between Japan and the United States. We stationed part of the fleet in Hawaii, where it had gone on maneuvers in 1940, and we made a number of very stiff diplomatic protests to the Japanese government in regard to the occupation of Indo-China.

So I think at that time the Navy much have concluded that any additional advance southward was almost sure to involve even stronger American reaction. And I think another thing was that the Navy as well as the Army were impressed by the dramatic changes in the war situation in Europe and the brilliant German victories in France in the summer of 1940. I know that the Japanese military in Germany were of the belief that Germany would eliminate Great Britain and win the war in a comparatively short time, and that this estimate was transmitted to Tokyo with the urgent recommendation that Japan make the most of this situation and take every advantage of the German victory.

It was apparent then that many of the Army general staff officers, and not only the Army but the Navy general staff officers, too, were convinced by this argument. It's probable that some of the cooler heads in the Japanese Navy, such as Admirals Nomura, Yonai, and Toyoda -- Admiral Nomura being sent to the United States as Ambassador, and Toyoda was Foreign Minister in the Cabinet for a while -- still urged caution, and I think they were sincere in their efforts to reach a settlement with the

United States that would be satisfactory to Japan and satisfy the Army. Still, they became more and more a minority.

Q: Captain, I get the impression, and correct me if I'm wrong, that your theory is that the Japanese Army was bogged down in China. Therefore, they wanted to go into French Indo-China to stop supplies from going into China, and therefore, the Navy was dragged in with unforeseen consequences. Can you review the bidding on that for me?

Smith-Hutton: Yes. It seems to me that the Japanese Army, as I say, which had been fighting all these years in China without positive results, was getting tired and that the country was over-extended. So the Army was anxious to bring an end to the war in China as soon as possible. They were searching for ways to do that. They decided that since certain supplies, comparatively large amounts of supplies, were going into southern China via French Indo-China, they could be stopped by a Japanese occupation. And the plan was to use that as the first step and then to go from there to Malaya and then to the Netherlands Indies. They were astonished by the fact that the United States protested so strongly their occupation of French Indo-China, and they were then convinced that if they continued with their program, American opposition would be even stronger.

In any event, they must have the assistance of the Navy in a war with the United States. The result was that the Army began pressuring the Navy to prepare for a war with the United

States. Meanwhile, they were preparing moves against the British in Malaya and the Netherlands Indies. The result was the beginning of World War II and Pearl Harbor.

Q: It was about this time specifically, as I understand the picture, that the Japanese Navy, being pressured by the Japanese Army, decided that they had better come up with a plan to strike the U.S. Navy where it hurt, meaning the U.S. fleet. Is this correct?

Smith-Hutton: That is correct. Because it was early in 1941 or possibly late 1940 that the Commander-in-Chief of the Japanese combined fleet, Admiral Yamamoto, instructed his staff to make a plan for an aerial attack on our base at Pearl Harbor.

Q: And Yamamoto actually probably did this against his better judgment because he knew of the strength of the U.S. having served in this country?

Smith-Hutton: I believe that is so, and I think that the only reason he did agree was he realized that the Army which had more power in the nation was adamant. He felt that the Navy could not successfully oppose the Army politically, and that the only thing the Navy could do would be to go along with the Army plan no matter how reluctantly.

Q: That a very interesting and plausible theory. Thank you,

Captain.

Captain, in the latter 1930's the U.S. and Japan were building their naval strength up at a fast and faster pace. One of your duties was to report on the Japanese building program. Where did you get your information, and did you personally observe any of these ships being built?

Smith-Hutton: We were able to report the details of the Japanese naval budget, because the budget was debated in the House of Peers and the Diet, the National Assembly. They debated in considerable detail the names of the ships where they were building, the general characteristics and costs of the building programs.

These debates, however, did not mention the detailed characteristics of the ships. That is, we learned that a battleship was being built at Kure and another was being built at Yokosuka. We knew that a carrier was being built at Mitsubishi Yard in Nagasaki, for instance, but the size of the carrier or the size of the battleships or the characteristics of the guns and the number of planes they might have were closely guarded secrets.

For the last few months of the tour of duty of my predecesrot, Captain Bemis, the Japanese Navy Department had declined to allow him to visit the places that he had requested, and he was told informally that the Japanese Naval Attache had not been given permission to visit some of the yards and bases in the United States. So since visits were based on reciprocity, he could not visit as usual the bases and air fields. In turning over to me he advised that I not make the usual requests, because that that might induce the Japanese to try again in the United States. He had also understood informally from Washington that we would prefer not to give the Japanese permission to visit our yards and bases for some time, due to the fact that we were carrying on a big building program. The result was that the mutual inspection system which had existed for many years broke apart and we had no chance to visit Yokosuka, Kure, or Sasebo, the main building yards of the Japanese Navy.

Q: In 1940 when the U.S. Pacific fleet was stationed in Pearl Harbor, was there any reaction in the Japanese press or within the Japanese Navy?

Smith-Hutton: The Japanese press frequently carried news reports of aggressive attitude of the United States as shown by stationing the major portion of the fleet at Pearl Harbor. They considered that this was one of the first steps in bringing pressure on Japan to give up her gains in China. Of course, the Japanese Navy realized that we could station the fleet where we pleased, and Pearl Harbor was a naval base. There was no official reaction whatever. The Japanese press, however, was interested in bringing out Japan's difficulties not only in China but with the rest of the world, was nationalistic and the fact that our fleet was in Pearl Harbor was a good excuse to write anti-American propaganda.

Interview No. 25 with Captain Henri Smith-Hutton, U.S. Navy
(Retired)

Place: Stanford, California

Date: June 6, 1974

Subject: Biography

By: Captain Paul B. Ryan

Q: Captain, in our last session we were discussing Japanese-U.S. naval relations. As tensions increased between the two countries in 1940, how did this affect your relations with your friends, your official contacts, and the like?

Smith-Hutton: At first there was little change in my official or personal relations with Japanese naval officers I'd known for years. For instance, Admiral Nomura gave a luncheon in my honor shortly after I got back to Tokyo, and when Admiral Yarnell passed through Japan in late July 1939 after he'd been relieved as Commander-in-Chief, and the ship that he was taking passage on to the United States was in Yokohama, he was invited to come to Tokyo and was entertained by the Navy Minister who at that time was Admiral Yonai. They had a very elaborate luncheon for some twenty-five senior officers, and both the Navy Minister and Admiral Yarnell made brief speeches expressing the hope that the differences between our countries could be settled in friendly fashion. But that gradually changed, largely because the Japanese Military Police became very suspicious of all of our activities. Articles appeared in the press from time to time saying that the Japanese should be suspicious of all foreigners living in Japan, that there were many spies, and that they mustn't divulge national secrets. So that after parties or visits to our homes the police interrogated our Japanese friends at great length as to what went on, what we said, what we did and how we acted. Gradually they became discouraged and didn't like to be interrogated. So we lost our contacts in many instances, not because they didn't like us, but because it was too complicated if every visit was followed by a long session with the police. Gradually we lost our contacts with them.

Q: Now, what was the name of the Japanese official police?

Smith-Hutton: The Japanese police? They were the Kempeitai. They were military police and were part of the Japanese security system.

Q: It would be of interest to future historians to know who the members of your staff were, both the officers, enlisted men, and civilians. Would you describe them for us, Captain?

Smith-Hutton: I had two officers as assistants. When I reported for duty, the Assistant Attache was Lieutenant Commander McCallum of the class of 1924. He was an officer that I had known for many years, and he was Captain Bemis's assistant. He was a good Japanese language officer, competent, who read Japanese very easily. The Assistant for Air was Lieutenant Jurika, Jurika was in the class of '33. McCallum was a bachelor, and Jurika came with his very charming wife and they soon had a baby.

Lieutenant Jurika's duty was to observe and report on the Naval Air Force, but unfortunately, since the inspection system had broken down, he had very little opportunity for close-up observations. He could only catch glimpses of their planes flying and operating. But he read, translated, studied, and reported all the written material in regard to the Navy, and he did a good job. He and McCallum both left in the Spring of 1941, and at that time Lieutenant Commander Stone of the class of '27 came to relieve McCallum and Lieutenant Phares, in the class of '32, relieved Jurika. Stone remained until war broke out, but Phares went to do his flight time in the Philippines in October. Before he left I suggested to Admiral Hart that he not return because he had very little chance to observe Japanese naval air operations. He was an experienced patrol plane pilot, and it seemed much more worthwhile for him to be where he was needed more than in Tokyo. Lieutenant Phares was a bachelor and I told him what I was going to do, so when he left Tokyo, he took his gear with him, and was prepared not to return. We worked very closely as a team, and all of my assistants were very competent. In addition to the officers, there was a retired chief yeoman, Leonard Wagner, who had been in Japan for many years. He had learned to speak Japanese, and read it very well. Wagner was a bachelor, somewhat of a recluse, and he was most useful, because he was loyal, quiet, efficient, and in addition to that he kept the accounts of the Attache's office and was a good stenographer. He typed all of our reports so there was never the slightest question of security. We also got permission from the Navy Department to hire as a part time an American woman who worked in another office in the Embassy, who did not have sufficient work to do.

In addition, there were two Japanese employees. One was Mr. Iwamoto. He was graduate of Harvard University and a very superior person. He was married to an American lady and had a talented and charming daughter, who was an excellent violin player. The other Japanese was a younger man who came as a messenger and remained as office boy. Iwamoto was an excellent translator, because he spoke good English, was devoted and very useful. I was very fortunate to have a good staff.

Q: What happened to Lieutenant Phares?

Smith-Hutton: For the first part of the war he was in command of one of the PBY's in the Philippines. He survived the war, and I think he retired as a Captain. He was a fine officer.

Q: You mentioned before a Lieutenant (jg) Jurika, who was also an aviator and Assistant Naval Attache for Air. What happened to him?

Smith-Hutton: Lieutenant Jurika, who was there before Lieutenant Phares, returned to the United States in the late spring of 1941. Among other assignments, he was on the aircraft carrier from which Lieutenant Colonel Doolittle made his raid on Japan in the spring of 1942. Lieutenant Jurika was one of the officers who briefed the Army aviators on the carrier, the Hornet, and was the one who pointed out to them some useful targets. He retired after having commanded a small carrier as a captain. I believe he is teaching in this area.

Q: Yes, I believe he's a Ph.D. on the faculty of Santa Clara University.

Q: Do you have any conception of your production of intelligence reports during this period, Captain? Did you crank them out, or were they hard to acquire? How did it go?

Smith-Hutton: Actually our reports were voluminous, because we followed the Official Gazette very closely, and reported every mention of the Navy in the debates in the Diet or the House of Peers. They were published at length. There was considerable interest in the Navy among the civilian population so there were a number of popular naval publications and magazines. There was also quite a lot published in regard to the Merchant Marine and many pictures. Among other things, for instance, all the time I was there, we bought each week several very detailed maps of different sections of the country. By the end of a year and a half we had a very detailed topographic map of all Japan. We bound these together and sent them back to the United States.

They didn't give details of fortified areas or military bases, but they showed the cities, towns, rivers, railroads, and terrain and our pilots found them very useful during the war. We sent back a picture of every merchant ship that appeared in a magazine or paper, including detailed plans of the ships, which were not classified. So our reports, while they contained no startling information, were full of detailed non-classified data of interest to our Navy.

Q: I can say from personal experience that the pictures of the Japanese merchant ships that you sent back found their way to the U.S. submarine Silhouette as target books that we used in the Pacific for identification purposes quite a lot.

Smith-Hutton: Yes, the Office of Naval Intelligence did a good job in preparing recognition manuals using the materials we sent from Tokyo.

Q: In the days after World War II the U.S. Embassies had the custom, in fact the requirement, to send in a weekly report to the State Department that was known as a "Weeka" -- a simple weekly analysis. There was a section in there for the Naval Attache wherein you contributed the news of intelligence of the week. This was a classified report. Did you have such a thing as a Weeka" in Tokyo in the days before Pearl Harbor?

Smith-Hutton: No. The "Weeka" was not in existence during the time I was in Tokyo; that is, in 1939, '40, and '41. We sent very few of our reports by telegram. Almost all went by diplomatic pouch and were written. Since it cost quite a lot of money to send cables, we felt that our reports were not urgent enough to be cabled. There was no "Weeka."

Q: Captain, among the leading figures in the U.S. Embassy staff were the Counsellor, Eugene Dooman, and the Military Attache, Colonel Cresswell. I'm sure there were others, too. Would you care to comment on your impressions of these senior officers?

Smith-Hutton: I met Mr. Dooman in 1926, since he was the Japanese specialist in the Embassy and had been on the staff for years. He gave me my final examination in Japanese language in 1929. He spoke perfect Japanese, having gone to school in Japan as a boy. His father was a missionary and until he entered the university -- I think he graduated from Yale -- and then joined the diplomatic service, had spent most of his life in Japan.

Many Americans considered that he was pro-Japanese. I don't agree. He was a very diffident man and difficult to get to know. Sometimes he gave the impression that he was opinionated. I found him, on the other hand, to be very knowledgeable and we got along well. Perhaps it was because I was not a State Department official that he felt a little more free with me.

His great value to the Embassy was was that he had so many friends among the Japanese, that he spoke such excellent Japanese, and that he was a very hard working, intelligent man. He wrote beautiful reports and I thought that he was one of the very valuable men we had in the service in Tokyo. He was completely loyal to the Ambassador and they got along quite well. He said frankly that his job, he felt, was to prevent war and to try to make the Japanese understand our point of view. Perhaps he leaned over backwards in that connection, but I don't think so. I have very high regard for him.

Of course, in the old State Department precedence list the Attaches, the Army, Navy, and Commercial Attaches, were immediately after the Counsellor in the order of their rank, particularly as regards the Military and Naval Attaches. The third ranking official on the Embassy staff was Lieutenant Colonel Cresswell, the Military Attache. He was a bachelor about forty-five years old who spoke good Japanese. As a matter of fact he and a Japanese Army officer prepared a dictionary of military terms, and it was, until the middle 1950's, the standard work. His contacts with the Japanese Army were quite good. He was a methodical, careful, and thoughtful officer, and his reports were full of a great detail, perhaps too much detail. He had few outside distractions, and spent all of his time working. I think that if he had any weakness, it would be that he didn't see the larger picture as much as he saw the fine print and the details of his job, but that is only an observation. We got along very well, too.

The Commercial Attache was Frank Williams, who was a wealthy, socially-minded officer. He had awfully good contacts among Japanese business men, and he had a poor opinion of the Japanese. I think that he was somewhat biased, because he spoke no Japanese and didn't make any pretense of wanting to learn much about the people. His great value, of course, was that he did have contacts among Japanese businessmen, and also with foreign diplomats. He played excellent golf, was a very cheery fellow and well liked. His reports also were excellent. He had an assistant named Donald Smith who did most of the leg work and reporting. The two of them worked hard and their reports were outstandingly good.

There were two First Secretaries. One was Mr. Edward Crocker, and the other, George Mackenson. Crocker was of a very well-to-do New England family, and a cheery fellow from Princeton who got along well with everybody. Mackenson was an excellent administrator and worked hard. Two Second Secretaries spoke very good Japanese having been reared in Japan like Mr. Dooman. They were Mr. William Turner and Merrill Benninghoff -- excellent young men.

The third Second Secretary was Charles Bohlen, who came from Moscow to join the staff just a year before Pearl Harbor, so that there would be a better liaison between our embassies in Tokyo and in Moscow. He became very well known in the diplomatic service. He was Ambassador to Russia, later Ambassador to the Philippines, and finally Ambassador to France. He was one of the most likable and one of the ablest men in our foreign service.

There were three excellent young Third Secretaries, one of whom is now working here in Palo Alto, named John Emmerson, who is with the Hoover Institution. The others were Charles Cooper and James Espe. All were Japanese language specialists, so the staff was oriented toward technical competence and the reporting in my view was of a high order.

Q: Having described the officers in the Embassy, do you have any comments on the Embassy wives and their ability to contribute to their husbands' work?

Smith-Hutton: Yes. Beginning with Mrs. Grew. Mrs. Grew was very popular in Japan, since one of her ancestors had been Commodore Perry. That was well known, and she was well liked by the Japanese. Mrs. Dooman, the wife of the Counsellor, was a great help to her husband. She was a charming lady, and entertained very well. And there was Mrs. Crocker, the wife of the First Secretary. Unfortunately, except for Mrs. Dooman, Mrs. Grew, and my wife, there were few ladies left in the Embassy in 1940 and '41, because the State Department had a policy of not allowing the wives to return to Tokyo if they were in the United States, having gone home on leave. So that by the end of 1940 and through 1941 Mrs. Grew and my wife were almost the only officers' wives still in Tokyo. It was somewhat lonely for the husbands in Tokyo without their wives, but the State Department was inflexible and would not allow the wives to return.

Q: Tell me again now, why did Mrs. Smith-Hutton decide to stay?

Smith-Hutton: For one thing, Mrs. Grew asked her particularly to remain in Tokyo. That was because they were close friends, and Mrs. Grew felt that she needed the company of at least one American wife. Jane was chosen and didn't hesitate to stay. As a matter of fact, she wanted to stay, but her desire was strengthened by Mrs. Grew's request.

Q: You had a small daughter, did you not?

Smith-Hutton: Yes, our daughter was six when we finally left Japan. She went to the Sacred Heart convent on the outskirts of the city which was another reason why my wife wanted to stay.

Q: Captain, I'm looking at an old photograph which you brought back from Japan, taken somewhere around 1939 or '40, showing Ambassador Grew and yourself and your wives at a country party with some distinguished Japanese. Can you describe the circumstances?

Smith-Hutton: This is a photograph of a luncheon in a small town south of Tokyo called Odawara. It is about two hours from Tokyo by train, and we are in the summer home of Baron Matsuda, who had been the head of Mitsui Trading Company, one of the great companies in Japan. He was in his eighties when this photograph was taken. It shows the Ambassador and Mrs. Grew with the then Military Attache, a Colonel Crane. (This was before Colonel Cresswell reported.) It also shows Captain Martin, who was his assistant. Jane wasn't feeling well on that day and didn't attend.

In the photograph are Baron Matsuda and Count Kabayama, both well know, prominent in the America-Japan Society, and great friends of the United States. There is Admiral Uriu, who graduated from our Naval Academy in the class of 1881. Baron Matsuda asked the Ambassador to bring us to this luncheon party. We went by train, were met at the station, and were driven to

Baron Matsuda's home. We had a delicious Japanese luncheon on a summer-like day. Odawara is on the seacoast and considerably cooler than Tokyo. It was a country excursion and picnic party, refreshing and relaxing in a country atmosphere among friends, among Japanese who were obviously glad to have us and were being most hospitable.

Q: With the Mitsui Company being one of the huge corporations in Japan, and Baron Matsuda being one of the economic, industrial giants, what ever happened to him?

Smith-Hutton: He died just before the war broke out, since he was an old man. During the early days of the occupation, Mitsui Trading Company was broken up by orders of General MacArthur. It has, however, been reconstituted and is operating very much as it used to, because it was organized in such a way that it could be broken up or fitted together without too many complications. And that's what happened. The various subsidiaries came back together as if nothing had happened.

Q: This reflects rather well on the state of the Japanese economy when this move was made, I should say.

Smith-Hutton: Yes, it does, and it also shows that one of the great accomplishments of the Japanese is their ability to work together and to set up complicated companies and factories and have the parts fit neatly into place. The Japanese have an excellent way of cooperating and making large corporations or large factories operate smoothly.

Q: Captain, there's a special word in Japanese to denote these giant corporations. Would you repeat that word for us?

Smith-Hutton: One term used to indicate large organizations and its members is "zaibatsu." It's used by foreign officials and foreigners and literally means "plutocrat".

Q: Captain, I'm looking at a photograph obviously of a foreign attache group taken with the Chief of the Japanese Navy, and I saw a similar photograph, but this one is different. Could you comment on that?

Smith-Hutton: This photograph was taken at the Japanese Navy Club, about ten minutes from the Navy Ministry, in a beautiful park section of Tokyo. The occasion was the appointment of Admiral Zengo Yoshida, as the Minister of the Navy. He gave this luncheon which was unusual in that it was after war was declared in Europe in 1939. He invited the German, French, British and Italian attaches to the luncheon, and all came. On glancing at it I see that on the Navy Minister's right is the Russian Naval Attache, and on his left is the French Naval Attache. On the Russian's right is a German officer, and not far from him is an Italian officer. It was really a cosmopolitan luncheon.

One of the points I would like to make about the host,

Admiral Yoshida, is that he had the reputation of being the most intelligent officer in the Navy. He was a classmate of Admiral Yamamoto's, and Yamamoto was, of course, already Commander-in-Chief of the Combined Fleet. Admiral Yamamoto was a great admirer of Yoshida and said that he himself would be very happy to be the second in command or be Yoshida's assistant in any assignment that Yoshida might have been given. This shows that he was held in high esteem by the entire Navy. Shortly after he left this position as a Minister in 1940, he became ill and never played an active part in affairs after that. I know that many times my friend regretted that he was forced to retire from the service because of health. I'll take occasion to refer to this when I've had a chance to name a few more of the officers who were present at the luncheon.

Q: I believe you said that this was the last luncheon where all the Allied and Axis Power officers ever attended as guests of the Japanese.

Smith-Hutton: This is correct. After this we were asked to a number of official luncheons, but the British, French, and American Attaches were invited to one, and the Axis Attaches were invited to another. We were never all invited together as on this occasion.

Q: Captain, we know that our relations with the Russians were a bit on the murky side in 1940, '41. What were your relations with the Russian Naval Attache?

Smith-Hutton: Before '39 our relations had been confined to speaking politely and exchanging innocuous remarks. The Russian Attache was a member of the foreign attache group and attended our luncheons. We were friendly enough but I didn't care for him particularly. One of the problems was that he spoke little English and almost no Japanese or French, so I had difficulty communicating with him.

However, after one of the luncheons, he asked if he could come to my office and I said I would like that very much. When we got there he asked if we translated the Japanese "Notices to Mariners" which were published every week, and distributed to all the attaches and sent to hydrographic offices throughout the world. I said yes, we always translated them. He asked if it would be possible for him to get copies of our translations. I thought for a moment and said I didn't see why not. I didn't think that would be complicated. I would just have one additional copy typed. He said that would be of very great value to him, because he didn't have anyone who could do the translation. I was surprised at that, but made no comment. After that I sent him, through the mail, a translation of the weekly Notices to Mariners.

I didn't feel that it was necessary to report this. Apparently he appreciated getting the translations because from then on we received boxes of Russian cigarettes and caviar, which was appreciated very much by my wife. Sometimes he sent Russian champagne, which I gave to Iwamoto who did the translations.

I always believed that the Russians would have a very competent staff in Tokyo and was astonished that they were unable to translate documents as readily available as the "Notices to Mariners." I couldn't understand it, and must confess that my opinion of Russian Intelligence fell considerably.

Q: That is most interesting -- your relations with the Russians. How about your relations with the Japanese? Were there any attempts made to compromise you on security matters?

Smith-Hutton: Yes, I think that the same attempt was made on me that was made on almost all of our attaches, and it wasn't very subtle. It was rather clumsy, and may not have been a hoax, but it seemed to me that it was. One afternoon a man's voice came over the telephone and said in rather halting Japanese that he would like to come to see me, because he had an important proposal to make and would like to come in about an hour. I told him to come ahead, that I had no appointments. He appeared and was very nervous. I closed the doors to my office and sat down behind my desk and said, "What can I do for you?" He said that he had in his brief case some pictures and a map of a naval air station not far from Tokyo, and he'd like very much to sell them to me.

I knew that this sort of approach had been made to attaches before but as far as I knew none had ever accepted such a proposal. I immediately decided that it would not be worth compromising my office or the reputation of the Embassy by having anything to do with it; so I stood up and said I was not interested. He appeared very much flustered, but he made no protest, and almost ran out of the office. As I say, I'm not sure that he was sent, but at least it seemed to me that he was trying to compromise me. I've been very happy always that I refused his offer.

Q: Captain, that's most interesting. Did you report this to Ambassador Grew, and if so, what was his reaction?

Smith-Hutton: I reported it to the Ambassador, and he said that he thought I acted correctly. The Navy Department made no comment when I reported what I'd done. It is probable that the man was trying to test me but I will never know.

Interview No. 26 with Captain Henri Smith-Hutton, U.S. Navy
(Retired)

Place: Stanford, California

Date: June 13, 1974

Subject: Biography

By: Captain Paul B. Ryan

Q: Captain, in our last session we were talking about covert collection of information, and you recounted the episode of the presumed agent who came to your office. Did any other opportunity offer itself to you to gain information covertly?

Smith-Hutton: Only one which could have been important and which happened in a rather curious fashion. I played tennis almost every day at the Tokyo Tennis Club, only three blocks from the Embassy. This was a club where half the members were Japanese and half were Europeans. It was a fine club in that the Japanese were all good players or well-to-do or of noble families. There were one hundred members from the European community and one hundred Japanese members. Hundreds of Japanese wanted to join so among them there was keen competition, whereas there weren't more than a hundred Americans, British, French or other diplomats and businessmen who wanted to play. For us it was a very simple matter. A European applied and almost automatically became a member.

The Japanese were really very nice to us. They were anxious to learn European manners and customs, and they were also a splendid group of men and women. The standard of play among the Japanese was usually quite high. It was not nearly as high for us. The Japanese also enjoyed having tournaments and matches with other clubs.

Once in early 1940 there was a match between our club and a Yokohama club. After the match we almost always went to a restaurant for dinner, and this particular time I sat next to a young Japanese student -- a very personable young fellow. I got on well with him and occasionally after that he came to our club at the invitation of one of the members.

One afternoon, in the summertime I found him waiting at the club without a partner since a change in his partner's plans had made it impossible to play that afternoon. I didn't have a game so I asked him to play with me. We played and afterward, since it was summertime and my wife and daughter were in the mountains to avoid the heat, I suggested that we go to dinner at a restaurant. Several of us went, and after dinner, I strolled home with him since I lived nearby and he was going in that direction.

We were walking along a quiet street early in the evening, and he asked me if I'd be interested in learning more about the Japanese Navy. I said yes, and he said he thought he might be able to help me. I said, "Well, how in the world could you do that?" Then he told me, much to my surprise, that he wasn't Japanese, but Chinese, that his parents had been killed in the earthquake of 1923, and that he'd been reared by an uncle who lived in Yokohama, had taken a Japanese name and pretended to be

Japanese. He himself had done the same.

He and a number of his classmates at the University were much upset by the actions of the Japanese troops in China. He would like to do something "to get back" at the Japanese for their actions. I asked how he could do that. He replied that he was a medical student. The Japanese authorities were very anxious to have the students learn as much as possible about the military services so they had organized a club and frequently arranged visits to naval ships and bases nearby. Since he was thought to be Japanese, it might be possible for him to find out what I might want to know. I said I was interested, and would think about it.

Shortly after that we met again at the tennis club and he said his club was going to Yokosuka soon and they might go aboard a destroyer. He asked if there was anything about destroyers that he might learn. I told him to look carefully at the torpedo mountings and guns to see if he thought the torpedoes were larger than 21 inches. He asked how, and we figured out a quick way to estimate the size of the tubes. When he came back he said he estimated that the torpedoes were larger than 21 inches and probably they were 25". One of the torpedomen on the ship told him that the Japanese no longer used air in their torpedoes, that they used oxygen. I was astonished and reported this to the Navy Department. There was no comment, but it developed that the latest destroyers had 25" torpedoes and used oxygen. They were remarkably good and accurate torpedoes.

Sometime after that he had occasion to go on board a cruiser, and he came back rather surprised. He had visited a Mogami class cruiser, and saw that the guns were not like the sketch in Janes Fighting Ships. This sketch showed five turrets with three six inch guns in each turret. In fact each turret had two guns, which were not six-inch, but eight-inch guns. The ship had been modified. When I reported this to the Navy Department, the comment of the Bureau of Ordnance was that it was impossible for the Japanese to change a ship designed for six-inch guns to carry eight-inch guns, and the report was not accurate.

It turned out that the report was accurate. When the Mogami and the Mikuma were badly damaged at Midway, aerial photographs taken showed that they did have five turrets of twin mounts and we learned that they were eight-inch guns. The Japanese had altered the ships which were light cruisers under the London Conference definition and had made them heavy cruisers with eight-inch guns. My friend also gave me information about the aircraft carriers that he visited, but nothing important. I had a small amount of money to give him although he didn't want money except for his expenses. When I asked for an increased allowance for this purpose from the Office in Intelligence, I was instructed to discontinue this source of information, and that I would get word as to who would carry on with him. Actually, the word was that the Assistant Naval Attache in Shanghai, Major Greg Williams, Marine Corps, supervised such sources and he would get in touch with my friend to give him instructions. But before contact could be made, the war started and nothing further came of it. He might have been of more help to me if I'd been allowed to work with him.

Q: Your comments regarding the Bureau of Ordnance is certainly discouraging, and probably reflects the state of mind that prevailed in the U.S. Navy -- among certain people at least. Whatever happened to this young man?

Smith-Hutton: I don't know. I imagine that he was killed during the war, because when I went back to Tokyo in 1945, I made inquiries at the Tennis Club, which had been my only contact with him. I saw many of my friends when I returned, and I inquired about him, but none of them had heard of him since the beginning of the war. I fear he was killed.

Q: Captain, did any case come to your attention where the Japanese were successful in trapping a foreign attache?

Smith-Hutton: The only success that I know about was, I believe in 1938 when the Italian Air Attache was asked to leave Tokyo, because he had been caught buying information from a Japanese citizen who turned out to be an agent. As far as I know that was the only case of the kind. There may well have been others, but if so, I have forgotten about them.

Q: That is interesting, because a short time later Japan signed a tri-partite act with Germany and Italy, and here is one of its allies sending in spy reports on them.

Smith-Hutton: Yes, that's very true.

Q: Captain, one of the elements in the strategy of Japan was to maintain control of the Mandate Islands and to deny information to the U.S. on these islands. So we didn't get very much. Did you ever think about this problem and the ways and means we might have been able to solve the need for information?

Smith-Hutton: Yes, I did. By 1938 and '39, for instance, after numerous attempts to get permission for visits to the important Mandate Island ports failed, particularly those that were open to foreign commerce, such as Truk, Palau, and Saipan, where in theory foreign ships could enter and foreign nationals could visit. It seemed to me that the only way to get the information as to whether the Mandates were really fortified and if they were, the extent of that fortification, was to take aggressive, positive steps to obtain the information.

For instance, if a plan were well prepared for a carrier with high-flying aircraft to appear just before dawn off Truk and aircraft flew very high and made one or two passes over the island, photographed it completely and disappeared over the horizon, there would have been suspicions on the part of the Japanese that we had done it. But I'm not sure that they could have made anything more than a protest, and I think we would have gotten away with it. We would then have had the photographic information that we required. Or if an expedition had been prepared for a submarine to appear shortly before dark, launched several men on the beach to get information, I believe that could have been done with success.

Unfortunately, I didn't make such recommendations so I have no right to criticize the lack of aggressive attempts. It's easy enough looking back to think of what might have been done.

Q: Hindsight is always better than foresight, Captain.

In April of 1939 the cruiser, Astoria, with Captain Kelly Turner in command, arrived in Japan and it was quite a successful visit. You came in June, I believe. Was there any reaction still existing as to how Captain Turner and the Astoria visit hit the Japanese people?

Smith-Hutton: Yes. The Ambassador and the Embassy staff were pleased and talked at length as to how successful the visit had been. They felt progress had been made in creating good will between the United States and Japan.

Of course, they were always very happy when this happened. Captain Turner and his ship had made a fine impression on the Japanese and we had done the dead Ambassador Saito great honor in bringing his remains back to Japan in the Astoria. It was one of the very successful events of that period when relations were almost always strained between Japan and the United States.

Q: Kelly Turner later became the Chief of the Plans Office in the Office of the Chief of Naval Operations, prior to Pearl Harbor, and as such he tended to belittle the evaluations and reports of ONI and to assume full responsibility for intelligence. He could do this because he was in the operational business and ONI was in a staff function. Do you have any thoughts upon this arrogance on the part of Captain and later Admiral Turner?

Smith-Hutton: Yes, of course. There was always rivalry, and the planners always had a stronger hand in the Department than the Office of Intelligence. It's quite possible that Admiral Turner, because of his contacts with the Japanese (Rear Admirals Yokoyama and Nakamura became friendly to him during the Astoria trip to Japan and gave him information) felt that he had the same good sources that the Office of Naval Intelligence had. This is quite possible.

Q: Captain, in looking at the history of the Japanese Navy before Pearl Harbor, there was a small group of officers who were Japanese Naval Attaches in Washington who later formed an informal group which tended to oppose war with the U.S. Navy.

These included Admiral Yamamoto and Captain Yokoyama who was Admiral Kelly Turner's friend. Do you have any comments or thoughts about the breadth of knowledge of the USA and its industrial potential as it existed in the body of the Japanese officer corps in the Navy? In other words, was the average naval officer in Japan informed about the industrial might of the USA?

Smith-Hutton: No. The average officer had a tendency to look on the United States and to judge us in a special way. They were apt to judge the United States and to estimate us as a potential enemy not from the point of view of our capabilities, but from the Japanese conception of their special spiritual strength. The average officer believed that Japan and the Japanese spirit would prevail over any opposition as it had for many years.

The officers who had been in the United States as attaches, such as Hasegawa, Nomura, and Yokoyama knew from the actual figures that the United States had great capabilities and terrific potential and they also knew, because they had read American history, that our conduct of wars, including our Civil War, our war against the Spaniards, and our conduct during World War I against the Germans showed that technically we were very competent, capable of organizing a powerful Army, Air Force, and Navy. They did not agree that one Japanese was equal to many Americans as the more unsophisticated Japanese warriors were inclined to think. And they cautioned their colleagues of all the Services against being over-confident.

Q: You may be interested to know that according to Japanese scholars your counterpart in Washington, Captain Yokoyama, in 1941 was sending back reports to Tokyo warning them of the industrial power of the USA, and that these warnings went unheeded, such as your reports evidently went unheeded on the armament of the cruisers.

In September of 1940, Japan signed a tri-partite pact with Italy and Germany, which in effect said that each agrees to attack jointly any power, the United States for example, if that power makes war on any of them. This must have promoted close relations with the German Attaches, and my question is, did Germany send any other naval officers to Tokyo to promote liaison and operations?

Smith-Hutton: About that time the new German Naval Attache was Rear Admiral Wenneker, who had been in command of the heavy cruiser, Deutschland, which had operated in the North Atlantic in the early part of World War II and had had spectacular success in sinking British merchant ships and capturing British equipment. He had become a world figure as far as the German Navy was concerned. He came to Tokyo as Naval Attache, and I must say that he was a very attractive man personally and apparently very competent as a naval officer. He spoke good English, but didn't speak Japanese. He was active in foreign diplomatic circles and I'm sure as a result of his efforts the German Navy became much more well known in Japan than it ever had been. The Japanese were inclined to think that the German Navy was a ultra conservative service, efficient perhaps, but un-interesting. So Wenneker's efforts to improve relations between Japan and Germany were effective.

I'm not sure, but I understand that he also made great efforts to prepare for the running of the submarine service between Japan and Germany whereby the Germans sent to Japan weapons, optical instruments and equipment and returned with rubber quinine and other raw materials that were needed in Germany. I'm sure that his efforts in Japan were successful and he was a popular officer.

Q: How successful was the submarine transport service they were running, Captain?

Smith-Hutton: It was not very successful, particularly when we got into the war, because we were able to follow the movements of those submarines without difficulty, and almost without exception they were sunk before they returned to ports under German control. We had a remarkable success there, so their entire effort came to nothing; but the plan was good and could have amounted to something if we hadn't been able to thwart it.

Q: Are you speaking from the experience as Operational Intelligence Officer in Admiral King's staff?

Smith-Hutton: Yes. That was one of our accomplishments between 1942 and 1944.

Q: Captain, in June of 1940, France fell and the Battle of Britain started. This must have made itself felt among your Japanese naval friends. What was their reaction to this development?

Smith-Hutton: My Japanese Navy acquaintances were astonished by the weakness of the French and British Armies in northern France and the ease with which the Germans had overrun France. As a result of the brilliant victories on the ground, they were also convinced that the German air offensive against Britain would probably be successful.

The naval officers were somewhat cautious about their predictions, because they realized that Britain was an island, and the tremendous potential of the German Air Force hadn't become apparent. The fact that the Germans might have great problems in invading England was recognized, and they weren't convinced that an invasion would succeed or at least they weren't as convinced as the Army was that Germany was going to prevail. On the other hand all of them did feel that German strength was tremendous and the situation for the British and their allies was a very difficult one.

Q: Perhaps this is the time to quote a short paragraph from your Fitness Report from April to December 1940, signed by Admiral Walter S. Anderson, who was the Director of Naval Intelligence. He said that "Lieutenant Commander Smith-Hutton is performing his duty as Naval Attache, Tokyo in an exceptionally able manner under particularly trying circumstances. His reports indicate alertness and an exceptional grasp of the situation coupled with mature, sound judgment which are rendering his services of outstanding value."

Smith-Hutton: That's very nice. I'm delighted to know that. I hadn't seen that report.

Interview No. 27 with Captain Henri Smith-Hutton, U.S. Navy
(Retired)

Place: Stanford, California

Date: June 20, 1974

Subject: Biography

By: Captain Paul B. Ryan

Q: We were discussing the situation in Japan in 1940. This is a time when the U.S. Asiatic Fleet had left Tsingtao and Chefoo for good. In Tokyo was there any perception of a crisis building up at this time, and when did the crisis mentality become apparent to you?

Smith-Hutton: Well, when the Army launched the attack in North China in the summer of '37, we knew that the situation was potentially very dangerous, and there were many periods of greatly increased tension; for example, after the Panay was sunk, and during the bombing of Chungking, when in '38 the Tutuila was almost hit. However, the Japanese government did appear to be trying to avoid incidents by keeping the forces in China under control.

It was the war in Europe, especially the fall of France in 1940, which moved the Far East toward a crisis. Japan's move into French Indo-China, the signing of the Alliance with Germany and Italy, the advance into south Asia toward Malaya and the Netherlands East Indies, and the increased emphasis in the press and in government statements about the "Greater East Asia Co-

Prosperity Sphere" all indicated that the situation was indeed approaching a critical point. It wasn't, however, until a year later, really, when General Tojo became Prime Minister that the crisis was recognized as such. All throughout 1940 the situation was bad, but it didn't seem hopeless.

Q: Captain, in the Embassy itself, what was your feeling along with the other naval attaches about the operational readiness of the Japanese Navy at this time? In other words, they were about to fight a war, although we didn't know it, and to fight a war you have to be ready. Were they ready?

Smith-Hutton: Frankly, we considered that the Japanese Navy was in operational readiness for war at all times after the Army attack began in '37. We realized that the Navy, while it wasn't completely mobilized since many Naval Reserves were not required for the operations in China, could complete mobilization in a very few days time. The other consideration for Japan was to keep her industries strong in order to keep up her foreign trade. Some Reservists were required on the farms to keep agriculture going, which was most important for a nation at war as Japan was in China.

As long as they were not needed in the Service and could be called up in a matter of hours, reserves were allowed to continue in their civilian capacities. As I pointed out, we felt that within very narrow limits the Japanese Navy was mobilized and was operationally ready for war at any time. That was true all through 1940 and '41.

Q: Captain, did the Embassy staff in 1940, early '41 recall how Japan had used surprise attacks successfully in other wars?

Smith-Hutton: Yes. We were all aware of Japan's use of surprise attacks, and we talked about it from time to time; that the Japanese had made initial attacks against the Chinese in the war with China in 1894 and that in 1904 they had sent their torpedo boats to attack the Russian ships off Port Arthur within forty-eight hours of breaking off the talks with the Russian government. There had been no formal declaration of war then either, but the talks had been broken off. We realized that the Japanese tradition was to try to catch an enemy by surprise, and for that reason we were well aware of the great importance of being on the alert.

Q: Did you have any particular U.S. bases in mind for possible surprise attacks?

Smith-Hutton: We thought that the bases that would most likely be attacked would be bases in the Philippine Islands. I'm sure that Admiral Hart felt that he must double his precautions, and, as you recall, our ships in the Far East were not surprised by the Japanese.

Q: That's quite right. In the summer of 1940 FDR made his agreement with the United Kingdom for destroyers for bases, which certainly indicated that we were becoming closely allied with the British. On the other hand we were drifting away from Germany and in fact our Navy in the Atlantic as the months went on was becoming more aggressive against German U-Boats. In this connection how did the German attaches work with the Japanese Navy in comparison with you, for example?

Smith-Hutton: Rear Admiral Wenneker, the German Naval Attache, got on well with the Japanese. While I have no way of knowing, I would guess that since Japan and Germany were allies, and since Wenneker had commanded a successful raider, the Japanese listened to his advice and paid attention to his observations.

However, during this particular period, I had no problems with my Japanese friends. We used to meet periodically for luncheons and dinners, and there seemed to be no real change in their attitude toward me. On the other hand, I do recall that none of them would accept an invitation to come alone. They always came in groups. Looking back I think that was for protection, because they could then tell anyone, including the military police and senior officers exactly what the conversations consisted of and could prove that they had passed on no secrets to me. I didn't realize it at the time, but I'm sure that was so. There was even among our Naval friends a desire to avoid anything that would get them in trouble with the security police.

I know of only one case of a friend who had come for years and was well known to us. That was Madame Hagiwara. Madame Hagiwara was in her late sixties, who had belonged to the court of the Empress Dowager. She told Mrs. Grew and my wife quite frankly that she had been called upon several times by the military police and they had asked about her conversations. She in effect told them to go to the devil, that she was old, she didn't know any military or political secrets, and she wouldn't tell anybody if she did. On the other hand, she was able to judge when Mrs. Grew or anybody else told her something that was interesting. So the gendarmes were wasting their time if they tried to interrogate her. She had such a high rank, was such an independent character and was such a fine person that they apprently dropped the matter. She's the only one I ever heard of who stood up to the security police and told them it was none of their business. Rather astonishing.

Q: Interesting story. Tell me, Captain, in your socializing with the Japanese Navy, suppose you asked them, "How's the war going in China?" What would be their answer?

Smith-Hutton: Before 1940, shall we say, they would be quite willing to go into details and to discuss even the most difficult problems. As time went on, however, their answers to questions became more and more vague, and while they didn't decline to answer, there was less and less substance to the answers and they gave formal replies which were meaningless. They are pastmasters at the art of keeping their thoughts to themselves, and giving as little information as possible. The language helps too, if the speaker wants to be vague.

Q: Historians in writing now in the 1970's point out that the

Japanese naval leaders were becoming convinced that the United States was trying to contain Japan by tightening a ring of bases, such as Hawaii, the Philippines, and the Aleutians around the home islands. Also, the United States was building up China and restoring diplomatic relations with Russia, and we were helping the British build up Singapore. All these elements were causing the Japanese Navy to become alarmed. What do you think about this? Are these historians telling it the way it was or not?

Smith-Hutton: I think that the historians are overemphasizing these moves. I feel that the Japanese weren't as impressed by these moves as they were by the embargo that we placed on oil and steel scrap exports and the freezing of Japan's assets. There was some build-up of our bases, but they were practically unchanged in 1939 and '40. We had recognized Russia in 1933, and this was a factor, but not an important one. The embargo on trade, however, showed that we were seriously opposed to their moves in Indo-China and the threats to Malaya and the Netherlands Indies. They knew that we were supporting Great Britain and Holland in Europe and they could see that we might support them in the Far East. There was no clear indication of that, but that is the natural conclusion.

Of course, negotiations with Washington in the '40's were centered on the Japanese actions in Indochina and on the withdrawal of troops and the general settlements with Indochina and China. There was also a question of how far the Japanese government, which was at that time Prince Konoye's government, could control the Army, and would the Army forces in the field obey instructions that were given from Tokyo. Prince Konoye assured Ambassador Grew that they would and that if he could meet the President and if they could arrive at an understanding on specific problems, the Prince felt that the United States and Japan could arrive at satisfactory agreements in regard to the Far East. On the other hand most of the solutions hinged on the fact that peace must be made with China after an understanding had been reached before any further progress could be expected.

Q: In summing up, then, you would say that China was paramount in their minds and all these political factors I mentioned were of distinctly secondary importance.

Smith-Hutton: That's what I meant, yes.

Q: In late May of 1941 FDR declared an unlimited national emergency in the United States. This was just one element in the crisis that was building up. Did you in Japan notice any change in the intensity of the crisis?

Smith-Hutton: While we knew that as long as Prince Konoye was Prime Minister, the Japanese would probably act rationally and perhaps avoid a break with the United States and even limit their actions in Indochina, we also knew that the Army was getting more and more influential. Especially after the limited emergency declared by the President, the Japanese would get weaker and weaker, because their source of supply of oil and iron, which came largely from the United States, was cut off.

We in Japan were very sensitive to anything that the President did and tried to follow the changes as Europe was affected, because we knew that the Japanese were paying very close attention also.

In the early part of the summer the custom is to leave Tokyo to go to the mountains or seashore to escape the rather oppressive heat of the rainy season in late June and July. That year I had nine language officers, all of them competent young officers. Before they left for the summer, I called them together for a conference and said that it appeared to me that the situation was getting to a dangerous stage, and while I realized that any move which would bring about a war would be taken by the Japanese rather than by us, we did not know exactly what was going to happen. I wanted them to be ready to leave Japan on a moment's notice.

Only one of them was married. That meant that all the bachelors had to do was to pack up, leave the places they lived and store their gear in our store room. They could be ready to go within a few hours. All of them did this. I had exchanged letters with the Office of Intelligence saying that it seemed to me that in the event of war it would be a mistake to run the risk of having the Japanese seize nine young officers who had a somewhat different status from the Embassy staff. They were attaches and had special passports, but they were not diplomats. I thought they could carry on their studies in Hawaii or any place where there were Japanese teachers and the opportunities for study were as good as in Tokyo.

I also recommended that I send to the United States the books, such as dictionaries, phrase books, and grammars that would be needed for an expanded program of study in Japanese. The answer came back very quickly from the Office of Intelligence. They agreed completely with that plan and by the middle of July all of the officers received orders to leave Tokyo. We got them to Shanghai and out within ten days. I also got permission to send back all the dictionaries we could buy and several hundred of these were shipped out in mail bags.

Q: That's a very provocative account, Captain. I know that the Naval Language School during the war was very happy to have all those text books and dictionaries that you had the forethought to send on. I think it would be interesting to name these language officers who were there and whom you sent home.

Smith-Hutton: There were seven naval officers and two Marine officers. They were Lieutenant (jg) Wilson, class of '32; Lieutenant (jg) R. L. Taylor, class of '34; Lieutenant (jg) Allan Cole, class of '34; Lieutenant (jg) G. R. Mackey, class of '35; Lieutenant (jg) Baird, class of '34; Lieutenant (jg) Bromley, class of '34; and Lieutenant (jg) Slonim, class of '36. The two Marines were Captain B. T. Holcomb, class of '31, and 1st Lieutenant Bishop who came in '39 at the same time as Holcomb.

Q: You mentioned that one of the officers was married out there. I thought that was against the rules.

Smith-Hutton: Yes, it was. However, in the case of Lieutenant (jg) Taylor, the Navy Department made an exception. Taylor was a very good language officer. While he was in Tokyo, he fell in love with a young Swedish girl whose father was Consul in the Swedish diplomatic service who had lived in Japan for many years. He requested permission to get married, and since he was keeping his studies up very well, we thought that this marriage would not detract from them. Permission was granted, and Rufus Taylor married Karen Gertz in the summer of 1940. They lived in Tokyo, left Tokyo together, and are still a happily married couple.

Q: Perhaps you should get on the record what rank he attained, some of the positions he held, and where they are now.

Smith-Hutton: He stayed on active duty longer than any of the language officers. He became a rear admiral in 1964, and was Director of Naval Intelligence. Shortly after he had completed a regular tour of duty, he was promoted to the rank of vice admiral and was Deputy Director of the CIA. He retired, I think, in 1970, and now lives in North Carolina. He is a very distinguished and able officer.

Q: Thank you, Captain. Did you stay in Tokyo during all of 1941?

Smith-Hutton: In the early autumn of 1941 I became more and more frustrated because I wasn't able to see anything and my Japanese friends were very non-communicative. The papers and magazines were heavily censored. I decided that I would get out of Tokyo to see whether I could learn anything first hand, realizing that it wouldn't be easy.

With the permission of the Navy Department and the Ambassador, I arranged for my wife and me to go first to Osaka and then on west to the Inland Sea area. It happens that not far from Kure, the great naval base in the Inland Sea, is a resort known as Miyajima, which has a large shrine on a beautiful island. They are accustomed to having many visitors -- Europeans and Japanese, so we made reservations at a famous hotel there. I should have known after the short stay in Osaka that it wasn't going to be easy to get around. We wandered about the city then on to Kyoto, and were followed by a policeman wherever we went. We didn't care, because we felt that he was some protection, although there was no apparent need for protection.

When we got to Miyajima we were met at the station by two policemen, one in uniform and one in plain clothes. I should mention that the train passes through Kure before arriving at Miyajima. The Japanese had built a high wall around the entire base, so that it was impossible from the train to see inside. The train attendent lowered the window shade in our compartment and said that we mustn't raise it, so we were completely enclosed. When the train stopped at Hiroshima, which is the large Army base just east of Kure, we were also instructed not to leave the compartment, and the curtains were lowered. They were being sure that we did not see anything.

We got to our room and saw that it faced a beautiful park, but did not overlook the harbor or the Inland Sea. We went out for a walk -- it was a pleasant day -- and in the distance saw Kure which we could catch glimpses of through the trees. There were obviously many ships in port. We could see much smoke from them. Kure is a flourishing area, but it was about fifteen miles away, too far to see very clearly, and our escort of two policemen were right behind us. They were cheery and willing to talk, but not particularly communicative. After two or three days of this, we decided to return to Tokyo.

I saw the Ambassador and made my report, and sent a message to the Navy Department outlining what had happened, saying that there were restrictions to travel, and that under the circumstances it would be a mistake for the Navy Department to depend on me to forecast what might happen even in the Tokyo area, which was not in the papers or on the radio; that the censorship was very strict and my movements restricted.

Interview No. 28 with Captain Henri Smith-Hutton, U.S. Navy
(Retired)

Place: Stanford, California

Date: July 18, 1974

Subject: Biography

By: Captain Paul B. Ryan

Q: Captain, in the last session we were discussing events in Japan, the environment of the summer of 1941. About this time there was a report from a Latin American diplomat to the effect that Pearl Harbor might be suddenly attacked. Can you give the background on that?

Smith-Hutton: In January 1941 Ambassador Grew heard the rumor circulating in Tokyo that in the event of a break between the United States and Japan, the Japanese would make an all-out surprise attack on Pearl Harbor. He talked to me about it, and said that he understood that one of the main sources of the rumor was Dr. Rivero-Schreiber, the Peruvian Minister in Japan. I said that rumors like this had circulated from time to time, but that I hadn't heard this one. When he said he was reporting it to the State Department, I understood why even though it was impossible to verify it, and I added that with all the talk of war there was always the speculation among diplomats and newsmen about what each country might do.

Q: Captain, did you base your opinion on the history of previous surprise attacks by the Japanese Navy?

Smith-Hutton: Yes. I said that the Japanese could act very quickly and make a surprise attack, whereas our country had to have a vote of Congress before we could go to war and that while I thought this rumor was just a rumor, since it was most unlikely that the Japanese planners would let their real plans get out of the secret category, it was logical for them to concentrate an attack on our fleet no matter where it was, whether it was in Hawaii or on the west coast, and that our commanders must be very vigilant. I said that the Japanese had a history of making surprise attacks. Naturally, such rumors could not be confirmed nor traced to any particular sources, but surprise was a favorite Japanese method and we should remember it. We all knew that.

Q: I appreciated that the ONI was receiving copies of Ambassador Grew's dispatches to the State Department. Did you find it necessary at any time to parallel his dispatches with information of your own?

Smith-Hutton: Occasionally I did. In this particular report, I didn't feel it was necessary. I knew the report would reach the Navy Department and the Office of Intelligence. Once in a while I sent a report when I thought it was desirable to emphasize the Ambassador's original report. I did from time to time send parallel reports because I thought it would be useful just to make my opinions known. In this particular case I didn't, as I felt it wasn't necessary.

Q: I'm sure the message was really read in the Navy Department.

Smith-Hutton: Yes, it was. I understood that from later conversations.

Q: Captain, you probably know that in early '41, I believe, the U.S. Government made a very secret agreement with the British and Dutch governments to come to their aid in the event of trouble in the Far East. Were you or Ambassador Grew aware of this secret agreement?

Smith-Hutton: No, we weren't aware of this agreement, and we did not realize we were so committed to the support of the British and the Dutch.

Q: That confirms Ambassador Grew's diary when he said on October 19, 1941, "Why on earth should we rush headlong into war? When Hitler is defeated, the Japanese problem will solve itself." He obviously didn't know about it either.

Captain, in 22 June 1971, Admiral Toyoda became the Foreign Minister in Prince Konoye's cabinet. Did you know Admiral Toyoda?

Smith-Hutton: Yes, I knew him quite well. He was a soft-spoken officer, who spoke English well, having been in England as Assistant Naval Attache and as Naval Attache. He was one of the group of senior naval officers which included Nomura and Yonai, who were pr Anglo-Saxon not pro-German. He was well known in Tokyo for his moderation. So when he became Foreign Minister, we were all very pleased. I think Ambassador Grew found him pleasant to work with and liked him as a Foreign Minister.

Q: When the Konoye Cabinet fell, Admiral Toyoda was forced to resign. What happened to him then?

Smith-Hutton: He was put on the inactive list as was his good friend, Admiral Nomura. Nomura had been sent as Ambassador to the United States by Prince Konoye but was continued after Tojo became Prime Minister. Nomura and Toyoda were of a kind. There was no question of disgrace in being placed on inactive duty since they were subject to recall to serve in the Navy.

Q: Did Ambassador Grew ask for your evaluation of Toyoda?

Smith-Hutton: Yes, I gave him my opinion of Admiral Toyoda and we agreed that he was a pleasant, straight-forward man.

Q: On the 7th of December, or probably the 8th of December in Tokyo, can you describe the chain of events that brought you to internment?

Smith-Hutton: I got up a little earlier than usual and went downstairs to have breakfast in our dining room where we had a good short-wave radio, because the day before we'd had some unusual reports from the United States and also from the south.

I'd heard on San Francisco radio the news that the Ambassador was getting a message to be delivered to the Emperor, and I'd also heard that there were Japanese ships sighted along the coast of Malaya headed south. I'd conferred briefly with the British Naval Attache and with the Consuller of the British Embassy. About 10 o'clock on Sunday night I called the code room at the Embassy and found that the message the Ambassador was supposed to deliver had just been received from the Japanese telegraph office and he hadn't yet had a chance to take it to the Emperor. That morning I was wondering whether anything had happened, during the night.

I had discussed the situation with Jane, my wife, and we decided that we weren't going to send our daughter to school Monday morning. I couldn't get San Francisco on my radio because of static, so I shifted to Shanghai radio which came in clearly. The announcer was just saying that Americans were asked by the Consul General in Shanghai to stay off the streets and not to be excited. The Consul General would inform them of events later in the day, and in the meantime they should remain as calm as possible. I told Jane, who was just getting up, that apparently something unusual had happened in Shanghai, that I didn't know what it was because the radio report was indefinite, but if she'd hurry we might go to the Embassy to see whether we could learn more there.

This was just before 8 o'clock. She came down very soon. It was a two-minute walk, a short distance down to the street and then about fifty feet to the entrance to the Embassy garage.

There was a police kiosk there that had been put up a few months before. The policeman on duty didn't look at us, didn't pay any attention to us. Usually he smiled and said good morning.

We walked into the Embassy garage and then toward my office. Before we got there we passed the office of Lieutenant Commander Stone and saw that it was full of people. We had the office radio there. When my friends saw me they said, "Have you heard? San Francisco radio says the Japanese have attacked Pearl Harbor!" I said, "No. I hadn't heard that." I went to my office to telephone the Ambassador. I told him of the KGII San Francisco report. He said he couldn't believe it, so I repeated the radio report. He said he'd left the Foreign Minister about fifteen minutes before. Mr. Togo hadn't mentioned an attack. I said I only knew what the radio report was.

He told me to go to the Japanese Navy Department to find out if there was truth in the report, and if so, when could he expect official notice of a declaration of war. My car which was in the garage came soon. The streets were deserted although it was after eight. I went to the Navy Department, which was only about three mintues in the car -- about four blocks away. I asked for Rear Admiral Nakamura, the senior aide to the Navy Minister, and was taken to the usual waiting room where Rear Admiral Nakamura, whom, incidentally, I had known for several years, soon appeared. I told him that my Ambassador had sent me. I asked about an attack by Japanese planes on Pearl Harbor, whether there was truth in the report and if so, when we could expect to get a notice of the declaration of war. He looked rather sad, because I think he was really a friend of the United States. He said yes the report was true. He had just learned about it himself, and could verify it. As to the declaration of war, he couldn't say, because that would have to come from the Foreign Office and was not a Navy Department matter. The embassy would soon hear from the Foreign Office, he was sure. He said I could report to the ambassador that the attack had taken place, and that he personally was not happy about it. I told him I wasn't either, and I said this might be the last time I would see him. I hoped he would survive the war. He said he hoped the same for me. He usually said goodbye in this room, but this morning he came down the staircase and saw me to the car.

I got back to the Embassy and found the gates already closed. There was a policeman on guard, but he let me pass. I believe other cars later had difficulty getting in, but I had an Ambassy license. I called the Ambassador and told him that Nakamura had confirmed the attack, that he would get information later from the Foreign Office, but there was no doubt that the attack had taken place. He thanked me and said that as a matter of fact he had been notified by the Japanese post that the State Department was calling him and he was going to talk to someone there momentarily. In the meantime he'd given instructions to burn all confidential and classified papers and codes. He knew that I had already done this because I had reported to him on Friday that I had. The other officers in the Embassy were soon busily engaged in burning. I went to see what was happening in my office, and by that time the electricity in the

Embassy had been shut off and we couldn't operate the radio.

The police soon arrived and they confiscated the receiving set of the Embassy which was operated by a Navy radioman. We had no sending equipment in the Embassy, but could receive State Department Bulletins and news reports from Washington. This naval radioman was attached to the Embassy State Department staff not to my office. The police confiscated the main receiving set, and within a matter of minutes they also had our office short wave receiving set. Ours was one of the few in the Embassy. I'm not sure whether the Military Attache had one, but there were one or two in addition to ours. We couldn't use them, though, because there was no power, so we were entirely cut off from the world. I looked in the garage area and the staff was engaged in burning papers in big trash cans, dousing the papers with kerosene. It was a smoky, dirty place. That was how Pearl Harbor Day started for me.

Q: That was an interesting account. Did these Japanese invade the Embassy? What about diplomatic immunity and all that?

Smith-Hutton: Actually, they came right in, but they weren't rude at this time although they were a little bit later. The police closed the Embassy gate and stationed a police guard. There was no way to keep them out, so they walked in and announced they wanted to take our radio sets and walked off with them. They confiscated the Ambassador's set too.

Q: It would be interesting what the Washington police did with the Japanese Embassy there.

Smith-Hutton: I'm not sure. I don't know what our police did. We had incidents during the months of internment that were very trying and the Ambassador was very much incensed several times.

Q: Captain, did the Japanese police compromise any of the U.S. confidential publications?

Smith-Hutton: No. The police were entirely correct while they were seizing our radios. They confined themselves to the radios and made no attempt to seize confidential documents being destroyed.

Q: Captain, before we finish this session, I want to go back to September 1941. Ambassador Grew, in his daily diary which is on file at the Hoover Institution in Stanford University, has some correspondence between himself, that is, Grew and Mr. Matsumoto of Domei News Agency. The correspondence relates to an interview reportedly given by you to one of the Japanese reporters. This took place in September, 1941, and it appears in the Grew letter of 14 September, 1941. The gist of it is that on the 13th of September, Domei radio broadcast from Shanghai and from San Francisco alleged that Lieutenant Commander Smith-Hutton had given an interview in which you had commented on the President's recent speech. The speech in question probably had to do with the President saying that we would tolerate no attacks on our shipping. In other words we were fighting at this point. This refers to the war in the Atlantic. The story went on to say, or at least the letter went on to say from Ambassador Grew to this editor-in-chief that you had been approached by a reporter to comment on the President's speech, you had refused to do so, but you did, in response to some background questions which the reporter asked, say that you would comment, but this was not for publication. It was merely to be helpful in giving them background. The reporter then went out and published the report, which went on the radio and in the press. Is this your recollection of the incident?

Smith-Hutton: Yes, it was exactly that. The reporter came to my office and asked for any comments that the Embassy or I could make on the President's announcement in regard to convoying ships in the North Atlantic and aiding the British. I replied it would be absurd for me to comment on the President's speech, which speaks for itself. The President says what he wants to say, and it's all quite clear. The reporter then said that Mr. Matsumoto had hoped that we would comment. I replied that since I knew Matsumoto well and since he was a good friend of America and the Embassy, it was understandable that he would like a comment, but I could only repeat that the President had made it quite clear to the world and particularly the Germans, what we planned to do, and that we were within our rights. I said again that this was not for publication, but was completely off the record. He said he understood. Then much to my amazement, the Ambassador and I heard it on Shanghai radio, and he said I believe, that it was on San Francisco radio. When the Ambassador asked me about it, I told him exactly what had happened, that the reporter had said that Matsumoto particularly wanted a comment but that I'd declined. However, I had talked to him off the record. The Ambassador was very good about it, as he wanted to protect me. He felt that maybe the Embassy might be queried by the State Department because we never made comments on statements by the President or the Secretary of State. So he wrote to Matsumoto, and Matsumoto, who was very straightforward replied I believe that we were quite correct, and that he was sorry that the reporter had violated my confidence by publishing the off-the-record comments that I'd made.

Q: That's correct, Captain, Matsumoto replied on the 16th of September, and said that the reporter was under the erroneous impression that you had spoken for publication, which obviously was a lie, but Matsumoto said that it was not a deliberate attempt to violate a confidence, that it was unintentional and so sorry.

Smith-Hutton: It all ended well, but Matsumoto was a clearcut fellow, and I liked him. He was a graduate of Harvard, I believe, and a good man. My recollection is as the Ambassador has recorded it.

Q: The dispatch in question on the President's speech related to an incident wherein a U-Boat had fired two torpedoes at a convoy en route to Iceland and had sunk two U.S. merchant ships. FDR then broadcasted a radio message to the U.S. people saying that the U.S. Navy would defend the freedom of the seas by striking at all Axis rader ships in American defensive areas. That's the defensive area he established around the United States.

Smith-Hutton: Yes, I remember it now and exactly as it is recorded in the diary.

Q: Thank you for clearing that up, Captain.

Smith-Hutton #29 - 335

Interview No. 29 with Captain Henri Smith-Hutton, U.S. Navy
(Retired)

Place: Stanford, California

Date: July 25, 1974

Subject: Biography

By: Captain Paul B. Ryan

Q: Captain, we left the last session when you were in internment with the rest of the Embassy staff. In this period did Ambassador Grew hold a staff meeting, a postmortom session on the Pearl Harbor attack?

Smith-Hutton: If he did, I wasn't included, and so I'm quite sure that none were held. Of course, no analysis of the Embassy reports was possible at that time, because the Embassy papers had all been burned on Pearl Harbor Day. We all knew that the Ambassador had warned the State Department many times that the Japanese were capable of swift and even suicidal action, and that we should be prepared for it. Incidentally, by an actual later count nine such warnings were made over the course of a year of so. Except to report the rumor about a possible attack on Pearl Harbor, no mention was made in Embassy reports of Pearl Harbor. However, defense against surprise attack is such an elementary military precaution that even inexperienced commanders could have been expected to take precautions.

Lieutenant Commander Stone and I both knew that our Naval intelligence organization was reading Japanese radio traffic, and monitoring Japanese fleet traffic at Pearl Harbor. We were trying to track the movements of all important naval units, and I felt confident that radio intelligence would give warning of an attack on our fleet. It didn't occur to me that our fleet could be surprised under any circumstances.

This was a U.S. Navy secret operation and both of us had been part of the service in previous years, but we didn't mention it in the Embassy. The Ambassador, the secretaries and the Army personnel did not know that we were doing it. The Navy had long followed a policy of informing only those who needed to know of our secret activities. However, the Japanese were very clever in masking their fleet movements, in setting up dummy radio traffic to make it appear that the carriers were still in the Inland Sea, and in maintaining radio silence by the carriers at sea. So in spite of our intelligence efforts, we were surprised at Pearl Harbor. Also there was a big element of luck in the Japanese operation, although it was very skillfully executed.

Q: In retrospect, Captain, how do you view your period of internment?

Smith-Hutton: The conditions of our internment in Tokyo were not bad. We did not suffer, but when you remember that the Japanese in Washington were sent to luxurious White Sulphur Springs until they were exchanged, there was no comparison in the treatment. We were crowded into the Embassy compound and the gates were locked. About six secret police were on guard at all times and we were crowded but not mistreated. The senior staff with two exceptions lived in the Ambassador's residence and had their meals there.

Q: What were your berthing arrangements in the Embassy compound?

Smith-Hutton: In the residence, of course, Ambassador and Mrs. Grew were there, and they had two personal servants. There were three guest bedrooms. In one bedroom were Dooman and Williams. Dooman was the Counsellor and Williams was the Commercial Attache. My wife, our small daughter and I had the second, and Crocker and Bohlen had the third. Crocker was the First Secretary and Bohlen the Second Secretary. The Smith-Huttons, Crocker, and Bohlen shared a bathroom. Lieutenant Colonel Cresswell, the Military Attache, and Mackinson, the Consul General, used their large offices as bedrooms and they slept in the Chancery. They took their meals with the rest of the senior staff at the Ambassador's.

There were two apartment houses with several apartments, which were filled up with part of the personnel. The others lived in the Chancery in the offices. For instance, Lieutenant Commander Stone lived in our office. We had adequate space since we were allowed to bring beds and bedding from our homes to the Embassy. These were installed in the Chancery building, and in the apartments so they were fairly comfortable. Each of us had a place to live. It wasn't luxurious, as I said, but it was not uncomfortable.

Q: This was a trying time, Captain. Did Ambassador Grew take firm charge of the situation within the compound?

Smith-Hutton: Yes, he did, and in my opinion the Ambassador showed remarkable leadership. The whole internment was proof that we Americans can get organized and do well under trying conditions. Within twenty-four hours of the time we were locked up we had a system of Officer of the Day with a desk and internal telephone at the main entrance. The Officer of the Day could get a stenographer and typist if needed, and he kept track of the Japanese police. When the Swiss Minister was allowed to come in, the Officer of the Day did the honors and escorted him to see the Ambassador or other officials.

It was the Japanese police, of course, not representatives of the Foreign Office, who had final word in regard to our internment. If the Ambassador had not stopped them firmly during the first few days, they would have made a real prison camp out of the compound. They even resented our having the Officer of the Day system.

Q: Did you ever have a confrontation with the Japanese police?

Smith-Hutton: Yes, that was when the Ambassador stopped them. We were in the large reception hall in the residence. One evening we found that a policeman was hidden in the window curtains, observing us and listening to us. About six of us rushed at him and in very rough Japanese told him to get out. He did, and the next day the Ambassador sent a very stiff note to the Japanese government through the Swiss Minister protesting this violation of our diplomatic status. After that the police were more circumspect.

Q: Would you describe the messing arrangements in the compound?

Smith-Hutton: There were about sixty-five of us and each was assigned to a mess for meals. The Pearl Harbor attack was shortly before Christmas. Japan had been on a war status for several years, because of the hostilities in China. Many food items were impossible to obtain so the staff had gotten together in September 1941 and sent a large order for staples to a San Francisco wholesale grocer. This order had been delivered in the middle of November, and consisted of items no longer available in the stores, as well as things we wanted for Christmas and for gifts to friends.

For instance, we had ordered a big supply of coffee, as my wife had found that our Japanese friends appreciated a gift of coffee at Christmas time. I don't remember the exact figures, but I think we had ordered about one hundred and fifty pounds. We and others had also ordered canned hams, meats, and fish and vegetables since these were also impossible to get.

Q: Did you have a commissary set-up at this time?

Smith-Hutton: Yes. We were allowed to bring the provisions

which we had at home into the Embassy when we were moved from our houses. These were all put together and made into a commissary. Several ladies took charge, and the foods were given to the various messes on a fair and equal basis. Unfortunately, we used up our provisions faster than we might have if we had realized that we were going to be interned for a long time. In 1914, the German Embassy staff left Tokyo a week after the declaration of war, and we thought we might not be permitted to leave 'til after Christmas. Actually it was the middle of June, 17 June 1942, to be exact, before we left.

Q: Do any particular events stand out in your memory during this period of internment, Captain?

Smith-Hutton: There were several highlights. The first was certainly the visit of the Swiss Minister some ten days after war started. We shouted and cheered as his car came in the gate. This reception made the Japanese police very angry. They refused to let him say a word to us and took him almost by force to the Ambassador, who was waiting at the residence. He was there an hour or so, and on his way out the police refused to let him say anything to us again.

However, that evening the Ambassador called us together to tell us what had been said. Unfortunately, there wasn't much that he could tell the Ambassador. The war news was bad -- almost as bad as the Japanese press was reporting -- and up to that time there had been no progress in talks about the exchange. He couldn't tell the Ambassador when we were to leave or where the exchange ships would go. We'd just have to be patient, which wasn't easy. He promised to keep us informed and to visit us frequently in the future.

The Swiss Minister in charge of American affairs was a Mr. Hausherr, a typical Swiss gentleman, very meticulous and careful in everything. We got to like him, although he was not a very outgiving sort of person.

Q: Two and a half weeks after you went into internment Christmas came. How did you celebrate the holidays?

Smith-Hutton: Christmas celebration was certainly the second highlight of our stay. The ladies did a wonderful job. They made pretty decorations out of very little, and we still had a supply of good food and we enjoyed that. Also, a group of ladies practiced in secret and the night before Christmas, after we'd had dinner and were sitting in the large reception room talking, about ten of them appeared out of nowhere singing carols. There certainly wasn't a dry eye among us after that. It was exceptionally beautiful. I recall that among these carollers was Miss Arnold, the Ambassador's secretary, Mrs. Scanlon, Miss McMahon, the secretary of the Military Attache, Mrs. Fujimoto, and my wife, among others. Their voices were very sweet.

Q: Did you have a Christmas tree, Captain?

Smith-Hutton: Yes. Much to the dismay of some in the Embassy, we cut down one of the spruce trees in the garden. It was a perfect Christmas tree. Many who found out where it came from objected, but it was Christmas, and we had a tree. Of course, it was so long before any of us got back to Tokyo that it really didn't matter.

Q: How did you decorate the tree?

Smith-Hutton: The ladies made stars and figures out of bright paper, and made popcorn strings. We had a few lights. It was all homemade, but it looked genuine and would have been a pretty tree under any circumstances.

Q: It sounds like rural America, Captain.

Smith-Hutton: It was indeed. They showed much ingenuity and imagination to make the tree as pretty as it was.

Q: What about religious ceremonies? Did you have divine services in the compound?

Smith-Hutton: It was impossible to have formal divine services, but many of us were church members. The Ambassador himself frequently read the Lesson. Services were held every Sunday morning in the main library of the Chancery, which had been made into a gathering place -- they called it the "Lido", the name of fashionable night clubs in Paris and Shanghai. The "Lido" substituted as a chapel on Sunday mornings, and we sang hymns, and the Ambassador frequently gave talks. Dooman, the Counsellor, also gave talks as did Benninghoff, whose father had been a missionary at Waseida University. He was Third Secretary. Anyone who wanted to sing, meditate, and pray could do so on Sunday morning in the Chancery.

Q: Captain, did any particular individuals stand out during this six-month internment as giving of themselves more than others?

Smith-Hutton: In addition to the Ambassador who was, of course, at the heart of everything and really outstanding, I might mention Edward Crocker, "Ned" to everybody. He looked like one of the Marx brothers. He came from a prominent New England family. In addition to being an excellent golf player and a good bridge player, he could tell wonderful stories. He did a great deal to cheer people up.

Bohlen, who had reported early that year from Moscow, was a great help. He was a very cheery fellow who was always ready to organize and assist people. Those two were certainly outstanding. One of the Army language officers named Gould -- a chubby man whom everybody called "Pop" -- was Santa Claus at the Christmas party. He was a great help in cheering people up too.

Another who was excellent was the Ambassador's personal secretary, Robert Feary. He did a good job of seeing that we had our laundry done properly. There was a small laundry machine which he set it up in the Chancery. He made regular rounds collecting soiled clothing and making it clean. He was an excellent man. Those are the individuals that stand out in my memory.

Also, one or two or us got ill during the internment, including Mr. Dooman, who had an attack of phlebitis. He needed regular care, which he got from Miss Arnold and my wife. However, anyone who needed attention got it. It was a time when we all helped each other. My wife had to go for a brief stay in a Catholic hospital and was well cared for there by the sisters.

Q: On the 18th of April the famous Doolittle raid took place in Tokyo. What are your memories of this raid, Captain?

Smith-Hutton: The Doolittle raid was certainly another of the highlights of our internment. On 17 April it was announced that there were going to be air raid drills. These drills started in the afternoon and lasted for three days. There was a blackout, and we had complete blackout curtains in the Embassy, the Chancery and in all buildings. We were careful to see that lights didn't show outside the buildings. The drills held up to that time had not been very interesting.

On 18 April, the day after the drills had started, air raid sirens were tested in the morning, and there were a few fighter planes flying about. About 12:30 p.m. we heard several explosions. The air raid sirens sounded again. My wife and I were sitting in my office waiting to go to lunch at the residence when we heard the explosions. We went out into the compound and an Army language officer who was on the roof of one of the apartment buildings called to me to say that the drill was certainly the most realistic ever held. He could see smoke from two or three fires, apparently caused by the explosions. He added that another fire was starting.

On the path to the residence from the lower compound we met the Swiss Minister who had been to see the Ambassador that morning, and we asked him whether there was any possibility that this was a real raid. He said he didn't think it possible. Shortly after we saw the Minister, we all gathered waiting for lunch to be announced. It was a beautiful sunny day, warm and pleasant, so that the dining room was open into the garden. The residence is on a hill and we could see the smoke in the distance. Then we noticed policemen on the roof of a building across the street. We all went in to luncheon, sat down, and suddenly heard another loud explosion.

When this happened, my wife and Ned Crocker dashed out into the garden. They were sitting on the garden side of the table. Just as they got out, a plane flying a little above the treetops passed over head and they got a glimpse of it. Neither of them have good eyesight, and they couldn't describe the plane or the markings. It passed out of sight in a few seconds flying in a westerly direction and still very low. This happened before the rest of us got outside. We believed the Japanese anti-aircraft was firing at this plane.

Q: Were you convinced that these were U.S. aircraft?

Smith-Hutton: No. We resumed our lunch and there was a warm discussion about the events of the morning. Half of our group thought it was a genuine air raid, but no one could be sure of the nationality of the planes, because there had been two or three other planes that had passed earlier which had apparently started the fires, before this last plane flew over the residence. We had not the faintest idea where they came from. The other half of our group still thought it was a drill.

However, that night, Tokyo radio announced that there had been a raid by ten aircraft which came from the north of Japan. The nationality was not mentioned. The radio said that the planes had dropped bombs but had damaged mostly hospitals and schools, and that all planes had been shot down. It wasn't 'til much later that we heard from the Swiss a few more details about the raid.

Q: How did you learn about the Tokyo radio report?

Smith-Hutton: By that time the Japanese had returned one of our small radios so that we could listen to local Tokyo broadcasts in Japanese. We were also allowed to get Japanese papers. We received the English language Japan Times, among other papers.

Q: How did the Embassy people view the consequences of the Doolittle raid?

Smith-Hutton: At the time we felt that since the raid did very little damage, it wasn't important. No one in the Embassy, even after we got home, realized that the raid really was very important. As a result of the raid, the Army Air Defense Command kept a much larger force of fighter aircraft assigned to the defense of the main island than had been planned originally. These aircraft therefore, were not available for assignment overseas as they would have been if the raid had not taken place.

We did realize that it was important for the morale of our own people after our long series of defeats. But in addition it was very important from the strategic point of view, that is, keeping aircraft tied up in the main islands.

Q: What did the staff do for recreation? For example, did you have a wine mess?

Smith-Hutton: In the more than six months we were there we played bridge and poker every day. The poker game went without interruption every day of the internment. The Ambassador, Mr. Dooman, Lieutenant Commander Stone, and from time to time Crocker and Bohlen, played, and also there were two Army officers who were enthusiastic players. They played for rather high stakes. Several won or lost two or three thousand dollars, which was more than I cared to risk, but I'm not a poker enthusiast. However, we also had a bridge tournament. The Ambassador gave a silver plate engraved for the winner of the "Greater East Asia Bridge Matches." I gave the second prize, and there was a third prize.

Incidentally, I won the first prize, the Ambassador's plate, which I still have and cherish as the champion of the "Greater East Asia Bridge Meet."

We also played badminton, and finally Lieutenant Commander Stone laid out a very ingenious nine hole golf course around the apartments and swimming pool. They had three or four good golf tournaments. I am not an enthusiastic golfer and played only occasionally, but many played almost every day. We were well organized as far as sports and recreation were concerned. I advanced in the badminton meet and was defeated in the semi-finals which was won by Merrill Benninghoff, who incidentally was the best tennis player in the Embassy. There was keen competition, and a good place to play in the Embassy garage. So we had plenty of things to do. It was too cold to swim, of course, so that was out.

The Ambassador had a fine assortment of wines. He was very fond of wine, having been in Germany and Austria in 1914, before World War I. We had his wine occasionally and we all put our whiskey and hard liquor in the mess to be divided, but again we didn't have nearly enough to last the six months we were interned.

Q: When did you run out?

Smith-Hutton: We ran out of liquor about the 1st of February.

Q: Does that include tobacco also?

Smith-Hutton: The tobacco lasted a little longer, but in the end we were smoking coffee grounds in our pipes. The Japanese arranged for us to get ration cards for cigarettes after a certain period, so we received Japanese cigarettes. "Cherry" was the brand that most of us smoked, since they were much like American cigarettes. The winter was a rather severe one for Tokyo, but my wife and other ladies who could sew made clothing out of drapes and curtains. We used much of our limited allowance of fuel oil to have hot water for several hours every evening before dinner rather than to heat, so that we could all have warm baths and keep our clothes clean.

Q: How did you learn about the diplomatic exchange, Captain?

Smith-Hutton: Finally, about 7 May, the Swiss Minister, Mr. Hausherr, told us that the Japanese Foreign Office had proposed that Lourenco Marques in Portuguese East Africa be the exchange point; that the Asama Maru take Americans from Japan, Hong Kong, Saigon and Singapore, and that an Italian liner, the Conde Verde, which had been caught in the Far East, take Americans and South Americans from all other places in China. They had made this proposal early in May. The State Department accepted the plan after some discussion, and 10 July was set as the target date for the exchange in Lourenco Marques.

So we knew early in May that we had a little more than a month to go before we were to get on board the ship. That last month we had several occasions to get together. We had a birthday party for the Ambassador on 29 May, and on Memorial Day we had a meeting the Ambassador organized. He made a moving speech that brought us all together, and it was one that we would never forget. On 17 June we left the Embassy to go to Tokyo station. Curiously enough, the few Japanese in the Embassy (those that were made to stay at first, but who finally seemed to welcome staying), the janitors, the cooks, one or two maids and caretakers all lined up to wave goodbye as we drove out of the Embassy compound and they were really rather emotional about it. We shouted farewell and bon voyage, then we drove through the streets to the station.

The police had cleared all the streets which were completely deserted. The station was almost deserted also. When we got there, there were a number of officials on the platforms. Among them was Rear Admiral Nakamura from the Navy Ministry who had come down to say goodbye to me and Commander Stone. We went on the short ride to Yokohama -- about twenty miles, a quick ride -- and went directly to the dock where the Asama Maru was tied up, arriving without incident. After we got on board, the Asama moved out and anchored in the harbor, and there were certain delays. It wasn't until 25 June, more than a week, before we finally sailed. I think the delay was largely because of changes in routing instructions and questions of the clearances.

Some of the civilians who joined the ship, that is, American and South American civilians, missionaries, and others, felt that possibly the exchange negotiations had fallen through. Some of them, including the newspaper men and the managers of the large oil companies had been very badly treated. I found out later that they were very much worried. One of them told the Ambassador that rather than go back to the internment camp and the brutal police treatment, he would commit suicide. Others felt they could not stand any more, because they were rather elderly, and they had been very roughly treated by the Japanese police. The police had tried hard to make them confess that they had been spying on Japan, which of course was not the case.

Interview No. 30 with Captain Henri Smith-Hutton, U.S. Navy
(Retired)

Place: Stanford, California

Date: August 2, 1974

Subject: Biography

By: Captain Paul B. Ryan

Q: Captain, when did you learn of your actual departure date from Tokyo?

Smith-Hutton: We learned early in May through the Swiss Minister that we would leave Japan in June. Sure enough, on 17 June, the Japanese moved all of us and the other personnel -- about five hundred people who were to embark on the Asama Maru -- to Yokohama where the Asama was tied up at the pier. The Embassy staff left the Embassy about 9 a.m. and were driven to Tokyo station in automobiles. Other diplomats, that is, Canadians, Brazilians, and other South Americans arrived at the station about the same time. The train was a long one and only a few cars were needed for the diplomats, so we assumed that businessmen, newsmen and others were on the train. But we weren't allowed to mingle with them. It was good to see old friends from the other embassies that we hadn't seen since Pearl Harbor Day. We all had experiences to talk about.

Q: Was this train well guarded?

Smith-Hutton: It certainly was. We left Tokyo station in about half an hour and there were guards and police all around. There were police in each car, but they didn't say anything to us. The general public obviously knew nothing about our departure because there were no sightseers. We got to Yokohama in about thirty minutes, because the train didn't stop and we went directly to the pier where the Asama was tied up. Our walk to the Asama was a short one. We got on board with our hand luggage and were told that our other baggage would be delivered to our rooms. In about an hour I had my family well settled. It was very much like taking a steamer trip in peace time.

Q: How were your accommodations, Captain?

Smith-Hutton: They weren't bad for an exchange ship. Our stateroom was small but comfortable. There was a bath and we were really in luck, because families, such as mine, had been given precedence. Some of the senior officers, that is, Crocker, Bohlen, and Cresswell were in third class in the hold; and even Dooman, who was next to the Ambassador in rank, had an inside stateroom without a port. Although he was alone, he was ill with phlebitis. His quarters were not luxurious.

Q: Did the ship actually get under way?

Smith-Hutton: Yes. Having got my family settled, I decided to go on deck to see whether I could be of assistance to the Ambassador, and to learn what was going on. About that time the ship left the pier and headed for the harbor entrance. I thought we were sailing for Hong Kong which was to be our first stop, and said to myself that this was a very efficient operation. After many months of delay we were finally going. Much to my disgust, we anchored about two miles from the Yokohama pier. We merely cleared the pier and severed connections with the beach. The Ambassador had no instructions for me so I wandered around the deck looking for old friends.

Q: How long did the ship remain at anchor, Captain?

Smith-Hutton: We sailed on the night of 24-25 June, a week after we got on board.

Q: How did you occupy your time during this week at anchor?

Smith-Hutton: One of the first things I wanted to do was to see about the five Navy nurses who'd been captured when Guam fell and who were supposed to be on board the Asama Maru. Early in 1942 the Swiss Minister asked the Ambassador if the Embassy ladies could give some warm clothing and bedding to five Navy nurses who had been sent to the Japanese military prison camp at Zentsuji from Guam. They had only white uniforms and summer clothing, and the winter weather was quite severe.

The Japanese Red Cross was helping, but it had limited means. The Ambassador told Dooman and me about it, and my wife collected a considerable supply of bedding and clothing which we turned over to the Swiss Minister to send to them. In discussing this problem with Dooman, I said that usually medical-personnel weren't treated as combattants, and yet the nurses were in a military prison camp. This seemed to me to be a violation of international law. Dooman said he hadn't thought of it but he'd look into it, which he did. It developed that the Japanese did not want to hold them, and Dooman arranged with the Swiss to have them repatriated with us.

Q: Did the Japanese impose any conditions on their release?

Smith-Hutton: The Japanese said that if they released them, the nurses must not make public statements about their capture or the occupation of Guam or about the treatment of Navy personnel or of the natives of the island.

I soon found Miss Olds, the senior nurse who had the rank of Lieutenant Commander. (The others, Miss Lorraine Christiansen, Miss Doris Jedder, Miss Leona Jackson, and Miss Josephine Fogarty were all Lieutenant (jg's)). They were all in good spirits and in fair physical condition, and were soon very popular on board ship. They did all they could to help the children and the older passengers, and were indeed a great help. I asked Miss Olds to be very careful about telling stories of Guam. She said she'd warn everybody. They took over the care of Mr. Dooman from my wife and did other things that nurses would normally do.

Q: As I understand your account, if you had not mentioned this to Counsellor Dooman about the nurses, they never would have been repatriated, would have languished in a prison camp perhaps.

Smith-Hutton: That's possible, because normally only naval and military personnel realize the difference between combattants and non-combattants. They were Navy nurses and to State Department official or civilian, a Navy nurse is the same as a Navy officer, but that isn't so under international law. When you point this out to them, they understand right away.

Q: Do you recall any nurses in particular?

Smith-Hutton: Well, I remember one of them particularly, Miss Fogarty. She was especially pretty and a tireless worker, and soon attracted the attention of many people on the ship, including young Frederick Mann, who had been Vice Consul in Kobe. It wasn't long before they were walking together on deck, playing cribbage with my daughter's cribbage board, holding hands, and not long afterwards they became engaged.

A problem did come up. When the newsmen started to interview all the passengers before the ship got to Lourenco Marques, it seems that Miss Fogarty and one of the other nurses had been slapped by Japanese sentries who gave orders in Japanese which they didn't understand. The word got to the newsmen about this, and they wanted to publish it. But Miss Olds and I both knew about the conditions of their release and the nurses did too, but had forgotten it. When the newsmen asked for a press conference with the nurses, Miss Olds notified me, and asked me to come. She told the nurses that she would do all the talking. When the newsmen asked if any of them had ever been slapped, she said no. The newsmen knew better, but they already had many atrocity stories by that time and this was a relatively mild one so they accepted her answer.

Q: What happened to nurse Fogarty?

Smith-Hutton: In Lourenco Marques, Frederick Mann got orders to Brazzaville in French Equatorial Africa, the State Department allowed him to take a month's leave and Miss Fogarty was released by the Navy Department, so the young couple were married in Lourenco Marques. The Portuguese waived the thirty-day residence requirement. By the time we had left the Asama Maru and were on board the Gripsholm, the people who had followed the romance of this popular young couple were very happy with them. I heard from the Manns for several years after they got to Brazzaville. He continued a successful State Department career and their marriage was a success.

Q: That's an interesting story. Were there any other delays getting under way, Captain?

Smith-Hutton: We'd hoped to leave Yokohama shortly after we'd gotten on board, but there was another delay. This was caused by the insistence of our government that several American teachers who lived in northern Japan, who had been found guilty of espionage, be released and exchanged with us, since they weren't in fact spies and had been found guilty on trumped up charges. This firm attitude produced results, the teachers were released, and the ship did sail on the night of 24-25 June, as I've already mentioned.

Q: Was the assignment of cabins on board made by U.S. personnel?

Smith-Hutton: Yes. The head of the committee was Counsellor Dooman, who worked with the Swiss. The idea was that families should be together, and women would be given the best cabins. The result was that many of the senior State Department officials and men whose wives were already in the United States were given third class accommodations. This was generally acceptable, but the food in third class was very mediocre.

Q: Why did the ship not serve a standard menu to all passengers?

Smith-Hutton: I think it was because the Japanese have a routine and couldn't change from this even though the passengers were not usual third class passengers. We men in first class wanted to take turns with our friends in third class every other day so we could all have first class meals part of the time. The Japanese stewards soon noticed this, and declined to serve men in first class and who weren't regularly assigned there and in third class they wouldn't serve men assigned to first class, so our plan fell apart.

Q: That was an unfortunate thing. I understand that the crew of the other exchange ship, the Gripsholm, treated their Japanese passengers from Washington in a royal fashion. What else can you tell us about the Asama Maru?

Smith-Hutton: The officers certainly did as little as possible to help us. For example, we all thought the case of one of the newspaper men, Ray Cromley, the Wall Street Journal man in Tokyo was sad. He was married to a Japanese woman and in spite of his pleas and her pleas and wishes, she was not allowed to leave Japan with him. He did have his three-year-old son on board and they were put in third class.

My wife saw him one hot afternoon walking on deck with his little boy, and suggested that she take the boy to our stateroom to give him a shower. Ray and Donald agreed that was a nice idea, and while she had him in the shower she discovered that his head was covered with a very infectious skin disease. From her experience in the tropics she knew that unless it was treated quickly, that infection would spread to all other children on the ship and there were many on board. After drying him, she took him at once to the ship's doctor. The doctor was a Prussian type and after she explained her mission, he told her in very rough Japanese to get out of his stateroom. She not only declined very hotly, but told him in no uncertain terms that no Japanese doctor was going to talk to her like that, and she was going to stay right where she was until he took care of the boy. Apparently he was so astonished at this response from a foreign woman, that he did exactly that, and although Donald was given pretty rough treatment -- rougher than necessary -- he was treated, and soon he was on the road to recovery.

Q: I suppose the moral there is never underestimate the reaction of an American woman.

Captain, how did the American newsmen on board react to the treatment they were receiving?

Smith-Hutton: Many of the newsmen and teachers who came on board in Yokohama told stories of very bad treatment at the hands of sadistic Japanese guards. These were almost insignificant in many cases compared with the stories of the three hundred Americans who came on board in Hong Kong when we got there about 30 June.

They told us that some of the Japanese troops who had captured Hong Kong in 1941 about Christmas time were from southern Japan and apparently they had been specially indoctrinated to hate British and Chinese. When they captured Hong Kong, they bayonetted some of the British prisoners in cold blood and raped the Chinese nurses in hospitals for hours on end. Several Americans told the same stories of these atrocities. There was apparently no exaggeration, but fortunately these acts did not include large numbers of the British garrison nor did it include all of Japanese troops.

Q: Captain, did you eventually find out the itinerary of the ship?

Smith-Hutton: Yes. The Asama Maru made brief stops in Saigon on 4 July and Singapore on 6 July before continuing to Lourenco Marques in Portuguese East Africa. We passed through Sunda Straits between Java and Sumatra and looked for wrecks of the battle in which the Houston was sunk late in February, but we couldn't see any. When we left the ship in Portuguese East Africa, we went on board the Swedish liner, Gripsholm to return to the United States.

Q: Captain, the ship had a very cosmopolitan group on board. Is that the way you would describe it?

Smith-Hutton: Yes. There were many different groups. We Americans were by far the largest, but almost every country in North and South America was represented. The diplomatic group was a large one, and again the American was the largest, including the Tokyo Embassy staff, the staff of our legation in Bangkok which came on board in Saigon, and the Consulate in Hong Kong. There were numbers of Canadians, Brazilians and Chileans, with a few from other Central and South American countries.

In general the diplomats hadn't been treated badly. I remember two with much admiration. They were outstanding men.

D'Arcy McGreer was the Canadian Charge in Tokyo. He was among the distinguished members of the Canadian Foreign Service. He spoke perfect English and French among other things, had great charm and a keen political mind. He was probably the best informed chief of a small mission in Tokyo. He knew what was going on. The Brazilian Ambassador, Branco Clark, was also a distinguished well informed gentleman. I saw him often years later in Paris where he was the Brazilian Ambassador. I always admired his keen sense of humor and his perception.

Although they weren't a numerous group, the U.S. newsman from Tokyo, Hong Kong, and Saigon included some well known names. For instance, Otto Tolischus was the New York Times man in Tokyo. He had covered the Nazi takeover of Germany until the Nazis expelled him. The Japanese sentenced him to eighteen months in prison. There were six other correspondents in Tokyo including Max Hill of the A. P. Bureau and Ray Cromley, the Wall Street Journal man. Relman Morin (everybody called him "Pat" Morin) was the A.P. man in Saigon, and four newsmen in Hong Kong were also on board. The Hong Kong contingent included Joseph Alsop, who had been interned there. Almost without exception they had been badly treated, beaten, and tortured and they were very bitter.

Q: Which was the biggest group in this passenger list, Captain?

Smith-Hutton: The biggest group numerically at least, was the teacher group. This was a very mixed group in that there were almost three hundred and fifty Maryknoll priests who'd been in Korea and Japan. Most of the priests were graduates of Notre Dame, some had been football players, and many were returning to be chaplains in the Armed Services. They were a stout group of fellows, very admirable. There were about twenty nuns, Marymount Sisters, who had been in Manchuria and Korea. Many had been badly treated by unruly soldiers and had been raped, but they declined to say anything about their treatment and made no attempt to change their normal habits. You wouldn't have known that anything unusual had happened from their talk or their deportment.

Q: So far, Captain, all of the passenger groups were admirable types. Were there any difficult people on board?

Smith-Hutton: Unfortunately, there were. There were some Protestant missionaries, and these included a small group who were against the war. They tried to form what they called a "Fellowship of Reconciliation", that is, a group which would refuse to participate in war or sanction military preparations. They received no support from the majority of Protestant missionaries on board or from the government boards of their home organizations. There were in all ten or twelve men and women with their own feelings quite unsupported by most of us.

Q: You've been very complimentary of the priests and nuns and critical of Protestant missionary pacifists. Would you mind telling us your religious affiliation?

Smith-Hutton: I'm an Episcopalian and I don't mind saying that one of the finest missionaries on the ship was an Episcopalian who had been head of a school in Tokyo, who was going back to join the Army Reserves. His name was Paul Rush. The group I just mentioned was not representative of the Protestants in general. They were a very small minority.

Q: You mentioned the U.S. businessmen aboard. Why hadn't they left Japan earlier in view of the dangers looming?

Smith-Hutton: Most American businessmen who could go had left Japan, but there were a few representatives of large companies which still had extensive interests that they weren't able to dispose of to the Japanese or anybody else. Therefore, they remained to act as caretakers. There was little or no business after July '41 when the President ordered all Japanese credits in American banks frozen, which stopped American exports to Japan. At this time American ships began to avoid Japanese ports to go direct to China or the Philippines.

Thus, there were a few who were caught at the time of Pearl Harbor. For instance, Mr. Thomas Davis, who had been head of the Tokyo branch of the National City Bank of New York, and Mr. Charles Meyer, the head of Socony Vacuum. Both had been arrested by the gendarmes on Pearl Harbor Day, taken to prison and questioned endlessly as to how they'd engaged in industrial espionage.

Both of them were tortured and threatened with death. Mr. Davis had been sentenced to eighteen months in prison, and Meyer was still awaiting trial when the exchange ship sailed. Actually, both were bona fide businessmen and the industrial espionage of which they were accused was the normal activity of a businessman, that is, reporting on economic conditions and potential business opportunities.

Interview No. 31 with Captain Henri Smith-Hutton, U.S. Navy
(Retired)

Place: Stanford, California

Date: August 9, 1974

Subject: Biography

By: Captain Paul B. Ryan

Q: During our last session the Asama Maru was about to enter Lourenco Marques. Could you describe this occasion of entering a neutral port?

Smith-Hutton: After a long hot voyage across the Indian Ocean, the Asama Maru arrived in Portuguese East Africa on 23 July. All of the passengers who could be were on deck, because they knew that within a few hours we would be out of Japanese control for the first time in seven months. It seemed too good to be true. The Swedish liner Gripsholm wasn't in the harbor, but the sight of an American cargo ship with our flag flying, lying along side of one of the piers thrilled all of us and cheers went up. Some passenger on the Asama shouted across to the cargo ship, "Which team is going to win the National League pennant this year?" And again there were cheers from all over our ship.

Q: I can see that it was a very happy occasion. What kind of city was Lourenco Marques?

Smith-Hutton: It is a sleepy Portuguese city with a small population of Europeans and many Africans, and has an excellent harbor.

It is a flourishing port with large coaling facilities. From the sea it's a beautiful sight. The coast and wide beaches are of reddish sand, the water and sky in the tropics are deep blue, and the buildings and houses of the town are pure white as they are in Portugal. It is a picture in red, white, and blue. Even some of the passengers who'd been beaten and tortured began to feel better. In about two hours the Italian liner Conde Verde with Americans and others from China came alongside the same pier ahead of us.

Q: Did you observe pratique as you were coming through?

Smith-Hutton: Yes, of course. As usual, the health and immigration officials of the port were the only persons who were allowed on board, and we were not permitted to go ashore. Late that afternoon the Gripsholm entered and tied up at the pier astern of us. This ship had brought the Japanese diplomats and residents in the United States and South American countries who were to be exchanged for us. So it was evident that the exchange was indeed in the final stage.

Q: What was the exchange procedure that had been set up?

Smith-Hutton: That night we were told to be up and ready to leave the Asama by 9 the next morning as we were going on board the Gripsholm during the forenoon. A strict count would be made to assure that one Asama or one Conde Verde passenger was exchanged for one Gripsholm passenger. We could carry small amounts of luggage, but our heavy luggage should be plainly tagged so that we could get it when we went aboard the Gripsholm. We were ready at the appointed time, but it was actually somewhat later when the exchange got going. It was conducted by representatives of the Swiss Foreign Office, our State Department and the Japanese Foreign Office.

Each passenger's name was checked on the list carried by each of these representatives and when his or her name had been called, the passenger was allowed to leave the ship, go down the accommodation ladder to the pier, and walk along the pier some five hundred yards and then get on board the Gripsholm. As we walked along the pier in more or less single file to the Gripsholm, another file of Japanese was moving from the Gripsholm toward the Asama Maru.

Q: Did you have a chance to see any Japanese whom you knew?

Smith-Hutton: Yes. I saw a few of my former friends in the Japanese line, including Ambassadors Nomura and Kurusu and Captain Yamamoto, the Naval Attache, but I didn't make any attempt to greet them. I understood later that Ambassador Nomura tried to arrange a meeting with Ambassador Grew, but Ambassador Grew declined.

Q: Did the Ambassador explain why he didn't meet with the Japanese officials?

Smith-Hutton: He felt it wouldn't do any good; that we were enemies and the countries at war, and he didn't want to see Japanese officials under any circumstances without the authority of our government.

Q: I'm sure that was the right decision. How were the accommodations on board this new ship?

Smith-Hutton: It was wonderful for us to get to the Gripsholm. My wife and daughter and I found our stateroom which was comfortable, and then we went to the main deck where a beautiful Swedish-style smorgasbord was available for all of us. Many of the Asama and Conde Verde passengers were already there doing honors to a delicious meal. After the best meal many of us had had in months, we began to look around, and much to our dismay we found that while we were indeed well taken care of, all of our shipmates were not so fortunate. The State Department had arranged with an official of the American President Line to take charge of the assignment of rooms on the Gripsholm, and this had been done in a most inefficient and haphazard way.

The result was utter confusion. Most of the senior officials, as I was lucky to be, were well taken care of, but some were assigned two bunks and others weren't assigned any. Families were split up for no apparent reason, others who went to the berthing office found that their names were unknown and they weren't supposed to be on board.

Q: You mentioned the poor diet aboard the Asama Maru. What was the diet?

Smith-Hutton: There was nothing wrong with the contents of the diet or the original ingredients, but the Japanese were poor cooks and didn't know how to make good meals out of meat and vegetables as the Swedish cooks on the Gripsholm did. It was the way in which the meals were prepared.

Q: Going back to the confusion on the accommodations. I suppose all this made some people very unhappy.

Smith-Hutton: Yes, it certainly did. To some of the passengers the confusion didn't matter, as when the newsmen learned they hadn't been assigned bunks, they decided to go ashore to see the town. They investigated almost all the places in Lourence Marques where drinks were served. The older passengers and the women couldn't do this. They wandered around the decks of the Gripsholm looking for a place to sit down and even that wasn't easy.

That night about 9 o'clock, my wife was coming back to our cabin and she found Lieutenant Commander Olds, the senior nurse, leaning against a stanchion crying. When asked why, Miss Olds said she'd decided that the only thing to do was to jump overboard -- to commit suicide. It developed that they hadn't assigned her a berth, and she'd been wandering around for hours looking for a place to go. My wife thought that a bit drastic and told Miss Olds to come with her. Miss Olds was too weak to protest. When they got to our cabin, my wife told her to undress and get in the shower. After the shower she gave her a pair of my pajamas which were several sizes too large, but covered her up.

Then they started down the deck looking in every door. My wife would open the door and look inside, and if there were five bunks and five people in them, she'd close the door and go on. Finally they found a room with two bunks, and nobody was in the lower bunk. She shook the occupant of the upper bunk who came to slowly. It was a young State Department language student who'd been interned with us in Tokyo. He told her that no one had been assigned to the lower bunk, so she told our State Department friend that she was putting another good friend in the lower bunk, and if anything happened to her, he'd have a lot of explaining to do to the Ambassador. Our friend nodded sleepily and my wife thinks that both of them were asleep by the time she got the door closed.

Q: That's quite a story, I must say, and a very resourceful measure. Were there any other similar cases of confusion?

Smith-Hutton: Oh yes, there were plenty, but this confusion finally disappeared, and by the following afternoon it was largely corrected with the help of several Embassy secretaries. By the following evening it was evident that the Gripsholm was a crowded ship, but the passengers could make it to New York, as they were supposed to do.

Q: Do you recall how many passengers there were, Captain?

Smith-Hutton: A little over fifteen hundred.

Q: Was there any need for medical treatment for some of the passengers who, for example, came from Shanghai?

Smith-Hutton: Yes, indeed. Particularly some of the passengers of the Conde Verde, who had boarded that ship in Shanghai. They'd been very badly treated during their internment. Perhaps the worst of all was J.B. Powell, former editor of the China Press, who'd been very critical of the Japanese. The Japanese had locked him up in a small unheated cell and his feet had been badly frostbitten -- they were so eaten away with gangrene, that he'd never be able to walk on them again. The Navy nurses undertook to take care of him and some of the other passengers. They did a fine job especially with J.B. Powell.

Q: Did you observe any Japanese newsmen during this exchange, and how did they carry on having spent years in America?

Smith-Hutton: I saw them, and I heard from some of my friends among the American newsmen about them. In general, we Gripsholm passengers had no contact or relations with Japanese who had come from the United States. But there were some exceptions, particularly among the newsmen, who knew most of the Japanese newsmen who were returning to Japan. They met in bars as newsmen are wont to do, to exchange experiences and swap yarns. Without exception, the Japanese were ashamed when they learned how the Americans had been treated by the police in Tokyo and Shanghai, and they could contrast this treatment with that which they themselves had been accorded in New York and Washington, and at White Sulphur Springs.

Q: I suppose there was no way of making reprisals in Lourenco Marques against these atrocities, if you can call them that.

Smith-Hutton: No, unfortunately there wasn't. My wife had an experience, a last brush, with the Japanese about two days after we'd moved to the Gripsholm. About three o'clock in the afternoon she was coming back to the ship with our young daughter after a shopping expedition, and when she arrived at the accommodation ladder, she found a prominent American missionary member of the "Fellowship of Reconciliation" in conversation with a young Japanese man. The upper deck of the Gripsholm was full of spectators and my wife is a firm believer in direct action and she told our daughter to get on deck. Then she shouted at the missionary and the Japanese to get away from the accommodation ladder, saying they should be ashamed of themselves. They were startled, but upon recovering they told her they had every right to be there, that the pier was Portuguese, and that they didn't have any intention of moving. My wife shouted at them, "Well, I'll show you how much right you have!", and she started for them swinging a heavy handbag as a weapon. The Japanese took to his heels running toward the _Asama_, followed rather closely by my wife.

Fortunately she didn't catch him, but her foot slipped on the railroad rails and she fell heavily to the ground. The _Gripsholm_ passengers on deck had been watching this and shouted encouragement to her, but when she couldn't get up, an old friend of ours, Major Frederick Munson, who had been Assistant Military Attache in Peking and who had seen everything, quickly ran down the accommodation ladder to help her. It turned out that in some way she had cut her foot very badly when she fell, and her summer costume was soiled. Munson helped her up to the deck and to the doctor, who gave her an anti-tetanus shot and bandaged her foot. She limped to our cabin where I was working. I comforted her but when I heard what had happened, I suggested that she might think twice before chasing some young Japanese on the pier!

Q: That's a fascinating story, Captain. What happened to Major Munson who rescued Mrs. Smith-Hutton?

Smith-Hutton: After Major Munson got back to the United States, he had a brief stay in military intelligence and was sent first to Admiral Halsey's command in the South Pacific and then to General MacArthur's command in the southwest Pacific. He served with General MacArthur during the campaign in the Philippines, and ended up in Tokyo as assistant to the intelligence officer on General MacArthur's staff, Major General Willoughby. After the war he went to England as Military Attache and then to France as Military Attache. He's been retired about three years. He is a very distinguished Army officer and a great friend of ours.

Q: Where does General Munson live now?

Smith-Hutton: He lives in Washington at the present time.

Q: Going back to the Gripsholm, did you have a chance to bring back any intelligence material from Japan?

Smith-Hutton: Actually I did. That was really my first task in getting on board the Gripsholm -- to assemble and collect in the proper fashion the material I had brought out. The Japanese had told us that we mustn't take anything written out of the country, but I decided that perhaps they'd be too busy with other things to bother with a thorough inspection of the passengers.

In any event, I had collected a complete file of the English newspaper, the Japan Times, and also the Japanese newspaper, the Tokyo Nichi Nichi, from Pearl Harbor Day until 17 June. These were quite bulky, but I divided them among our numerous boxes and suitcases and hoped they would escape inspection. In a way I was helped by the fact that my wife always travels with many pieces of luggage which are almost always completely filled and this trip was no different from the others. She said I could distribute my materials as I wished, so I had many pieces of luggage to investigate. I also had a card index file of every Japanese naval officer of the rank of Commander and above with his duty stations and remarks on his personality. And I had several shipping yearbooks with details and sketches of Japanese merchant ships. And on my person I had a diary of important events and observations while we were interned. Fortunately for me, there had been no inspection of any kind before, during, or after our move from the Embassy to the Gripsholm, so these papers arrived on board safely and in a comparatively short time I'd reassembled them.

Q: That was a great find for ONI to receive all these materials and your diary.

Smith-Hutton: Yes. I turned everything over to the Far East section on my return to Washington.

Q: I hope they are in the intelligence archives, but one wonders. Sometimes these things are burned.

Smith-Hutton: I'm not sure, but I stayed there such a short time that I don't know.

Q: Captain, I recall in our previous conversations that you had a camera at the Embassy compound during internment. Did you have any chance to take any pictures?

Smith-Hutton: Yes, my wife and I took a number of pictures. As a matter of fact I had many Leica rolls of pictures. There were perhaps two hundred very good pictures of our internment. A most complete pictorial record. When the word got to the newspaper men that we had these pictures, they suggested that instead of putting them in a newspaper or trying to sell them to a news agency, my wife should see whether a magazine was interested and they published about a third of them after getting the whole collection in early September of 1942. There were pictures of the Embassy staff, the Ambassador, and many others. This created quite a lot of interest in our interment, all done at the initiative of my wife.

Q: That was a tremendous coup and of great historical value. On the voyage from Lourenco Marques, did you have an opportunity to do any intelligence work in the way of preparing reports or interrogating people?

Smith-Hutton: Shortly after we got to Lourenco Marques, the Ambassador sent for me and handed me a message from the State Department. It was a secret message sent to the American Consul there stating that one of the Chilean newsmen was known to be carrying a roll of 35 millimeter film which had been given him by the Japanese military and which showed pictures of the Japanese triumphs in Saigon, Singapore, the Philippines, and the Dutch East Indies. The Chileans were going to use them in South America to go with Japanese propaganda stories. The State

Department said that the Navy Department agreed that I be directed to search for this film and to bring it back to the United States. I was authorized to select one officer to help me, but only one, and suggested Major Greg Williams, a Marine Corps officer, who had been Assistant Naval Attache in Shanghai. I knew Major Williams well and admired him very much.

Two or three days after the Gripsholm left Lourenco Marques, we identified this Chilean newsman and located his stateroom, which was in the lower deck of the ship. He was in a room with three other Chileans, and I decided to enlist the help of my wife. I told her we wanted to investigate this man's luggage and didn't want to be interrupted while we were doing so. She agreed to stand guard on deck and warn us if any of them started down to their room. Fortunately, it was very hot in the stateroom and the men were seldom there during the day. We took turns searching and standing guard in the passage way and on the second attempt Major Williams found the film. It was rolled up in a tube normally used for a stick of shaving soap.

When the Gripsholm arrived in Rio, Lieutenant Commander Stone and I got dispatch orders to return to the United States by air and while we didn't know the reason, it developed that our radio intelligence service was swamped with important Japanese fleet traffic. The Commander-in-Chief Pacific Fleet was in urgent need of Japanese specialists to increase his staff in Pearl Harbor and Australia.

These needs had been met by sending all available officers from Washington which was now understaffed. Stone and I were experienced in this work, and they said we were urgently needed in Washington. The Chief of Operations had approved our travel by air. Unfortunately, it turned out that before we arrived in Washington, the Japanese Navy changed their codes and we couldn't begin work until much radio traffic had been intercepted and we could begin decrypting and translating. However, we arrived several days before the Gripsholm and were available if we were needed.

INDEX

For Series of Interviews with

CAPTAIN Henri SMITH-HUTTON, USN (Ret.)

Volume I

AROUND-THE-WORLD FLIGHT (1924); account of naval escort
and supplies, p. 41-2.

SS ASAMA MARU: takes Americans to Lourenco Marques
for exchange, p. 349-50; the embarkation, p. 353
ff; the navy nurses, p. 344 ff; conditions on
board, p. 354 ff; a description of the evacuees,
p. 361 ff;

ASIATIC FLEET: training, p. 34-35; ships ordered to Canton
(Dec. 1923) because of incident, p. 38 ff. Condition of dependents in Far East in time of crisis,
p. 253-5.

ASIATIC FLEET - Fleet Intelligence Officer: reasons for
such a billet, p. 110 ff; value of the French
Navy as source of information on China, p. 122;
evacuation plan for U. S. citizens in China,
p. 123; p. 209; sources of intelligence reports,
p. 210 ff; trips with Yarnell to North China,
the Yangtze and Peking, p. 212 ff.

USS AUGUSTA: flagship of Cinc, Asiatic Fleet, p. 197-9;
Felix Gygax is skipper (1936), p. 199; communications organization on the AUGUSTA, p. 200;
special group on board for experimental radio
intelligence, p. 201-2; overhauls in Cavite,
p. 207; p. 211; steams to Shanghai with outbreak
of hostilities between China and Japan - p. 223;
p. 225; damage to AUGUSTA - protest to the Japanese, p. 227-8; p. 242-3; p. 260.

BALLENTINE, Adm. John J.: Served as Assistant Naval Attache
for Air in Tokyo in early 1930s - visits Japanese naval installations, p. 73-4; his manner of
inspection of Japanese facilities, p. 74-7; p.78.

BOHLEN, The Hon. Charles: joins embassy staff in Tokyo,
1940 - p. 290.

BOONE, Capt. R. A.: Intelligence officer for the 4th
Marines in Shanghai (1937), p. 237-8.

CHENNAULT, Gen. Claire Lee: his experiences with the Japanese Zero and his advice to Washington, p. 79.

CHIANG kai-Chek: p. 114; p. 123-4; Admiral Yarnell calls
on him in Nanking, p. 212. Col. Stilwell's
report on his command (1937), p. 236; his Chinese
armies, p. 240-1.

CHINA: Revolution in the 1920s, p. 28 ff; opportunities to meet Chinese people, p. 30-2; health problems, p. 32-3; customs and revenues under international control, p. 40-1; military actions with Japanese (1930s) around Shanghai, p. 114 ff; p. 121 ff; interest of Admiral Taylor in China, p. 124; (see additional entries under: Chungking; Fourth Marines; Japanese Policy in the Far East; Shanghai; Tsingtao; Admiral Yarnell).

CHUNGKING: Admiral Taylor flies from Hangkow to Chungking, p. 126-8.

COMMUNICATIONS: Japanese Intercepts (Shanghai, 1937); p. 238-9.

SS CONTE VERDE: a former Italian ship - used to exchange prisoners of war, p. 367; p. 369; p. 372.

DEYO, Vice Admiral Morton L.: Plans and Operations Officer on staff of Admiral Yarnell (1937), p. 233; member of Board of Inquiry on PANAY singking, p. 244.

DIERDORFF, RADM R.A.: skipper of the LAWRENCE, p. 186 ff; p. 191-2.

DOOLITTLE RAID ON TOKYO: p. 344 ff.

DOOMAN, Eugene H.: U. S. Counsellor of Embassy (1939) in Tokyo, p. 275; background, p. 288-9; p. 354-6;

ETAJIMA: site of Japanese Naval Academy, p. 92

U. S. FLEET: ships moved from the East Coast of U. S. to Pacific - growing threat of Japan, p. 49 50.

FOSTER, Vice Admiral Paul: p. 101

FUSHIMI, Admiral Prince: cousin of the Japanese Emperor - made Admiral 1933 - becomes head of Naval General Staff, p. 153-4.

GALLERY, RADM Dan V.: First Division Officer on Idaho (1926), p. 51-3.

GERMAN SUBMARINE TRANSPORT SERVICE: planned by German Naval Attache in Tokyo - thwarted (1942-44) by U.S. efforts, p. 308-9.

GREW, The Hon. Joseph C.: U. S. Ambassador to Japan (1932), p. 135 ff; his routine in Tokyo, p. 158-9; p. 162-3; p. 171; his remarks in commendation of Smith-Hutton, p. 177-8; p. 267-8; home leave (1939) - his conferences and preparation for speech on U.S. policy, p. 271; his speech in Japan - its impact, p. 273-4; members of his embassy staff, p. 288-90; the wives, p. 291; p. 314; hears rumors Japanese would launch surprise attack on Pearl Harbor, p. 323; p. 325; his correspondence with Matsumoto of the Domei News Agency, p. 331-2; p. 337-8; the first visit of the Swiss Minister to the U. S. Embassy after Pearl Harbor, p. 340-1; p. 368-9.

SS GRIPSHOLM: The Swedish exchange ship, p. 367; p. 369.

GYGAX, Rear Admiral Felix Xerxes: skipper of the flagship AUGUSTA, (1936), p. 199.

HALLETT, Abend: New York TIMES correspondent in Shanghai (1937), p. 245; his articles on PANAY sinking, p. 246-7.

HANKOW: p. 36-7; p. 125-6.

HART, Admiral Thomas C.: p. 233-p.313.

HASEGAWA, Vice Admiral: Japanese naval commander (1937) in Chinese waters, p. 227; p. 242-3; offers his resignation over incident - Tokyo does not accept, p. 245; p. 250;

HOLTWICK, Capt. Jack S., Jr.: Replaces Wenger on the AUGUSTA, p. 202; p. 210.

HORNBECK, Stanley: p. 89.

USS HOUSTON - CA: Smith-Hutton becomes communications officer, senior watch officer, p. 106; flagship of Cinc, Asiatic Fleet (1931), p. 9-10.

USS HURON: First duty for Smith-Hutton with Asiatic Fleet, p. 18; p. 21-22.

USS IDAHO: Smith-Hutton ordered to her, p. 49-50.

USS ISABEL: yacht and relief flagship of the Cinc, Asiatic Fleet, p. 206-7.

IZUMO - BB: Japanese flagship at Shanghai (Aug. 1937) - target of Chinese bombs, p. 226; Smith-Hutton visits ship and lodges protest, p. 227-9.

JAPAN: (1932) p. 140 ff; relations with Japanese navy
personnel, p- 142-3; naval view of the prevailing policy in Manchuria and elsewhere,
p. 143-4; political assassinations, p. 144-5;
attitude towards Lytton Commission (1932) and
Secretary Stimson, p. 147 ff; Japanese efforts
at navy build-up, p. 151; role of military in
government, p. 154-5; suspicions of foreigners
with cameras, p. 163-4; policy in Manchuria
and China (1934-5), p. 169-71; views of Japan
in 1940-1, p. 311 ff; situation grows critical
after FDR's declaration of a limited national
emergency - events as they unfolded in Dec. 7,
1941 p. 326 ff. outbreak of war - as seen from
the U. S. Embassy in Tokyo, p. 327-30.

JAPANESE ATTITUDES (prior to WWII): pro-American feelings
of high ranking naval officers, p. 70-2; feelings
towards westerners, p. 86-7; towards action in
China, p. 89-90.

JAPANESE COAST PILOT: Smith-Hutton translates the revised
edition into English for Hydrographic Office,
p. 67-8.

JAPANESE COMMUNICATIONS: p. 198; p. 201-3.

JAPANESE EXCLUSION ACT - 1924: p. 71-2.

JAPANESE LANGUAGE STUDY: Smith-Hutton ordered to Tokyo,
p. 54-5; Smith-Hutton becomes guinea pig for
new approach to study of language, p. 58-63;
p. 66-7; translates into English revised edition
of Japanese COAST PILOT, p. 67-8; results of
Smith-Hutton's three years of study, p. 97-8.

JAPANESE MILITARY ACTIONS IN CHINA (1930s); p. 114 ff;
p. 121 ff.

JAPANESE NAVAL BUILDING PROGRAM: p. 280 ff.

JAPANESE NAVAL INSTALLATIONS (pre-WWII): U. S. Naval
Attache visits, p. 73 ff; Smith-Hutton accompanied Lt. J. J. Ballentine, p. 73-4; list of
U. S. Assistant N. A.'s in Tokyo until WWII,
p. 74; Smith-Hutton comments on Japanese naval
aviation prior to 1941, p. 77-8; N. A. reports
from Tokyo on Japanese aviation at variance with
concepts in Washington and the Fleet, p. 78-9.

JAPANESE NAVY - Pre World War II: p. 91-3; the division
of opinion among senior officers, p. 93-4; their
Public Information Bureau, p. 167-8; small group
of former N.A.'s opposed war with U. S. - warned
of U. S. industrial might, p. 306-7; p. 312;
p. 315-6.

JAPANESE PATRIOTIC SOCIETIES: Black Dragon Society, p. 81-2;
Uchida, p. 82-3; Jimmukai, p. 83; Koku Honsha,
p. 83; Dai Nippon Koku Suikai, p. 84; attitude
of Embassy officials on Patriotic Societies,
p. 84-5.

JAPANESE POLICY IN FAR EAST: p. 249; Yarnell's idea of
an economic blockage of Japan in case of war,
p. 250; Mandated Islands - refusal by the Japanese for U. S. visits, p. 253; the 'rape of Nanking' - slaughter that followed, p. 256-8; changed
attitude of Japanese towards captives, p. 256-7;
Yarnell works with Japanese navy for protection
of U. S. lives and property on the Yangtze, p. 259;
war requirements and their effects on the Japanese
homeland, p. 270-1; a change takes place in policies - autumn 1940 - decision to go into Indo-
China, N.E.I. and Malaya, p. 276 ff; Japanese
reaction to German victories in 1940, p. 277 ff.

JAPANESE RADIO INTERCEPT STATIONS: p. 96; Japanese Naval
Inspector offices entered, p. 101.

JOHNSON, Capt. A.W.: Direction of Naval Intelligence (1929),
p. 99-100.

JOHNSON, VADM Felix: flag lieutenant to Cinc, Asiatic Fleet
(1931), p. 108-9.

JURIKA, Captain Stephen: Assistant Naval in Tokyo p. 74.
p. 283-5.

KASUMIGAURA: location of Japanese naval training facilities,
p. 75-6

KATO, Admiral Kanji: pre-World War II outspoken advocate of
a large Japanese fleet, p. 93-4.

KING, Fl. Adm. E.J.: In command of N.A.S. Hampton Roads
(1930), p. 105.

KONOYE, Prince: Prime Minister of Japan (1940-1), p. 317.

KRULAK, Lt. Gen. Victor: Assistant to Capt. Boone as Intelligence Officer with the 4th Marines in Shanghai (1937), p. 237-8.

KUOMINTANG: launches a violent anti-British propaganda campaign (1925) in South China, p. 44-5.

USS LAWRENCE: Smith-Hutton reports as Executive Officer (July 1935), p. 184-9; recreation program, p. 191; in the Atlantic, p. 193.

LEAHY, Fl. Adm. Wm.: p. 232-3.

LeBRETON, Rear Admiral David: Commander, Yangtze Patrol (1937), p. 248.

LONDON NAVAL CONFERENCE: p. 104-5.

LOURENCO MARQUES: p. 349; p. 366-7.

LOVETTE, Vice Admiral Leland P.: author of Naval Customs and Traditions, p. 23-25.

McCOLLUM, RADM Arthur H.: p. 97; p. 163; head of Far Eastern Section, ONI, p. 180-1; p. 197.

MAGIC: code name for efforts to break Japanese codes, p. 198; normal designation for this came to be ULTRA, p. 198.

McVAY, Admiral Charles: Cinc, Asiatic Fleet, p. 108 ff.

MARCO POLO BRIDGE INCIDENT: p. 214-5; p. 217.

MASUDA, Baron: his home in Odawara, p. 69; Smith-Hutton entertained there, p. 70.

MANCHURIA: The Tanaka Memorial on Manchurian policy, p. 80-81 attitude of Japanese military men, p. 88-9.

MANDATED ISLANDS: Smith-Hutton discusses lost opportunities for obtaining data on Japanese installations there, p. 304-5.

USS MARBLEHEAD: p. 95-6.

U. S. MARINES: Fourth Marine Regiment - sent to Shanghai in 1932, p. 115-7.
Smith-Hutton visits headquarters ashore to get details for Yarnell, p. 226; Yarnell gets 6th Marine Division as reinforcements in Shanghai - they return home in Jan. 1938, p. 234-5; Capt. R. A. Boone is intelligence officer for Marines, p. 237-8; sources of intelligence in the Chinese community, p. 237-8.

MARFIN, Admiral Orin: Cinc, Asiatic Fleet - relieved by
     Adm. Yarnell, (Oct. 1936), p. 203.

NAGANO, Admiral: p. 176.

NAGANUMA: Japanese language instructor in Tokyo - develops
     a new successful method of teaching, p. 58-60;
     p. 98.

U. S. NAVAL ACADEMY: p. 5-7; Smith-Hutton and demerits,
     p. 6-8; work on the LUCKY BAG, p. 9; midshipman
     cruises, p. 12 ff.

NAVAL ATTACHE OFFICE - Tokyo: Capt. I. C. Johnson serves
     as N.A. in Tokyo (1932), p. 137; Smith-Hutton
     returns as Assistant Naval Attache, p. 133 ff;
     description of office/organization, employees,
     p. 138 ff; Capt. F. F. Rogers as N.A., p. 141-2;
     Smith-Hutton farewell round of parties, p. 176-9;
     Ambassador's commendation, p. 178; Smith-Hutton
     relieved by Lt. Ethelbert Watts, (1934), p. 178.
     Smith-Hutton sent as attache in April 1939, p.
     263 ff; changed economic situation in Japan,
     p. 269-70; Naval Attache not permitted to visit
     naval yards, p. 280; the staff when Smith-Hutton
     took over, p. 283; the nature of the intelligence
     reports sent back to the department (1939-41),
     p. 286-8; Smith-Hutton's relations with the Russian
     Naval Attache, p. 296-7; a possible Japanese attempt
     to compromise the Naval Attache, p. 297-8; a young
     man who supplied naval information, p. 299 ff;
     Smith-Hutton recommends (summer of 1941) to ONI that
     nine young language officers be sent home - also
     that he be authorized to purchase textbooks, dic-
     tionaries, for shipment home, p. 318-9; visit to
     Miyajima in fall of 1941 (near Kure naval base)
     prohibited from seeing anything of military in-
     terest, p. 321-2; speaks about Japanese history
     of making surprise attacks, p. 323-4; his account
     of events of Pearl Harbor Day, p. 327 ff: plans for
     diplomatic exchange, p. 349 ff; brings back in
     GRIPSHOLM a file of Japanese newspapers, p. 375;
     intercepts propaganda pictures on GRIPSHOLM, p.
     377-8; Smith-Hutton ordered to Washington from Rio
     (enroute) by air, p. 378;

NAVAL COMMUNICATIONS: establishment of OP 20G, p. 102-3.

U. S. NAVAL LANGUAGE OFFICERS in Japan (1932-35); p. 173ff;
     Redfield Mason, p. 173; A.D. Kramer, p. 174.

NOMURA, Admiral Kiskisaburo: p. 84; Japanese Naval Commander at Shanghai (1932), p. 115; p. 118-9; p. 156. p. 277; gives luncheon in honor of Smith-Hutton when he returns to Japan as Naval Attache (1939), p. 282.

OFSTIE, Vice Admiral Ralph: his reports on Japanese naval aviation, p. 268.

OLDS, Lt. Comdr.: Senior Navy Nurse - on board the GRIPSHOLM, P. 355-6; p. 370-1.

ONI (Office of Naval Intelligence): Smith-Hutton returns to U. S. and ONI in 1929, p. 98-99. ONI in 1935 when Smith-Hutton returns to Washington for duty, p. 180 ff.

PANAY Incident: p. 241 ff;

USS PEARY (DD 226); Smith-Hutton assigned duty on her (Aug. 1923) - ship on Yangtze Patrol, p. 36; with the Around-the-World Fliers (1924), p. 42-3; at Shanghai because of anti-British propaganda campaign, p. 44-8.

PHARES, Rear Admiral Everett L.: p. 284-5.

SS PRESIDENT HOOVER: Smith-Hutton takes passage on her with wife (July 1936) for Tsingtao and duty on the AUGUSTA, p. 196 ff.

PULESTON, Capt. W.D.: Director of Naval Intelligence, 1935, p. 178; Smith-Hutton reports to him, p. 180; p. 181.

REEVES, Admiral Joseph Mason: conducts Fleet Problem 17 - (1935) attack on the Panama Canal, p. 189 ff.

RICHARDSON, Admiral J. O.: with South China Patrol in 1920s, p. 39, p. 41.

RICKOVER, Admiral Hyman: p. 7.

ROBERTS, Comdr. David Wells: relieves Smith-Hutton (Nov. 1932) as Intelligence officer on staff of Adm. Taylor, p. 132-3; lost his life in the USS HOUSTON in the battle of Java Sea, p. 133-4.

ROCHEFORT, Captain Jos.: p. 103

ROGERS, Captain Fred: Naval Attache in Tokyo (1933), p. 141-2; p. 161-2; lack of rapport with Ambassador Grew, p. 162.

SAFFORD, Captain Lawrence: head of Op 20G, p. 102.

SETTLE, Vice Admiral Thos. G.W.: Fleet Communications officer on board the AUGUSTA, p. 205-6.

SHANGHAI INCIDENT: (Aug. 1937) Chinese-Japanese conflict breaks out, p. 225 ff; Yarnell's concept of his mission, p. 230-1; Yarnell requests 6th Marine Regiment to reinforce troops at Shanghai, p. 233-4;

SHANGHAI VOLUNTEER CORPS: p. 45; a description of its purpose, p. 47.

SHIGEMITSU: Japanese ambassador in Shanghai, 1932, p. 118; has leg blown off in bombing of review stand, p. 118-119; Smith-Hutton makes some arrangements for him to board the BB MISSOURI where he represented the Japanese Emperor in the surrender ceremony, p. 119-20.

SHIRAKAWA, General (Japanese): in command of Japanese troops at Shanghai, p. 117; killed while reviewing parade, p. 118.

SMITH-HUTTON, Captain Henri: personal data, p. 1 ff; early interest in naval academy, p. 2-3; Columbia Preparatory School, p. 4; first duty after graduation, p. 18; detachment from Asiatic Fleet - examinations for Lt. j.g., p. 48-9; makes a decision to study Japanese, p. 51; p. 54; examination for Lt., p. 95; has short course in aviation at N.A.S., Hampton Roads, p. 105 becomes Intelligence Officer on staff of Cinc, Asiatic Fleet (1932), p. 110-1; his social life in Tokyo as Assistant Naval Attache, p. 156-7. sent as Naval attache in Tokyo in 1939, p. 263-4; living quarters in Tokyo, p. 266.

STILWELL, Col. Jos.: military attache in China (1937) - his reports on the situation, p. 236.

STIMSON, The Hon. Henry L.: Secretary of State - directs that State Department efforts in cryptography be discontinued, p. 102; p. 104.

SUGIYAMA, RADM: Chief of Staff to VADM Hasegawa, senior Japanese naval commander in China (1937), p. 227-8; p. 242.

TAISHO - Emperor of Japan: his death (Dec. 1926) and funeral ceremonies, p. 64-5.

TAKARABI, Admiral: Japanese Navy Minister - a moderate in terms of navy development, p. 93-4.

TAYLOR, Admiral Montgomery: succeeds McVay as Cinc, Asiatic Fleet - Smith-Hutton becomes his intelligence officer, p. 110 ff; his special interest in China, p. 124-5; successful visit to Japan (1933), p. 156.

TAYLOR, Vice Admiral Rufus: young language student in Tokyo (1941) - gets permission to marry a Swedish girl, p. 320.

TORPEDOES: Their use and readiness prior to World War II, p. 190-1.

TOYODA, Baron: becomes Foreign Minister (June, 1941) in Prince Konoye's cabinet, p. 325-6.

TSINGTAO: base for the summer operations of the Asiatic Fleet, p. 129 ff; Smith-Hutton joins the flagship AUGUSTA there, p. 198; p. 215-6. Japanese return after Shanghai fighting subsides (1937-8), p. 259-60; p. 263- .

TURNER, Admiral R. Kelly: his visit to Tokyo in the USS ASTORIA (Apt. 1939), p. 305; his later efforts to belittle ONI reports on Japanese military preparedness, p. 305-6.

USS TUTUILA: gunboat - station ship at Chungking, p. 127-8.

VLADIVOSTOK: Yarnell's visit to the port (July, 1937), p. 217-8; p. 220.

WENGER, Rear Admiral Jos.: on staff of Cinc, Asiatic Fleet (1931), p. 112-113; assigned to staff of Admiral Yarnell (1936) as assistant communications officer, p. 197; his special project on board the AUGUSTA (1936-7), p. 201-3.

WENNEKER, Capt. G. W.: German Naval Attache in Tokyo before WWII - later skipper of the DEUTESCHLAND and then again Naval Attache in Tokyo, p. 166-7, p. 308; arranged for submarine transport service between Japan and Germany, p. 308-9; p. 314.

YAMAMOTA, Admiral I. (Japanese): p. 71; returns to Tokyo (1925) from U. S. - takes charge of naval aviation training, p. 76; said to have been air oriented and paid little heed to use of submarines, p. 150; p. 176. Cinc Japanese Combined Fleet - orders a plan developed for aerial attack on Pearl Harbor (late 1940 - early 1941), p. 279; p. 295.

YANGTZE PATROL: difficulties with anchors in river silt, p. 37-8.

YANGTZE RIVER: Admiral Taylor's trip in the USS HOUSTON, p. 124-129; p. 212.

YARDLEY, Herbert: establishes a crytographic office in New York for State Department and U. S. Army, p. 102-3.

YARNELL, Admiral Harry E.: cinc, Asiatic Fleet, 1936, p. 203 ff; his get-acquainted trip to Singapore, Dutch East Indies, etc., p. 203 ff; discovers lack of joint defense plans with British, p. 204; a characterization, p. 205; Smith-Hutton becomes Fleet Intelligence Officer, p. 209; p. 211 ff; visits Vladisvostok, p. 217-227; incident involving shrapnell inflicting damage on AUGUSTA, p. 227-8; Yarnell's concept of his mission with Fleet Units at Shanghai, p. 230-1; difficulties with Secretary Hull and State Department-his realism, p. 230 ff; his relations with British and French Naval Commanders in Far East, p. 241; Admiral Hasegawa calls to express regrets over PANAY, p. 243; his view of the Far East situation as a result of PANAY, p. 249-50; his idea for an economic blockade of Japan, p. 250; p. 251; p. 259-60; Yarnell visits Peking, p. 260-1; his praise of Smith-Hutton and approval of his assignment as Naval Attache to Tokyo (1939), p. 264; Japanese Navy Minister entertains Yarnell enroute home (July, 1939), p. 282.

YOSHIDA, Admiral Zengo: Japanese Minister of the Navy (1939) p. 294.

ZACHARIAS, RADM Ellis: Assistant Naval Attache in Tokyo, p. 95-6; takes first steps to establish radio intercept stations in Guam, Philippines, Shanghai, p. 96; p. 99; p. 101-p. 104 p. 264.

www.ingramcontent.com/pod-product-compliance
Lightning Source LLC
Chambersburg PA
CBHW082149070526
44585CB00020B/2144